WEST AFRICAN DRUMMING AND DANCE
IN NORTH AMERICAN UNIVERSITIES

WEST AFRICAN DRUMMING AND DANCE IN NORTH AMERICAN UNIVERSITIES
An Ethnomusicological Perspective

GEORGE WORLASI KWASI DOR

UNIVERSITY PRESS OF MISSISSIPPI • JACKSON

www.upress.state.ms.us

The University Press of Mississippi is a member of the Association of American University Presses.

Copyright © 2014 by University Press of Mississippi
All rights reserved
Manufactured in the United States of America

First printing 2014

∞

Library of Congress Cataloging-in-Publication Data

Dor, George Worlasi Kwasi, author.
West African drumming and dance in North American universities : an ethnomusicological perspective / George Worlasi Kwasi Dor. — First printing.
pages cm
Includes bibliographical references and index.
ISBN 978-1-61703-914-0 (cloth : alk. paper) — ISBN 978-1-61703-915-7 (ebook)
1. Drum—Instruction and study—North America. 2. Drum—West Africa—Influence. 3. Dance—Study and teaching (Higher)—North America. 4. Dance, Black—Africa, West—Influence. I. Title.
MT662.D67 2014
786.90966'0973—dc23   2013028812

British Library Cataloging-in-Publication Data available

FOR STEADFAST LOVE AND SUPPORT, I DEDICATE THIS BOOK TO Rose Ama, Yawa Nyuiemedi, Mozart Nuku, Joana Dziedzom, and Shelter Senyoagbe, my beloved family living here in Oxford, Mississippi.

To the virtuosic custodians of African indigenous knowledge who have originated and planted the various dance drumming genres that our students learn to perform. You have given the world some of its most sublime artistic expression. Even kings cannot resist taking regal steps to the vitality and affect from the vibes of your ingenious creativity.

CONTENTS

Acknowledgments IX

Introduction 3

1. Historical Overview of West African Drumming and Dance in North America
   From the Period of Slavery (1619–1863) until the Early 1960s 14

2. Selected University Ensembles
   History, Resources, Repertoire, Teaching, Learning, Performance(s), and Reception 44

3. Pedagogical Approaches of Dance Drumming Instructors 98

4. The Impact of West African Drumming and Dance on the Participating Student 131

5. Path-finding Agency of Administrators and Ensemble Directors 156

6. A Transplanted Musical Practice Flourishing in the African Diaspora 188

7. World Music and Globalization
   West African Drum-Dance Ensembles 225

Postscript 254

Appendix A. Interviews
   Consultants and Field Sites [University Campuses and Conferences] 267

Appendix B. A Survey for Student Members of Ensembles 269

Notes 280

Glossary 284

References 292

Index 301

ACKNOWLEDGMENTS

Projects such as this book begin with ideas. As such, I thank Adam Gussow, professor of English at the University of Mississippi, a passionate blues musician and a friend, who suggested to me to consider exploring the Ole Miss African Drum and Dance Ensemble as a possible theme for my University of Mississippi Faculty Research Fellowship proposal. I gratefully received the idea, expanded it to cover similar ensembles in North America, and that proposal positively yielded the award of the fellowship.

I am indebted to the Office of Research and Sponsored Programs for the award of the Faculty Research Fellowship that empowered me to conduct my ethnographic field trips to university campuses where I interviewed consultants and other informants. Also, I thank the University of Mississippi's Office of Multicultural Affairs (Don Cole), the Department of Music (Charles Gates), and again the ORSP for financially sponsoring other travels including conferences during which I interviewed other informants.

Furthermore, I thank the University of Mississippi for granting me a sabbatical leave during which I wrote most of the chapters of this book.

My next and profound acknowledgment goes to all the research consultants for their shared knowledge, time, and other resources, but above all, the special hospitality that most of you accorded me. Dance drumming directors/teachers: Kobla and Beatrice Ladzekpo, Gideon Alorwoyie, David Locke, Christopher Ladzekpo, Kwasi Dunyo, Anna Melnikoff, Modesto Amegago, Elikem Samuel Nyamuame, James Burns, Patricia Tang, Kofi Gbolonyo, Ama Aduonum, Kwasi Ampene, Robert Simms, Frank Gunderson, Damascus Kafumbe, and Charles Lwanga. Also, I am grateful to members of the Society for Ethnomusicology's (SEM) African Music Section for organizing activities that resonate with this book's theme.

I sincerely thank the following administrators for their support for my project: Olly Wilson, Jacqueline DjeDje, Russell Hartenberger, Glenn Hopkins, Charles Gates, and Eric Charry. The invaluable insights you shared from your expertise and rich experiences phenomenally enriched this study. I was really touched and humbled by you.

For their professional support and/or encouragement, I am thankful to Kofi Agawu, Ruth Stone, Jacqueline DjeDje, Alan Spurgeon, Sister Marie Agatha Ozah, Bode Omojola, Denise Seachrist, and Amanda Johnston.

I would like to acknowledge technical assistance offered by Deborah Purnell (proofreading), UM's Faculty Technology Development Center, University of Mississippi Communications Photography, Tufts University Photography, University of Colorado Photography, Binghamton University Photography (ensemble photos), Kemi Alabi, Buki Alabi, and Yawa Dor (permission to use photo for cover page). John Price and Ethan Fox, Yeko Ladzekpo, Kobla and Beatrice Ladzekpo, Charles Lwanga, David Locke, Patricia Tang, Don Cole, Ama O. Aduonum, Kofi Gbolonyo, Casey Cass, Kwasi Ampene, Annette Holloway, Nii Yartey and Dance Department, School of Performing Arts, University of Ghana: thanks for giving me the permission to use your photos for this book.

What inspires me most and sustains my passion for this book project is the Ole Miss African Drum and Dance Ensemble (OMADDE). Accordingly, I thank Elizabeth Payne, Steve Brown, John Samonds, and Charles Gates for their respective roles in the founding and sustenance of the ensemble. Ricky Burkhead and David Carlisle deserve my profound gratitude as faculty and professional percussionists who have unflinchingly remained regular members of OMADDE since its inception. To all ensemble members, aficionado, co-sponsoring university departments, and the larger Oxford cultural community, I say, Ayekoo! (Well done!).

I sincerely acknowledge the support that my Ghanaian family in Oxford has given me. You all—Rose, Mozart, Shelter, Joana, and Yawa—have played leading roles in OMADDE as singers, dancers, and/or drummers. Cate Aboaku, thank you for your leadership role as well as for being an extended Ghanaian family member. Edward Tana and Akos Anku, thanks for your hospitality when I came to Toronto in 2010.

My sincerest gratitude to the readers for the time and exceptional intellectual acumen that they have evidently expended in their meticulous attention to detail and positive recommendations for both the revision and publication of this manuscript. As the Ewe adage goes, "Wisdom is but like a baobab tree that one man's hands cannot surround."

Finally, I thank Craig Gill, editor-in-chief and the assistant director, as well as other members of the assiduous editorial/publishing team of the University Press of Mississippi who worked on this book.

WEST AFRICAN DRUMMING AND DANCE IN NORTH AMERICAN UNIVERSITIES

INTRODUCTION

West African Drumming and Dance in North American Universities: An Ethnomusicological Perspective explores the strong existence of a world music ensemble and genre in the American academy. For, ever since Mantle Hood's introduction of world music ensembles into the ethnomusicology program at the University of California at Los Angeles in the early 1960s, West African drumming and dance have gradually become part of the soundscapes and cultural lives of other institutions. Beginning in 1964 at both UCLA and Columbia University,[1] a good number of North American universities have vigorously and wholeheartedly embraced the teaching, learning, promotion, support, performance, and reception of West African dance drumming over the years. These institutions include Wesleyan,[2] Berkeley, University of Toronto, York University, Pittsburgh, North Texas, West Virginia, Florida, Tufts, Brown, Ohio University, Colorado, MIT, Bowling Green State, Illinois State, Binghamton, Arizona State, Alberta, British Columbia, and the University of Mississippi. It is no exaggeration that no less than twenty North American universities and twenty other colleges in the United States and Canada have West African drum-dance ensembles.[3] Certainly, a body of factors explains the dynamism of this genre for almost half a century in American universities. Exploration of these underlying meanings is a major task of this book, which draws heavily on the rich and diverse perspectives of ethnomusicologists, ensemble directors, student ensemble members, administrators, and audiences of diverse racial backgrounds.

This book offers a unique salience to the fields of African music study in particular, and ethnomusicology in general. Specifically, this study contributes to the area of world music, and also provides insights on the newer forms of African music in the diaspora, a young but growing focus of African music scholarship. While some authors and/or editors of world music textbooks, Bakan ([2007], 2012), for example, have privileged the traditional and/or popular music genres or styles of distinguished migrant West African artists as a part of the text on Africa, a paper panel session sponsored by the African Music Section at SEM 2010 in Los Angeles, for instance, was on the music of Senegalese and Ivorian migrant West African musicians living in major U.S. cities.[4] And yet, the promotion and projection of the study, performance, and reception of contemporary African art music in the diaspora and beyond has been the foremost scholarly and creative preoccupation of a few Africanists, of whom Akin Euba[5] is a classic example. Seminal publications on the lives and works of prominent African art music composers by Denise Seachrist,[6] Cynthia Kimberlin and Akin Euba,[7] Chapman Nyaho,[8] and Bode Omojola[9] also add to the discourse on other forms of newer African music in the diaspora. Furthermore, the African church in North America is another revealing ethnographic site for the study of African music in America. In her *Soundscapes*, Shelemay (2006: 360–379) provides a critical and contextualized discussion of the Ethiopian Christian chant in America, but not without comparatively situating the practice within its homeland landscape. Similarly, I have made the study of the art choral music performed by the choir associations of Ghanaian churches in North America my next major research project.[10] As can be seen, the preceding emerging areas of interest should explain the centrality of this book on West African dance drumming to diasporic African music studies.

With the exception of a few followup interviews I conducted in 2012, I did the core of the ethnographic work from 2007 to 2010. But given the cost involved in air travel, I could not make multiple trips to all my field research sites that could have provided diachronic perspectives on changes in the ensembles. And yet, the book does not completely lack diachronic insights, especially in chapter 2 on the narratives of the various ensembles. Indeed, I returned to some of the field sites and conducted followup interviews during conferences, which provided a sufficient body of data on which this book is based. I have listed the field sites in the appendix, have quoted and distilled the narratives of my key research consultants in the body of the text, and hope that readers would appreciate the outcome of my research methodology.

For example, I visited Los Angeles/UCLA on three occasions, and when they first gave me the opportunity to familiarize myself with the relevant resources—instruments, space, and so on—I interviewed DjeDje, an administrator, in July 2007. My second visit served a dual purpose whereby I went to L.A. a day ahead of the Africa Meets North America (AMNA) Symposium in October 2009 to interview Kobla and Beatrice Ladzekpo. During AMNA I presented a paper on this same project for feedback from the audience, observed a class session by Kobla Ladzekpo, and attended a concert of which UCLA's West African Music and Dance Ensemble was part. Finally at SEM 2010, I attended the African Music Section's roundtable session, during which Ladzekpo led the discussion on/of pedagogical issues regarding African drumming and dance in the American academy. As part of the same conference, Kobla Ladzekpo's professional group ZADONU performed in a concert that I observed.

Similarly, after I visited Middletown/Wesleyan in December 2007 to interview Eric Charry and Samuel Nyamuame, observe their resources, and attend a semester-ending concert, I returned to Wesleyan during SEM 2008. In a concert that the African Music Section organized, I noted the musical roles of Abraham Adzinya and Samuel Nyamuame as they co-directed the university's African music and dance ensemble as part of a program that David Locke and many Wesleyan alumni returned to organize and perform. Eric Charry led the organization of this concert.

Mindful of the difficulty of returning to some of the sites for followup interviews, I spent two, three, or four full days at each field site in order to avoid rushing my field activities. For example, while I was in Toronto for three days in January 2010, I interviewed Kwasi Dunyo, Anna Melnikoff, Modesto Amegago, and Robert Simms all of York, inspected their resources—space and instruments—and attended two class sessions that Melnikoff led, and another session by Dunyo. At the University of Toronto I interviewed Kwasi Dunyo and Dean Russell Hartenberger, observed two class sessions and inspected their resources.

Furthermore, I have given presentations on aspects of this project at the University of Colorado, Boulder in November 2009, and also at St. John's, Newfoundland, during ICTM 2011, in addition to my paper at AMNA in 2009. Accordingly, I am confident that I have based this book on data that is sufficiently representative of the scope and is an outgrowth of good sampling. As may be evident in some chapters, my personal cumulative knowledge that informs this book spans about three decades. Chapter 1 is primarily based on secondary resources.

As an advocate for indigenous African knowledge, I have privileged the use of African conceptual metaphors, conception and perception of music related phenomena, ontologies, and ethos as aspects of indigenous epistemologies. As will be evident in this book, conceptual metaphors, for example, have heuristic, authenticating, phenomenological, and other hermeneutical values. This is a trend to which I hope this book is going to contribute. Finally, this book is historically expansive, hence the difficulty of ensuring a single overarching theoretical thread throughout the text. And although I have suggested the interplay among structure, practice, discourse, and agency, while emphasizing multiple voices, the Ewe metaphorical conception of planting a musical genre serves the purpose of an encapsulating interpretive framework.

Although the history of West African dance drumming in North American universities only spans approximately five decades,[11] the scope of this book is historically expansive. Chapter 1 thus situates the study within the context of drums and drumming traditions in North America retrospectively from the period of slavery. The evidence of the continuity or disruption of drums and drumming traditions in parts of the African diaspora constitutes an interesting subject matter worthy of lasting hermeneutical engagement. Factors that militated against an immediate reinvention of West African drumming traditions in North America even after Emancipation also receive critical examination in chapter 1. Further, the changing historical, socio-political, cultural, and intellectual landscapes, as well as the agency of individual personalities—Asadata Dafora Horton, Katherine Mary Dunham, Pearl Primus, Babatunde Olatunji, and Kofi Ghanaba—and key-player groups responsible for the revitalization or resurrection of the genre under discussion concludes the chapter. Strategically, this opening chapter, which I have called the "absence," prepares readers for the novelty that the "presence" of the genre, the subject matter of subsequent chapters, may offer them.

Chapter 2 privileges a selected number of West African dance drumming ensembles in North American universities by focusing on their histories, programs, repertoires, symbolism, unique challenges, and lessons they can offer the larger academic and cultural communities. UCLA, Wesleyan, Berkeley, York, Toronto, Pittsburgh, and Tufts were the institutions I was able to visit; but because I have interviewed other ensemble directors during conferences, this chapter also discusses MIT and Binghamton, as well as Ole Miss African ensembles. As may be seen, the institutions covered have some of the most enviable programs in West African dance drumming, and my sampling was based on personal foreknowledge and technical advice from well-informed Africanists. Regrettably, I could not cover some notable universities with great West African dance drumming ensembles in this book because of the unavailability of either funds to visit them all, or of their directors for interviewing during busy summer months and other schedules. On the other hand, several other ensemble directors had very fruitful conversations with me during Society for Ethnomusicology and other conferences that have complementarily enriched this book in a significant way.

It must be pointed out that the predominance of Ghanaian phenomena discussed in this book is the true reflection of the ethnic drumming traditions that are mostly practiced in the American academy. Frankly, Ghana is nowhere near the entirety of West Africa, and the question of "Why Ghana or Ghanaian?" is a legitimate one that must be interrogated. And although Locke (2004: 186–187), after even narrowing it to "Why Ewe?" has partly answered the question, I have given my personal perspectives on this predominance. Hopefully, readers will appreciate my inclusion of the perspectives of instructors on Mande and Wolof drumming traditions in this book, though still disproportionately. Truly, other West African national drumming traditions are stronger outside the American academy, but the universities are my ethnographic focus. Furthermore, I am aware of a few East African dance drumming traditions and ensembles associated with Pittsburgh, Florida State, Kent State, among others. However, I have chosen to focus my research on West African dance drumming traditions. I encourage readers to take a quick glance at Table 1 on ensembles and the repertoires.

More tellingly, this book offers compelling insights on a myriad of issues, processes, challenges, and themes inspired by my desire to examine the presence of West African dance drumming in America beyond concerns of the specific origins of the dances (Ghana). The agency of American ethnomusicologists, administrators, ensemble directors, motivation of students, collaborations that nurtured the ensembles, as well as interpretive frameworks and hermeneutical fields and tools appropriate for discourse on world music, enrich the perspectives in the following chapters.

Chapter 3 examines the pedagogical approaches of instructors of West African drumming and dance in the American academy. But before getting to the chapter's main theme, I subsume the ensemble directors and instructors under three categories: (1) former master drummers of a West African national dance ensemble, (2) Africans who have pursued or are pursuing a graduate degree in American universities, and (3) American ethnomusicologists who have conducted ethnographic studies of West African ethnic dance drumming traditions in Africa. Also, I engage in some degree of semantics involving three labels often used in qualifying these directors, calling for the selectivity necessary in the application of "master drummer," "mother drummer," and/or "lead drummer." Due attention is paid to processes of enculturation or modes of training, degrees of competence in acquired traditional knowledge, musical roles of these leaders, as well as the exploration of the possible ontological sources of these labels as they might interact with other indigenous African ideas within their respective processes of discursive formation.

A challenge of representing African music in the American academy, a major subject matter of chapter 3, resonates with the overriding theme in the essays in Solis (2004). However, in addition to a brief review of Locke's essay, the only one on West African drumming and dance in Solis's collection, chapter 3 richly and freshly draws on perspectives of no less than ten ensemble directors, student participants' opinions, and my personal observations. Positions of Kobla Ladzekpo, Christopher Ladzekpo, Anna Melnikoff, Kwasi Dunyo, David Locke, Pat Tang, Lamine Toure, Gideon Alorwoyie, Samuel Nyamuame, James Burns, among others, constitute the core of data I distilled in invoking the so-called "authenticity" debate. This debate implicates the tensions between traditionalism and modernity, village and urban contextual considerations, and local and global cultural dynamics that confront ensemble directors beyond the stylistic content of dances they teach to include their attendant teaching approaches. Determinants of teaching approaches discussed include course and program objectives, caliber of students—music majors or non-music majors, number of levels and sections available to students, teachers' resourcefulness, and directors' teaching philosophies on repertoire, interaction between academic and artistic goals and pedagogical processes and ends, as well as sensitivity to other variables. Furthermore, "The Debate on Repertoire: The Option of Multiple[12] or Limited[13] Dances" that teachers should teach within a semester is very revealing. As a springboard, I draw on Ricardo Trimillos's essay in Solis (2004: 23–52) and on the debate on "Teaching the Right Thing" led by Kobla Ladzekpo, David Locke, and Gideon Alorwoyie during SEM 2010 in Los Angeles, to contest what may be described as simplistic and overgeneralized binary oppositions implicated in the paradigms often used in framing the "authenticity" conundrum. I argue the complexities of the related issues and the extent to which these multilayered processes require more accommodating narratives reflective of the changing landscapes in world music.

Chapter 4 investigates the impact of West African dance drumming on the student participant. While the chapter shares pragmatic experiences of mature scholars and musicians who have benefited from West African dance drumming, it also reports reasons for current ensemble members' sustained membership beyond obtaining semester credits. Also, the chapter offers prospective students reasons for which they must seriously consider participating in this world music ensemble. Beyond having fun or aesthetic gratification, the consensus motivation for all students, the chapter opens with the discussion of Mantle Hood's concept of bi-musicality. DjeDje, Hood's student, throws light on multi-musicality, a concept that supported the founding of the earliest world music ensembles at UCLA. Multi-musicality has multiple ramifications for the areas of musical performance, music theory, music analyses, music education, and art administration. And yet, sharing his experiences, Olly Wilson stresses the importance of studying African music, including dance drumming, to his career as an African American composer and scholar.

Student participation may lead to the development of career and professional goals culminating in becoming future ensemble directors and repairers of West African drums, in some cases. For a deeper understanding of this specific impact, chapter 4 explores Russell Hartenberger's observation that knowledge in West African dance drumming is a quintessential hallmark of today's professional percussionist, given the abundance of repertoire that draw on resources (creative techniques) of this genre. The genre is not only a favorite of minimalist composers, including Steve Reich, but also a useful vocabulary of percussionists who are also composers.

Generally, however, the use of music and dance as a vehicle of understanding other domains of African culture has the greatest impact on numerous student participants who are not music majors. Accordingly, chapter 4 explores experiences of Kobla Ladzekpo, Christopher Ladzekpo, Anna Melnikoff, and Modesto Amegago to further elucidate the music culture model through West African dance drumming. Also, Oforiwaa Ama Aduonum sheds light on her didactic use of choreographed dances intended to correct stereotypical prejudices carried by American students about Africans and African Americans. The chapter concludes with the forum that rehearsals and performances offer student participants in building relationships through enhanced symbolic interactions—a major transformational impact.

Chapter 5 explicitly discusses the phenomenal agency of administrators as they relate to the lives of their respective institution's ensembles. These administrators are categorized into (1) ethnomusicologists who were not necessarily Africanists but were committed to founding multiple world music ensembles, including West African dance ensemble, (2) established percussionists and researchers of West African dance drumming traditions, and (3) personalities who did not participate actively in the performance of this genre throughout their educational experiences. The chapter also explores the general tendencies that the backgrounds of the preceding categories of administrators may reflexively have on the nature of their support for the ensembles. In addition to the importance of the administrative roles of deans of Colleges of Liberal Arts, the chapter also lists a number of cognate disciplines that often lend support to West African dance drumming ensembles.

The quintessential agency of ensemble directors is the next theme of the chapter. Discussed prerequisites of qualified directors include (1) their levels of knowledge and competence in the performance of African ethnic dance drumming, (2) good levels and command of the English language as a means of communication, and (3) an appreciable degree of formal Western education. The three categories of ensemble directors noted in chapter 3 are revisited in this chapter, but now for a more explicit discussion of the agency of these teachers. While the directors themselves reflexively tend to be overly conscious of their cultural backgrounds in the discharge of their roles, the chapter also examines possible student responses to leaderships that may be predetermined by such categories noted above.

Further, chapter 5 distills the narratives that selected directors have shared regarding the founding of their respective ensembles. These efforts range from well-planned or forethought departmental programs and projects to initiatives and considerations of the availability of African graduate students knowledgeable in the performance of particular ethnic dances, and innovative drives of newly hired African/Africanist faculty. After arguing for the suitability of the designation as directors as commensurate with what they do, the chapter dilates on facets including "Classes and Rehearsals," "Programming," "Performance Space and Other Arrangements," "Sponsorship and Support," "Publicity," and "Documenting the Event." The chapter closes with the examination of the sources and the challenges of securing financial support and funding for West African drumming and dance ensembles in the academy.

But considering the extent to which deliberate actions and calculated initiatives of path-finding individuals interact with prevailing landscapes—structures and discourses—in the founding of ensembles and practice of the genre of our focus, the success and effectiveness of the agency of administrators and ensemble directors discussed thus far are to a large extent influenced by the structures and systems operational in their individual academic institutions. As such, the interpretive framework for this chapter resonates with Anthony Giddens's (1984) theory of "structuration." To him, what knowledgeable individuals can achieve partly depends on the support and contributions they enjoy from their societies, and yet human agency can be enabled or constrained by structure and its emergent system within which human action is located. This duality also applies to other chapters of the book including chapter 1, though on a different contextual terrain. Regarding interpretive paradigms in general, I have encouraged multiple perspectives as deemed appropriate for each chapter. Thus after invoking a Western framework for this chapter, readers may find the African hermeneutic insights in the following chapter engaging.

Chapter 6 draws on the Ghanaian Ewe conception of "planting a musical genre"—*wudodo*. Accordingly, this chapter is predicated on the following premises: 1) a musical genre is metaphorically a plant; 2) West African dance drumming in the diaspora is a transplanted genre; 3) this genre ("plant") continues to flourish and "bear fruit" in the African diaspora; 4) a body of factors accounts for the strong presence of West African dance drumming in the American academy. After explaining the source and target domains of the preceding metaphor,[14] the chapter privileges the discussion of a) the genre as a university subculture; b) the unflinching following from audiences; c) African American perspectives; d) the circumscriptive and prescriptive role of the English language as a post-colonial imprint that enables or constraints the selection of dances, instructors, and countries in which the genre can be taught; and e) the influence of city/regional demography on the development of university ensembles, as factors that partly contribute toward the flourishing of the transplanted genre on a new "fertile cultural soil." In my opinion, this concept of a musical genre being conceived as a plant encapsulates the discussion of this book in its entirety. It is applicable to the changing landscapes,[15] agency,[16] and aesthetic consumption of the "musical fruit."[17]

The second Ewe metaphor that I have used in this chapter to serve as my partial interpretive framework is *Detsivivi yehea zipkui* (It is the sumptuous soup that draws the [eater's] stool [closer to the table on which it has been laid]). This figurative adage speaks to the power of aesthetic pleasure as the main factor that draws aficionados to West African dance drumming performances. In addition to the point on reception, this gravitation concept applies to the fun that sustains student participants' continued engagement with this world music ensemble. At a different level, the responses of informed audiences to my use of this adage then becomes another "stool puller" that suggests that my interpretive framework is like a sumptuous soup. In Atlanta,[18] Gainesville, Florida,[19] UCLA,[20] and Chicago,[21] my appropriate contextual usages of this saying instantaneously attracted visibly positive responses. Additionally, the aftermath discussions that this usage generated affirm the wisdom and appeal in exploring indigenous African concepts as partial interpretive frameworks in African music scholarship. Not only am I encouraged by these responses as a leading advocate of the preceding approach, I am also happy to prepare readers' minds toward such insights.

One other feature of this book is the substantial quoted dicta of my consultants, which I have done deliberately for two reasons. First, I want to acknowledge and emphasize the importance of the discourse of narration in African cultures. Second, rather than present myself as the omniscient author of this book, I want readers to access some of the rich insights of my knowledgeable research collaborators directly through their own words. However, I have reflexively balanced their perspectives with my own insights and ingenuity to a large measure, and I can only hope that readers for whom they may be new will not misconstrue these elements.

Chapter 7 focuses on external factors—terrains, institutions, groups, and personalities—that generally or specifically have fostered the development of West African dance drumming in North American universities. Beginning with globalization and its defining landscapes of ascendancy in transnational flows, circulations, and uses of ideas and goods as an environment that favors the embrace of a world music ensemble, the chapter also examines the extent to which ethnomusicological research on African rhythm and/or dance drumming has not only produced articles, dissertations, and seminal books, but also processes of training a category of lead drummers and instructors. The chapter further recalls how field research experiences offered windows of opportunity for future collaborations and preparatory arrangements that would be crucial to founding of certain university ensembles. The chapter notes that more recently, study-abroad programs have increased interactions among African and North American students and faculty, and West African drumming and dance is a major activity of such programs.

Included in this chapter are major cultural and academic institutions that have housed national dance ensembles, prepared future ensemble directors, canonized performance models, and served as sites for visiting researchers to affiliate with while learning about these genres within their original cultural sources and contexts. These institutions include the Arts Council of Ghana, Ghana National Dance Ensemble, and the Institute of African Studies, University of Ghana. Also, I have discussed the human agencies of Philip Gbeho, Albert Mawere Opoku, and J. H. Kwabena Nketia, selected key players who are associated with the preceding cultural and academic institutions as well as the development of dance drumming in Ghana. Additionally, I have drawn on Charry (2000); Polak (2000); Frieberg (2001); and Hill (2011) for perspectives on the case of Les Ballets Africans' contributions to the global popularity of the music of the Mande sub-region of West Africa. Yet those familiar with the intricate polyrhythmic designs of these dances, the beauty of the dance movements, songs, and costumes may support the advocacy to celebrate the imaginative creativity of those who originated these dances. Accordingly, chapter 7 concludes by valorizing the traditional knowledge of the indigenous musicians whose ingenuity engendered the sublime dance genres of West Africa. They remain some of the world's most creative people.

This book ends with a postscript that summarizes the broader issues discussed in each chapter and offers the consensus opinions of my collaborators. However, I have also provided my personal insights on the issues as well as the salience of this multi-purpose book to its diverse readers from the fields of African musicology, African studies, African diaspora studies, and ethnomusicology in general.

1

HISTORICAL OVERVIEW OF WEST AFRICAN DRUMMING AND DANCE IN NORTH AMERICA

From the Period of Slavery (1619–1863) until the Early 1960s

This book explores the strong presence of West African drumming and dance at North American universities, an ongoing process since 1964 that I describe as a resurrection. To offer a better understanding and appreciation of the reasons for calling West African drumming in the American academy a novelty, presence, and resurrection of a genre, it is crucial to situate this discussion by first evoking the broader a priori historical context that characterized the absence, disruption, and suppression of a symbolic musical tradition. Accordingly, I subsume this chapter under two historical phases: (1) Slavery (1619–1863), and (2) After Slavery until the Early 1960s. I will discuss drumming and dance in the North American academy from 1964 until the present day in subsequent chapters.

DRUMS, DRUMMING, AND DANCE DURING THE PERIOD OF SLAVERY

Although one cannot overlook the ethnic socio-cultural symbolic significance of specific African chordophones—Mande *kora* (Knight 1971, 1972; Charry 2000); the *goje* of the Fulbe, Dagbamba, and Hausa (DjeDje 2008); and tuned idiophones—Shona *mbira* (Tracey 1970; Berliner 1993), Chopi *amadinda* xylophones (Tracey 1948), Mande *balo* (Charry 2000), or Dagare *gyile* (Strumpf 1970; Mensah 1969), for example—I have observed elsewhere that "Drums are generally considered the most important musical instruments of Africans. . . . they are symbols of political power, . . . embodiment of black spirituality, galvanizing tools, uniting forces, speech surrogates, and exquisite artifacts" (Dor 2006: 356).[1] For the sake of sound historicity, it is important to emphasize that enslaved Africans were not only taken from West Africa during the transatlantic slave trade, but also from different parts of Central and Southeastern Africa, as evidenced in Philip Curtin (1969) and more recent works including segments of essays in Holloway ([1990] 2004). And although my preceding observation regarding the importance of dance drumming applies to all the aforementioned regional sources of enslaved Africans, I want to redirect my focus on the geo-cultural scope of this book, West African drumming and North America. Given that West Africa has some of the most vibrant drumming traditions in the world, and as most transatlantic slaves came from this region, one would have expected a steady and undisrupted continuation in drum and drumming traditions in all parts of the African diaspora. Contrarily, drumming was suppressed during the period of slavery in what is now known as the United States of America (Southern [1971] 1997: 172; Roberts 1998: 22, 173). I explore this historical backdrop under 1) dislocation and partial disruption, 2) Christian liturgy as embedded and indirect disruption, and 3) slaveholders' control as total suppression.

Socio-Cultural Dislocation as Partial and Natural Disruption of Drumming

Africa's myriad socio-cultural institutions, structures, and systems inextricably inform the organization of its respective traditional music genres. Nketia (1963; 1974), Bebey ([1969] 1975), and several other African music scholars in their writings have adequately thematized this axiomatic and symbiotic interaction between music and social, political, and/or cultural phenomena (Stone 1982; Euba 1990; Ames 1971; Hood 1964; Agawu 1995; DjeDje 2007). Also generally resonant with the preceding are the theoretical perspectives of Giddens (1977) and Monson (2007), which support the dialectical interplay between music cultures and socio-cultural structures and systems.

However, upon the migration of Africans into the New World, with completely new landscapes, all musical practices of the slaves became uprooted from the original social-cultural institutions, structures, and systems that previously underpinned their existence back in homeland Africa. As a result, specific musical traditions died out. A classic example is the music associated with the royalty or courts in Africa, whether dance, praise poetry, or what Nketia (1963) calls "state drumming." In addition to the nullification of socio-political structures is the centrality of the royalty—kings, chiefs, queen-mothers, or simply patrons, whose royal ancestry, political power and might, benevolence, and recompense the court musicians celebrated in praise poetry and regal dances. But in the light of the absence of the preceding rulers and the institution of chieftaincy in the diaspora, these court traditions that valorize rulers could not have survived. Thus, the replacement of the old African social terrains with new social formations and contexts in the New World engendered the natural extinction of certain drums and drumming traditions. I therefore suggest that the disruption of particular kinds of drumming in the African diaspora automatically and naturally started with this socio-cultural dislocation.

Yet, in critical discourse on the music culture of the African diaspora, specifically those that focus on African retentions, or the lack thereof, the contextual dislocation of musical practices from their African landscapes has not been given the attention it deserves. The circumscriptive and prescriptive authority of the slaveholder with reference to which musical types slaves were permitted or prohibited to perform is a common theme that authors often use in explicating the continuation or disruption of various domains of culture. Admittedly, the human factor and agency are central. However, I argue that the dislocation of dispersed Africans from their original homeland cultural, ecological, social, and political landscapes must be discussed along with how the people themselves were initially dislocated in their new lands. I think this geo-historical approach can complement the more habitual ways in which this topic has been approached.

Christian Liturgy as Indirect and Partial Disruption of Drumming Traditions

Religion is another important ambit under which the continuation or disruption of African drumming and dance in the diaspora can be understood. In homeland Africa, drumming and dancing are indispensable expressive and experiential domains of most traditional African religious practices, whether used as a means of invoking the presence of a divinity, inducing spirit possession in devotees, conditioning the momentary spirituality in an intermediary, a conduit of corporate expression of religious beliefs, or a vehicle for easy transition between different stages of worship, all which facilitates ritual efficacy (Rouget 1985; Nketia 1957, 1963; Friedson 1996, 2009; Kiehl 1999). Furthermore, Nketia (1968), Euba (2003), and Barber (2004, 2005) have discussed textual constructions in which a substantial amount of West African praise poetry is directed toward deities, whether sung or played on drums such as the Ghanaian *atumpan* or Yoruba *dùndún*. It is therefore legitimate to ask whether or not religious drumming traditions have been dislocated or discontinued like court drumming traditions and dances in the African diaspora. The answer to this question is the focus of the next few paragraphs.

The kind of intense indigenous praise singing, praise drum poetry, or dance that has survived among most identifiable groups within the African diaspora is that which lauds their objects of worship, within the context of continued practice of traditional African religions. Though transformed, drumming traditions within African-derived religious contexts in the diaspora have retained all the functions discussed in the preceding paragraph. Evidently, religious dances have preserved the traditions of drumming of which classic examples abound in Haiti, Cuba, Brazil, Jamaica, and also among the Sidi Indians, though with a different historical trajectory.

Contrarily, because most slaves in the United States converted to Christianity, they lost one of the major accesses to continued drumming and dancing during the time of slavery. Whether by intent or sheer coincidence, the volitional or coerced conversion of thousands of slaves in America to Christianity as their major religion can be viewed as an indirect, and perhaps unintended, perpetuation of the suppression of drumming in North America. At a time that African-derived religious practices of slaves in the Caribbean and Brazil, for example, remained a powerful medium through which religious dance drumming survived along with other Africanisms evidenced in cosmology and accompanying ritual behaviors, the Christian liturgy of some of these early Black converts in the USA, as Southern observes, was mainly European and without West African drumming.

Southern (1997: 178–179) has documented how the absence or extent of Africanisms in the black church before the Civil War (1861) depended on denominations of converted slaves, the degree of control or flexibility of white church leaders and slaveholders over the religious practices and expressions of slaves, and agency of black worshippers in the Southern colonies and later states. Not only did Eileen Southern stress the differences in attitudes of slaveholders in various colonies, but also those between the worship music of converted blacks in the urban and rural church. In European-African or black churches affiliated with Catholic, Methodist, Presbyterian, and Lutheran denominations, musical liturgy was desirably European, and for the sake of so-called authenticity, no room was allowed for Africanisms in regular worship services. "Negro worship music" was permitted for only a few special services. Given that the Protestant churches belonged to national conferences or societies, they ensured uniformity in liturgy. Writing on the beginnings of the religious folk songs of black Americans leading to the *Spirituals*, for example, Southern relates:

> First, there were the black Methodists of Philadelphia adding choruses and refrains of "their own composing" to the standard Protestant

hymns in Richard Allen's hymnal of 1801. Then a few years later, in 1804, a visitor to Allen's church ridiculed the "kind of songs" being sung at the church, implying that they were not orthodox hymns. Finally, in 1819 John Fanning Watson publicly aired the matter, protesting that the black members of the Society were singing their improvised hymns in public places and camp meetings. (Southern 1997: 180)

The preceding excerpt clearly articulates how uncompromising Protestant churches were regarding standardization of liturgy, perhaps aimed at enforcing church traditions including their related beliefs of efficacy in worship. It follows that such a landscape of regulated religious behavior was never a fertile site for even black Protestants' use of drum substitutes, let alone West African religious dance drumming.

Black independent churches, mainly Baptist, whose congregations were led by black preachers were autonomous, therefore "free from regulations of a national body," and rather controlled by local white church officers (Southern 1997: 178). Such a different and relatively more flexible atmosphere encouraged and enabled more black modes of worship and religious expression. No wonder the style of *lining-out*, especially of Isaac Watts hymns, has survived in black Baptist churches. But more notably related to this book's theme is the practice of drum substitutes as evident in the *ring shouts* in which handclapping and foot stomping provide the rhythmic synergy and accompaniment to singing and dancing. As by African conception in which a symbiosis exists between drumming, singing, and dancing, ring shouts contain call-and-response singing, subtle dance movements that are differentiated from black secular dance behaviors, and polyrhythmic structures that worshippers produce on/from their bodies, as well as intermittent ululation ubiquitous to many African ethnic communities. A classic example of this intangible knowledge and endangered heritage of the ring shouts can be found among the Gullah living in McIntosh County on the Georgia Sea Islands. The Gullah-Geechee Ring Shouters are a group committed to becoming the living repository and perpetuators of their ancestors' religious genre, though the Library of Congress has also documented performances of this genre by the Gullah group. Although the AME and AMEZ Churches also had black preachers, controlling national apparatuses made it hard for these churches to survive in the South.

Yet, as Southern observed, the majority of slaves were never permitted by slaveholders to convert to Christianity. However, the blacks of this category secretly formed the designated "invisible institution" or the "invisible church," and strategized ways and means to worship in secret, even within their rigidly controlled circumstances. Though one may not rule out the possibility of these secret churches also resorting to drum substitutes including handclapping, foot stomping, and beating parts of the body during worship, the secrecy with which they conducted their gatherings, to the extent of masking and muting the preacher's voice, leaves doubt with respect to any loud sonic outlets that might attract the attention and notice of slaveholders. Given that the intensity of the ring shouts or other singing and dancing might depend on where and when they worshipped, the main uncertainty that engulfs the religious practices of these secret churches is the secrecy itself. It is convincing for slaves to use songs with hidden transcripts such as "Steal away to Jesus" to cue themselves for times to converge for worship because, the use and evocation of such linguistic devices as situational knowledge expressions is a commonplace in black cultures. Also, the label of "secret institutions" superficially resonates with the closed religious societies such as the *Sande* and *Poro* of the Vai of Liberia (Monts 2000: 63–87), or the *Yewe* and *Afa* of the Ewe of West Africa. While future research may consider probing any possible Africanisms along such a geo-historical trajectory, it is abundantly clear that West African dance drumming might have been too loud for these secret groups and activities.

Contrarily, the eclecticism that characterized the religious practices of some blacks in Haiti, Cuba, and Brazil was more of a continuum than a revitalization of completely disrupted African-derived practices. In parts of the Caribbean and South America, the Catholic Church encouraged the continuation of some African cultural practices both within and outside worship. George Brandon discusses the formation and activities of Afro-Catholic fraternities in Cuba called *cabildos*, societies that were primarily ethnic-based that socialized and fellowshipped, among other things, through drumming and dancing outside of worship. These fraternities, according to Brandon, apparently enabled slaves of Yoruba descent to lay the firm foundations that nurtured the establishment of Santeria religion in Cuba, although not without the slaves' own agency (Brandon 1998). Further, Tompkins (1998: 491) notes that during the period of slavery, the Catholic Church in Peru also encouraged slaves to engage in drumming as a way of socializing in brotherhood groups called *cofrados*. Such freedoms were absent in the church in North America during the period under review.

On the other hand, while slaveholders in North America might not have believed in traditional African religion, one can posit that they might have been aware of the almost boisterous ritual behaviors of possessed devotees of Voudoun, Candomble, or Santeria, and of the fact that some of the deities were/are war divinities with wrathful attributes. And since it is dance drumming that partly induces this spiritual transference from the physical to the metaphysical realm of experience in the devotee, it must be counted a blessing in disguise, from the perspective of the slaveholder, that most slaves in the United States became Christians. Yet the Christian faith partly constrained the continuation of African dance drumming in religious contexts.

Slave Holders' Control as Total Suppression of African Drumming Traditions

Southern ([1971] 1997: 172), Roberts (1998: 22, 173), and several other scholars who have documented the outlawing of drumming during slavery, especially in the American South, all explain this suppression as a preventive strategy. Nketia not only discusses the diversity and symbolism of African drums, but also the three modes in which African drumming is done, namely, dance, signal, and speech (1963: 17). African drums' use as speech surrogates to serve as sensitizing, mobilizing, and galvanizing tools for warriors to be psychologically tuned up for war is a commonplace that could not have eluded the knowledge of pragmatic slaveholders. And yet the reinforcement of slave labor from Africa in the eighteenth century, for example, was equally a reinforcement of the African cultural presence in the United States,[2] not only in terms of the performing arts, but also of indigenous military knowledge necessary for resistance to subservience.

Writing on *Africanisms in American Culture*, Joseph Holloway mentions the Stono Rebellion of September 9, 1739, as a classic example of slaves' resistance to subjugation, which included suppression of their ancestral heritage of drumming. On the other hand, the rebellion exemplifies a vindication for the rationale behind slaveholders' suppression of drumming. This uprising took place in South Carolina when Jemmy, a slave believed to have come from Kongo or Angola, led other slaves in their agency for freedom. Compelling critical accounts on the Stono insurrection by Smith (2005: xiii), Shuler (2009: 3–4), and Kly (2006: 59) indicate that although the rebellion was relatively brief, the slaves' symbolic use of drums and drumming as both a tool and object of liberation is noteworthy.

Consequentially, the aftermath of this rebellion was marked by the passing of what is known as the Negro Act of 1740 in which slave behavioral codes were tightened with tougher controls. Among other things, the act prohibited slaves from South Carolina from drumming, assembling in groups, or relocating to neighboring non-British colonies that granted slaves

Figure 1.1 Sculpture at Congo Square, Louis Armstrong Park, New Orleans. [Photo by George Dor, November 2012]

some degree of socio-cultural freedom, and gave legal cover to slaveholders to kill any slave who engaged in future rebellious acts. Also, the Negro Act of 1740 influenced the passing of the Georgia Slave Code of 1755, for another English colony. However, beyond broader generalizations, one needs to acknowledge the nuances and realities of the practices in autonomous southern states. Historians have observed that slaveholders in Spanish Florida granted much more socio-political freedom to their slaves than was the case in the English colonies. It is then easy to comprehend why the ban on slaves' attempt to relocate to these neighboring states was part of the Negro Act of 1740. Furthermore, the cultural freedom of slaves in Louisiana in the eighteenth century deserves mention. At the same time that the Negro Act of 1740 prohibited slaves in South Carolina from assembling in groups, Southern writes on the practice of New Orleans slaveholders in the eighteenth century that they relieved their slaves from work on Sundays. This flexibility allowed them to gather at Congo Square, where they made music, danced, and generally interacted. While some may argue that such partial freedoms served as foundations of slave solidarity that later concretized and enabled the New Orleans slave rebellion in 1811 (after the French Revolution), the

Figure 1.2 Label describing the above sculpture at Congo Square, New Orleans. [Photo by George Dor, November 2012]

opportunity in any case allowed slaves the freedom at least to perpetuate their creolized culture, even though according to Southern, the drums that accompanied their dances were not African-derived.

In his book *Africa and the Blues*, Gerhard Kubik makes a relevant observation on the enduring effects that the disruption of African dance drumming has had on the musical structures of the blues. Specifically, Kubik (1999: 51–62) notes the absence not only of drums but also of complex polyrhythms and time lines, a subject he discusses in the chapter "A Strange Absence." As he explains, these absences should be bewildering not to Kubik alone, but also to anyone familiar with the drumming traditions of the Guinea Coast of West Africa that Richard Waterman, Alan Merriam, and several other scholars have written on. Moreover, the fact that a good number of slaves came from the same sub-region famous for its vibrant dance drumming makes the absence very conspicuous. However, citing Morton's contention that New Orleans is culturally a Caribbean space, although geographically part of the United States, Kubik notes a partial exception to his observations on some of the preceding "absences." Admittedly, proximity of New Orleans to the Caribbean facilitated cultural appropriations and domestications within the context of urban cultural hybridization.

Two competing accounts exist on whether or not slaves who were America-bound carried drums on ships across the Atlantic Ocean. While one

Figure 1.3 Historic Marker, Congo Square, Louis Armstrong Park, New Orleans. [Photo by George Dor, November 2012]

account holds that slaves were prohibited from carrying drums on board, the other maintains that they were encouraged to carry drums on board in order to make them happy, or to contain them as a kind of escapism from the realities of their Middle Passage and unknown destinations. This second account appears in an article published by and on a United Nations website as documentation of partial proceedings of an exhibition held in New York City on March 24, 2009, as observation of "International Day of Remembrance of the Victims of Slavery and the Transatlantic Slave Trade in New York," under the theme "Breaking the Silence, Beating the Drum." It reads: "During the Passage, slaves were encouraged to beat the drum. The hope was that beating the drum would keep their morale high as possible. But upon arrival in the Americas, beating the drum was forbidden for most slaves" (UN 2009).[3]

Personally, I do not find this second account very persuasive; it sounds like a reconstructed historical narrative that essentializes drumming while sacrificing the truth. For I cannot imagine how the slaves could drum in their shackles, even if they were allowed to do so. Citing Epstein (1973: 66–67), who has quoted from Bryan Edwards (1793), Kubik (1999: 6–7) discusses claims of slaves being encouraged to make music on ships during the Middle

Passage in the eighteenth century so that their levels of depression and dying could be reduced. This alleged calculated escapism through music making and dancing was reportedly possible because African instruments were supposedly collected before their departure from Africa. Also, Kubik problematizes and contemplates whether the presence and knowledge of West African types of chordophones in North America was a result of instruments carried along by captives from Africa on ships, or an outcome of the reinvention and construction of these instruments and their playing techniques based on captives' collective memories after arriving in the New World. In any case, the historicity of claims that the West African drums that the slaves played on the Atlantic route are now kept in British museums, in my opinion, remains questionable and most probably conjecture. Perhaps an isolated case happened in the eighteenth or early nineteenth century, but it has been made to sound as the normal practice. Relevant to this discussion, however, is how both accounts converged into a unitary position that slaves were not permitted to drum the moment they arrived at their destinations in the United States.

After the Period of Slavery (1863) until the 1960s

To answer the question of when exactly the practice of West African dance drumming was introduced in North America, one is tempted to revisit a number of possibilities even before 1863. Of course, historical accounts of the Stono Rebellion could not establish the use of any African-derived drums by the resisting slaves. Further, one is inclined to doubt the trustworthiness of the dubious claim that African slaves who later arrived in North America in the late eighteenth and early nineteenth centuries were permitted to bring along drums. The most probable window left to explore is the appropriation of Voudoun religious practices, including drumming, from Haiti. But writing on "The Case of Voodoo [*sic*] in New Orleans," Gaston (2005: 123) observes: "In Dahomey [current Benin] and Haiti a group of three drums served to lead and keep the rhythms. Voodooists in New Orleans proper were forbidden by law to use real drums in voodoo ceremonies unless they were part of the weekly public ceremony in Congo Square. Handclapping, leg patting, and foot stomping provided a handsome substitute." However, I have earlier pointed out Southern's report of slaves' use of non-African drums regarding drumming in New Orleans's Congo Square. Yet, while it may be hard to understand the reason for which Gaston could describe Voudoun without drumming as a "handsome substitute," especially given that dance drumming is a synergy behind spirit possession, a contextualized reading of the preceding Gaston statement within the landscape of laws and suppressed state of dance drumming makes her observations meaningful. I have discussed earlier that when drums were banned in the American South, slaves used drum substitutes including handclapping, foot stomping, and beating of parts of the body (i.e., hambone) to replace the rhythms and sounds of the drums, a theme I have explicitly discussed elsewhere (Dor 2006: 357–361). While one celebrates the ingenuity of the suppressed blacks in the diaspora in finding substitutes to express themselves in ways closer to their African cultural behaviors, the characteristic synergies of the drumming traditions that were prohibited are just different.

Deductive reasoning will suggest a higher degree of probability of an immediate revitalization or reinvention of West African drumming after the end of slavery by black Americans. However, that was not the reality, and perhaps only wishful thinking. In the next few paragraphs, I explore factors that could have encouraged the continued absence of West African dance drumming for almost another century. I will contextualize this prolonged absence within the church, social life, and the academy. But before I do so, it may be appropriate to explain the rationale behind spending more time on the absence of West African drumming in the United States of America.

Until the advent of post-structuralism, the study of the absence of a phenomenon was not a major research preoccupation of many intellectuals. Rather, researchers paid attention only to phenomena that constituted a defining element of a phenomenon or landscape—specifically in this context, music culture. Certainly, concerns for establishing homologies favor the prioritization of structural elements and idiosyncratic characteristics as hermeneutical objects and engagements. However, the awareness of the importance of human agency as capable of contributing to the absence of a phenomenon just as to its presence is at play here. Study of human behavior often reveals a body of circumscriptive, prescriptive, constraining, suppressing, and controlling tendencies and results, and I have earlier in this chapter suggested such trends with regard to West African drumming. Yet the paradox in question here is why some degree of change in social landscape after slavery did not immediately attract a corresponding freedom of expression in all domains of the lives of black Americans.

Absence of West African Drumming in the Black Church Defended

It is now common knowledge that after Emancipation, the black church became a site and space for the intensification of Africanisms in worship, especially in the churches founded by black Americans. These changes were evident in the preferences for practices and ritual behaviors including singing hymns without instrumental accompaniment, percussive sonic sensibilities, and dialogical modes of expression during sermon and/or congregational singing (Maultsby 2005: 326–355). And although most established churches, Baptist and Methodist for example, did not use drums and other percussion in worship, one would imagine that the deployment of drum substitutes in black churches of the nineteenth century intensified. More related to this book's subject matter was the use of bass drums and tambourines in many of the new denominations established by blacks in the late nineteenth century. These churches included the Holiness and Sanctified, some of which started in southern states of Alabama, Mississippi, and Tennessee in the 1890s (Southern 1997: 262). By the beginning of the twentieth century, all the Africanisms I have discussed thus far in the worship of the black church crystalized in Pentecostal churches where worship was characterized by playing of drums and idiophones, spirit possession, speaking in tongues, holy dancing, and improvisatory singing. Arguably, black worshippers' collective memory could have empowered them in the processes of reactivating these practices, but partly because they were also alive in certain black secular practices.[4]

Nevertheless, the wish for a profound revitalization and introduction of typical West African drumming in the black church sounds like a thought from an extreme Africanist, if not also Afrocentric. After more than three hundred years, black worshippers have reinvented and established their newer modes of expressive culture that did not need any revolutionized infusion of West African drumming in liturgy. I have already portrayed the European-African church as not a fertile ground for West African drumming because such a practice would have presented a conflict of doctrinal or liturgical positioning. Further, black Christians who had been influenced by assimilated Euro-American predilections carried the negative representation of African-derived religious practices, with their attendant drumming, as heathenish. Further, since Christianity was the religion of many educated blacks, it was often considered key to intellectualism and/or enlightenment. Accordingly, any consideration of a return to African cultural practices including drumming may have been considered a regression from an acquired state of "civilization." Not only was Africa referred to by the majority of Europeans and Americans as a "dark continent," a stigmatization that was popularized by Henry Morton Stanley's 1878 *Through the Dark Continent;*[5] as Okon Edet Uya observes: ". . . the challenge and responsibility of salvaging the ancestral homeland from presumed darkness . . . was most pronounced among [later generations of] church-oriented persons and groups" (1982: 71–72, 82). Uya further cites Alexander Crummell as the greatest advocate of the notion of Africa's "heathenism and benightedness." How then could converted black Christians in America yearn to reinvent a tradition from such a homeland continent?

As an African and a Christian myself I am very well informed about how Christian missionaries banned traditional African drumming and dance in the church: they were branded as heathenish, and converts who performed them were punished by excommunication. And until the 1940s, when drumming was introduced into the church in Ghana, for example, even educated Africans who were also Christians looked down upon such cultural practices. Yet Meyer (1999) has explored the diabolization of several African traditional practices by Christian missionaries in Ghana as an evangelizing tool. The preceding is a seeming diversion from the geo-cultural focus of this study (from North America to Africa) and yet thematically resonant and complementary, and aimed at providing further elucidation of a general mentality through which Christians anywhere in the world demonized African indigenous drumming and dance until the 1940s and 1950s, when radical changes in worldviews offered some degree of shift in the representation of African dance drumming in the church.

To return to America, West African dance drumming was never part of the black American church. While Southern (1997: 475) reports of the use of congas introduced into some black churches as late as in the 1970s, drumming and dance have become commonplace worship activities of more recent African immigrants living in major North American cities. For example, Kaufman Shelemey discusses the *kebaro* as one of the instruments the Ethiopian Orthodox Christian Church in America uses along with their peculiar chanting (2006: 360–379). Similarly, I have personally attended Ghanaian church services in Atlanta and Washington in which drumming was done to enable dancing during offertory.[6] Yet all these are newer developments that emerge out of another historical trajectory.

Absence of West African Drumming in the Black Secular Social Life Defended

Black Americans have developed and established their own unique musical heritage that comprises musical genres they continue to perpetuate. After centuries of disruption of drumming, this music genre of their remote ancestry was most likely lost in their collective memory. Furthermore, after Emancipation black Americans were confronted with several challenging social battles that they had to fight more urgently than thinking about the immediate revival of West African drumming, even if that was possible. Their primary concern was their agency toward complete freedom, equality, and restoration of respect, dignity, and pride, freedom from poverty, fear, discrimination, and their pursuit of total transformation from serfdom and social periphery to full and pragmatic citizenship, as well as resisting other social ills of the times. Preoccupied reactions to atrocities, disenfranchisement, and social injustices, simply categorized under racism, were more important to emancipated blacks than the reinvention of cultural traditions such as West African drumming.

Moreover, African Americans in post–World War II years historically witnessed a polarization regarding their positions and attitudes toward Africa and Africans. Elliot Skinner has explicitly illuminated this debate in his critical essay titled "The Dialectics between the Diasporas and Homelands," and I would like to take advantage of some of these factors as partial reasons that militated against the appropriation of any form of African culture (1982: 17–46). Later in the chapter I will argue how the change in the tide of the debate, especially during the peak of Pan-Africanism, correspondingly promoted African Americans' intensified identification with Africans in political, economic, and cultural spheres, eventually leading to a better reception of West African dance drumming in the United States of America.

It is important to point out that thousands if not millions of African Americans rather embrace the concept and agency of "Black Brotherhood" (Uya 1982: 70) through which the welfare of black people throughout the world transcends continental confines, although not necessarily within the framework of "return-to-Africa" advocacy. I have personally studied diasporic Africans' nostalgia for Africa and their love for Africans. And as I was partly schooled in the United States and work here, I am a lucky beneficiary of the goodness of several diasporic Africans—American and Caribbean—who know that I come from Africa. But in what may be described as a prolonged, generational, and perpetuated reaction, Skinner (1982) notes that a cross-section of black Americans, though relatively few, have held a strong bitterness against Africans for selling their ancestors into slavery. Whatever the deeper explanations of this rancor may be, this reason explained the position of some black Americans of not having anything to do with African culture. This very reason was enough for some not to consider Marcus Garvey's return-to-Africa call.

But for the black Americans on the other side of the debate, Africa remains their ancestral homeland to which they must be connected in some ways, in spite of the crimes committed against humanity during the transatlantic slave trade. Naturally, some have other legitimate reasons why the return-to-Africa advocacy did not appeal to them. These included the preference and choice to stay in America to demand that they were granted total freedom and equality so as to be able to enjoy the labor and toils that their immediate ancestors and themselves had expended in partly building the economy of their New World. Public self-declarations and affirmations of blacks as preferably Americans have even led to their fears of continued labeling of their associations with "Africa" or "Africans." To prevent possible denial of their requests from the American government, some African Americans, as Skinner (1982: 27) notes, not only desisted from the use of such labels but also denigrated their ancestral homeland in a body of dicta. Skinner thus cites, "Their spokesman declared that: [Africa was] 'without arts, without science, without a proper knowledge of Government, to cast into the savage wilds of Africa the free people of color seems to use the circuitous route through which they must return to perpetual bondage' . . . ." While there may be no need to unpack the preceding castigations of Africa and Africans, suffice it to observe that the claims sound like a rehearsal of Hegel's controversial slurs on Africa, as discussed by Campbell (2006: 228). But one may not need to go as far as to Germany in order to capture this pervasive worldview of the era on Africa. Kwame Appiah has discussed a similar assertion made by Alexander Crummell, an American missionary who lived and worked in Liberia during the post-Emancipation era, saying that ". . . his [Crummell's] theme that Africans 'exiled' in slavery to the New World had been given by divine providence 'at least this one compensation, namely, the possession of the Anglo-Saxon tongue'" downplays the richness of indigenous African languages[7] (Crummell 1862; Appiah 1992: 1).

It then follows that it was not only whites who stigmatized Africa and Africans in their discourse. In any case, such sentiments carried by freed blacks in post-Emancipation America are characteristic of assimilationists anywhere. For example, writing on "French and British colonial policy" in Africa, Kwame Appiah notes that "it is broadly true that the French colonial policy was one of assimilation—turning 'savage' Africans into 'evolved' black Frenchmen and women—while British colonial policy was a good deal less interested in making the black Anglo-Saxons of Crummell's vision" (Appiah 1992: 3–4). All assimilated people are normally careful in protecting their newly gained social status, doing so through a body of means including partial deployment of "public transcripts," in James Scott's terms (1990: 45–69). Again, the purpose of drawing upon these worldviews of freed African Americans is simply to argue for the reasons that explain the continued absence of West African dance drumming in North America. And even though a body of Africanist scholars contested some of Crummell's dicta, his work is unanimously acknowledged as foundational to African nationalism (Appiah 1992: 5).

In the next few paragraphs, I will discuss the leading roles played by three personalities from the late 1930s into 1950s as they introduced African or African-based dance into America, and then how the intensification of Pan-Africanism and the changes in the political climate of America in the 1950s and 1960s enabled and informed Babatunde Olatunji's phenomenal contribution to the presence of West African dance drumming in the United States of America.

The Beginnings of the Presence of West African Drumming and Dance in the United States of America (1930–60s)

The beginnings of the renaissance in West African drumming and dance in the United States of America can be traced to two major developments: (1) the immigration of African drummers to the USA, and (2) the founding of African-derived drumming and dance troupes or companies and, in some cases, schools. Although critical studies on the formative stages of the transplanted genre in the United States have been relatively scanty, the consensus reached in Emery (1988), Herd (1999), Perpener (2001), Herd and Mussa (2002), Sunkett (1993), and Charry (2005) recognizes Dafora, Primus, and Dunham as the most prominent key players who laid the foundations of African-based dance drumming in staged performances. Thus it turned out to be the ingenuity of an African male, an African American female, and a Caribbean female—all of whom are multi-talented, well accomplished, educated, and artistically astute personalities—that ignited a momentum that would change negative predilections that American audiences held about Africa, African culture in general, and dance in particular.

Asadata Dafora Horton (1890–1965) was born a Creole in Freetown, Sierra Leone, a grandson of a liberated African slave originally from Benin, as the name Horton suggests. Born into a well-educated family, young Dafora received a good Western-type education. However, he took a keen interest in the study of African culture, domains ranging from dance to languages, and as such, he could speak more than a dozen African languages/dialects. Dafora furthered his education in Europe, concentrating on musical training with special interest in opera, which he studied in opera houses in Italy. Consistent with his strong interest in choral music and to satisfy his nostalgia for African culture, Dafora attended a performance of West African songs in 1910 at a German nightclub, and as the singing moved him, he stood up and danced to the admiration of the audience. The appreciation of his dancing informed him of how Europeans were ready to receive African dance on a positive note, but most of them were ignorant about thousands of such dance traditions.

So when Dafora immigrated to the United States of America in the 1930s, he formed a dance troupe called the Shogolo Oloba, which he later renamed Federal Theatre African Dance Troupe. It comprised enthusiastic and talented drummers and dancers who were a great blend of Africans and African Americans that performed black dances, mostly ballets. Although the times were hard economically, he garnered support from influential people within the Harlem community. While the African-centeredness of the themes of his dance dramas served as a source of affect for the audiences, Dafora's typical costuming, in which parts of performers' bodies were exposed and decorated along African lines, appealed to the black audiences. For, beyond the beauty of body wear, the beautified bodies were deemed as closer to nature, whereas dance movements simulated specific gestures idiosyncratic of animals and humans. Accordingly, predilections of African "primitivism" gradually eroded as they gave way to audiences' experiences with refreshing dances that were considered to have arousing ideas about the sexuality of the body. His dances gave relief to aficionados who wanted something different from the concentration on dance themes of the individual heroine, as in Martha Graham's works, for example. Attendance for performances of his *Kykunkor* were reportedly overwhelming, necessitating the change to larger performance venues. Some think the masculinity of the male dancers and the general interest in the study of African dance among both American and European researchers informed both the reception and tone of critics' positive reviews.

Thus Dafora's trailblazing work in bringing African drumming and dance to the American stage was a result of many factors, including his combined musical training in opera and knowledge and interest in African dances, culminating in his desire to create awareness of African culture among American audiences. Certainly his ancestral background as a Creole and a descendant of an African slave and the pan-African composition of the group would have been inspiration to some of his fans. He certainly laid the foundations for future dancers and directors. For example, Pearl Primus was reported to have performed in his group, and his role in the establishment of an African Academy of Arts and Research was a feature that subsequent dancers, directors, and choreographers emulated. He traveled extensively with his group throughout the country in his mission to change the negative lenses through which Africa and Africans were viewed.

Katherine Mary Dunham (1909–2006), an American dancer, choreographer, songwriter, author, educator, and activist rose to prominence as the first African American to present indigenous dance on the concert stage and the first black who choreographed for the Metropolitan Opera. From the 1940s to the 1960s she founded and directed a dance company that she self-subsidized, choreographed ninety pieces, and became a leader in dance anthropology or ethno-choreology. To capture the magnitude of her pre-eminence in the field, the *Washington Post* once described her as "Dance's Katherine the Great."

Dunham showed early interest in dance and started dancing at a tender age. She was reported to have organized dance performances while in high school. She studied anthropology at the University of Chicago under Robert Redfield, A. R. Radcliffe-Brown, Edward Sapir, and Bronislaw Malinowski, very prominent scholars, researching the origins of American dances including the cakewalk, Lindy hop, and black bottom. After her graduate work, she received a Julius Rosenwald and a Guggenheim Fellowship to travel to the Caribbean, where she conducted an ethnographic study into their dances and later became focused on the Voudoun religion. Melville Herskovits prepared her for the fieldwork, and it is not surprising that her work bears some resemblance to Herskovits's with respect to her concepts of syncretism in Caribbean folk dance as a symbiosis of European and African dances. These studies engendered the sub-discipline of anthropology that combined intellectual and kinesthetic values and rigors.

Yet other major career determinants of Dunham's include her ballet studies with Mark Turbyfill of Chicago Opera and Ludtrilla Speranzeva of Russia, training that earned her the role of prima ballerina of Chicago Opera. Later Dunham formed the first black ballet company in the USA called Ballet Negres. Critics observed that Dunham had an admirable sense and gift of rhythm, costuming, choreography, dance, and stage presence that she developed to a stage and state of perfection. She danced for stage, clubs, and Hollywood films, and later established a school that perpetuated her dance techniques and aesthetics. Her own dance technique developed from a symbiosis of European, African, African American, and Caribbean dances. Although married to John Thomas Pratt, a rich white man who was her artistic collaborator, and in spite of her fame in America during a historical period characterized by racial discrimination, she never forgot her identity as an

African American. She had witnessed firsthand some degree of discrimination against her on performance tours. She gradually turned into a political activist, at times capitalizing on performance-related situations to voice her disapproval of social injustices of the times. Performing in the South, Dunham allegedly told an audience that if blacks and whites were segregated in the same performance space, then she would not return to that city. On another occasion she refused to perform because blacks were denied tickets. Her most well-known political act was her hunger strike that she took at the age of 82 for forty-seven days as her protest against the U.S. government's alleged discriminatory policies against the people of Haiti, the folk she studied and loved. Thus a degree of pan-Africanism informed her work and the interplay between musical practice, social structure, and discourse that Monson (2007) argues is exemplified by Dunham's career as well.

Pearl Primus (1919–1994), who hailed from Port of Spain, Trinidad and Tobago, was a dancer, choreographer, and ethnographer. These were the expressive modes through which she presented African dance to American audiences as she demystified stereotypical negative presumptions and prejudices about Africa's "savagery." But as Dafora noted earlier and Babatunde Olatunji would discover later, Primus realized that lack of knowledge about African people mainly accounted for these predilections. Accordingly, she presented African dance as worthy of intellectual engagement and artistic performance on the concert stage, also using her artistic and scholarly work to correct some exaggerated and misrepresented views held by Americans regarding waist-centered African dance motives. She thereby provided meaning to these cultural behaviors that she partly studied in Africa with their authentic aesthetic subtleties.

Primus can be described as a dancer by nature and nurture. She was born into an extended family of drummers and initiates of the eclectic Shango/Spiritual Baptist faith, and aware that her maternal grandfather was an Ashanti, from Ghana. Her family moved to New York when she was two. Growing up, she initially showed promise as a smart biology major at both high school and college, as well as an excellent track and field athlete. However, Primus discovered what would become her lifelong career after she joined a New York dance troupe and took keen interest in dances that expressed social criticism. She would soon combine her interest and training in dance with educational sociology and anthropology in her studies at New York University.

Her outstanding 1943 debut dance performance, in which she collaborated with other notable performers, received very positive reviews, including one in the *New York Times* that asserted "she was entitled to her own dance company." In June of the same year she performed to an audience of twenty thousand at the Negro Freedom Rally at Madison Square Garden. Her love for the black race is partially evident in her choreography of Langston Hughes's poem "The Negro Speaks of Rivers," while her earlier research project in 1944 took her to the American South where she visited seventy black churches, studying their dances and other expressive culture, and also identified with some of her informants by picking cotton on weekdays. After her rise to prominence, she was commissioned to choreograph a Broadway production, which she called the *Caribbean Carnival*.

In 1948 Primus was awarded the Rosenwald Fellowship of $4,000, which empowered her to do ethnographic work, studying African dances in Gold Coast, Cameroon, Liberia, Senegal, and Belgian Congo. But beyond the profound practical knowledge and experience she acquired on the dances was her appreciation for the affableness of the African people to her and the extent to which she enjoyed the communal warmth of her ancestral homeland. She rose to preeminence as a leader in the discipline, driven by a pan-Africanist spirit to educate, inform, and entertain through her performances and scholarship. Thus Dafora, Dunham, and Primus paved the way by providing the antecedents for Olatunji's cultural enterprises that would shortly be forthcoming.

Intensified Pan-African Consciousness and West African Dance Drumming in the 1950s into 1960s in the United States

In his introduction to the posthumously published *The Beat of My Drum: An Autobiography* by Babatunde Olatunji, Eric Charry sums up Olatunji's phenomenal contribution in the area of African drumming and dance in the United States: "He instilled pride in generations of African Americans, he stimulated a popular renaissance in African drumming and dance in the United States; he provided cultural education for black youth across the country; he introduced mainstream America to African drumming; and he spread worldwide message of peace and love through drumming" (2005: 19).

Michael Babatunde Olatunji (1927–2003) came to the United States of America in 1950 when he gained admission to Morehouse College, a black institution in Atlanta. After realizing the extent to which Americans were ignorant about Africa, especially its culture, he immediately resolved to embark on a mission to offer the necessary cultural education about his continent and the ancestral homeland of African Americans. Olatunji trusted his leadership strengths and innovative drive over and above his awareness of not coming from *Ayan*, a traditionally recognized lineage of drummers as a Yoruba (Euba 1990: 89–100), to popularize African drumming and dance, an enterprise that would define the rest of his life.

Olatunji relocated to New York with the intent of pursuing graduate study in public administration after graduating from Morehouse College in 1954. However, due to lack of funding he could not fulfill that dream. On the other hand, it was an opportunity for him to realize his ambition of becoming a cultural ambassador of Africa in America. He therefore formed a drum and dance troupe by recruiting a team of African American percussionists and dancers who were ready to experience African drumming and dance. His popularity was boosted by the 1958 job he got and featured in "African Fantasy" with the Radio City Music Hall orchestra. That marked a turning point in his career from the early 1960s on. For example, he had six album releases between 1960 and 1966; made several performance tours; regularly played at famous clubs in New York with jazz gurus including John Coltrane and Art Blakey; and performed at the New York World's Fair in 1964.

In the following paragraphs I discuss events that culminated in Babatunde Olatunji becoming the official pan-African cultural ambassador that he longed to be. Olatunji's life was undergoing transformation during a time of broader social and political processes of change that prized the liberation of all black people of the world. Pan-Africanism thus became a powerful underpinning ideological impetus for this cause, be it through the civil rights movement in America or the political independence of African colonial territories. Before Ghana's independence in 1957, Olatunji was president of the All-African Students Union in the Americas, and a friend to Kwame Nkrumah, a leading Pan-Africanist who studied partly in the United States. It was no coincidence that Nkrumah invited Olatunji to the First All-African Peoples Conference held in Ghana in December 1958. As Olatunji recalls in his biography:

> At the conference, I read my paper proposing the creation of an African cultural center in every major city in America, these would help destroy the stereotypes and ugly images of Africa that persisted in the minds of millions of Americans through Hollywood movies and incredible stories, of the kind that would not encourage anybody to embrace anything African. The cultural centers will disseminate information about the heritage, culture, and traditions of Africa through performances, presentations, classes, and other events. (Olatunji 2005: 137)

In a subsequent meeting Olatunji had with Nkrumah, the prime minister encouraged his friend to return to New York and begin there as the cultural ambassador of Africa. Nkrumah promised providing funding for the establishment of the center and shipping a set of drums that Olatunji requested. Thus during Olatunji's recording of his groundbreaking *Drums of Passion*, one sees his use of a variety of drums including those he received from Ghana and his friend Kwame Nkrumah. In a related conversation I had with Kobla Ladzekpo of UCLA, he remembered Olatunji's interest in the Ewe drums that their group was performing with during the 1958 conference and that he assisted Olatunji in acquiring the Ewe drums after he left for the United States (Personal Correspondence, November, 2010). The photo of the Ghanaian Ewe drums can be seen with the performers at a recording session on (2005: 127), and Olatunji's son Kwame, whom he named after his friend Nkrumah (2005: 128). An advertisement of a performance by John Coltrane held at the Olatunji Center of African Culture (2005: 128) provides another visual evidence of his realized vision. The preceding explains why Olatunji blended *ashiko*, *djembe*, and Ewe drums. Additionally, the release of his *Drums of Passion* in 1960 was timely as it added another dimension and dynamics to instilling pride in African Americans for the richness of their ancestral homeland's cultural heritage.

Today, the cultural diversity of Africa is a commonplace theme in a variety of culture-related discourse about that continent. This deliberate creation of awareness of the diversity and particularistic nature of African music cultures may be viewed as a reflection and result of an ethnomusicological methodology in which a shift occurred from a period marked by paradigmatic emphasis on universalities to that of cultural relativity. Also, the de-homogenization of African music cultures constitutes a correction of a previously and generally held perception of Africa by non-Africans, a necessary education about Africa as not a monolithic entity.

Naturally, one path to knowledge about ethnic diversity in African cultures is dance drumming; and consequently, the Pan-African spirit with which Olatunji perpetuated West African drumming and dance in the United States has been viewed by some as a constraint to the correct understanding of the plurality of African dance drumming traditions. Considering that some current ethnomusicologists expect dance drumming from different regions of the continent to be introduced and taught so that American students can learn more about the specificities of other traditions, and that they will not settle for the sufficiency of one or two ethnic groups representing Africa in a pan-African sense, it is reasonable for a pluralist to think along such lines. However, a historical contextualization of Olatunji's agency, as I have earlier explained, offers an understanding and a deeper appreciation of his role as a cultural bearer of the Pan-African mantle.

It is unimaginable for a passionate and patriotic African studying and/or working in America from the mid-1950s into the mid-1960s to be apathetic to the powerful movements and consciousness of Pan-Africanism, a discourse that informed the agency of many well-meaning blacks across the globe. As such, Babatunde Olatunji's cultural legacy was primarily underpinned by the philosophy and its emerging political landscape. Yet, he also contributed in noteworthy ways toward the process of pan-Africanism. Truly, all Olatunji's influences interplayed with Pan-Africanism: his staged African dance drumming performances; teaching drumming and dance to diasporic Africans; the establishment of the Institute of Culture; experimental and collaborative work with key jazz musicians; love for music and instruments from different West African groups, leading to his collaboration with Camara; and his recordings, especially *Drums of Passion*. Babatunde Olatunji is remembered as perhaps the greatest cultural vanguard of the Pan-African movement. He led a cultural renaissance in West African drumming and dance that affected both blacks and whites in America.

Africa Speaks, America Responds is not only the title of a 1956 album on Decca Records, but also the advocacy of another West African expatriate drummer whose forte was the use of African drums in jazz drumming. Kofi Ghanaba ("the Ghanaian child"), also known as Guy Warren and Odomankoma Kyrema ("the divine drummer"), did not contribute to West African dance drumming, the focus of this book. However, he deserves mention for his innovative experiments and collaborations with many preeminent American jazz musicians, the tenacity with which he lived and pushed his belief that jazz would become more African American if musicians could draw on African drums, and the fact that he is well respected in jazz circles even though his ideas were not fully embraced. He was a drummer par excellence, a composer, organizer, artistic and cultural visionary, and a friend of Kwame Nkrumah who shared similar views on the projection and revitalization of African cultural practices in Africa and beyond. Royal Hartigan, an American jazz drummer and a scholar who studied West African drumming at Wesleyan University, conducted research on Ghanaba in 1996 in Ghana and wrote a brief but a powerful article on him. Hartigan lists the jazz gurus with whom Ghanaba performed and gives information on his recordings: "[Ghanaba] had contact or performed with many jazz innovators, such as Duke Ellington, Billy Strayhorn, Charlie Parker, Lester Young, Thelonious

Monk, Billie Holiday, Max Roach, Buhaina Art Blakey, and Louis Armstrong. He subsequently recorded for RCA Victor, Regal, Columbia, and his own Safari label" (Hartigan 1999: 147).

Ghanaba replaced the normal jazz drum set with Akan (Ghanaian courtly) set of drums:

> two large *fontomfrom* placed on their side and played with foot pedals as bass drums, an *apentemma* directly facing him in the position of the snare drum, and two *fontomfrom* and two[8] *atumpan* to the right and left on stands as toms. *Fontomfrom* are huge, long, deep-toned master drums, *apentemma* are medium-sized hand drums, and *atumpan* are large deep-toned master drums, the talking drums of the Akan. Ghanaba uses the two long curved[9] wooden sticks that are traditionally used on *fontomfrom* and *atumpan* in this new context. (1999: 147)

There seems to be some symbolism in Ghanaba's choice of this set of regal drums rather than other Ghanaian drums.[10] I argue that they add a kingly aura to either the genre or its performers, and the artifacts in themselves would have been a spectacle for American audiences during performances. More importantly, the different kind of sonorities that these drums produced constituted a more likely reason for which jazz musicians recorded with Ghanaba. Yet for the purpose of this book and in the context of Ghanaba's knowledge about the suppression of drumming in the past history of African Americans, he could be making a silent statement as he advocated the use and resurrection of drums from Africa, although that would imply another suppression of all the innovations that have gone into the development of the jazz drum set.

The performance tours of national dance troupes of independent African nation-states made a phenomenal impact on American audiences beginning in the 1960s. The Les Ballets Africains of Guinea made the most profound mark regarding the beauty of choreographed dances, costuming, dancing, vibrant djembe drumming, and dazzling performances of other Mande instruments including the balo and kora. As noted by Charry (2005: 10–11), the migration of Ladji Kamara (1923–2004), the virtuosic master djembe drummer, to the United States of America in the late 1960s led to collaborations including those with Dunham and later Olatunji. Also, the move culminated in Kamara's founding of a djembe school in New York. Kamara is recognized as the "father of djembe movement" that has spread and laid the foundations for djembe becoming the most popular African instrument in the world. Performance tours of the Ghana National Dance Ensemble are also noteworthy, as some of the early master drummers later became founders and/or directors of a number of American university ensembles that I will discuss in subsequent chapters.

Absence of West African Dance Drumming in the American Academy until 1964

Writing on "Alternatives to African-derived Drums and Drumming" elsewhere, I noted "The appeal of step dancing as a characteristic Greek activity of black students can partly be linked to the strong presence of stamping in several African dances" (Dor 2006: 160). Also, the rhythmic sensibilities and expressions of black students during their performances of gospel music constitute both Africanisms—survival of handclapping, but a substitute for drumming. However, in her term paper for my graduate seminar on Diasporic African Music Cultures and a subsequent presentation at the Society for Ethnomusicology's Southeastern and Caribbean Regional Chapter conference in 2012, Kendra Jenkins, an African American, drew my attention to another form of drumming and dancing in the American academy: the drum lines of Historically Black Colleges and Universities. Drawing on her previous membership of both the Alcorn State University "Tower of Power" and the Ole Miss African Drum and Dance Ensemble, after comparing the two genres she recognized their common characteristic features to include polyrhythm, circular rhythm, repetition, call-and-response, the African conception of music and dance as a symbiotic art, and oral transmission of both traditions. But while the practice of drum lines in the American academy may predate the inception of West African drumming in American universities, drum lines are part of the marching band tradition that developed out of a different historical trajectory. Accordingly, I argue that drum lines are never a continuum of West African dance drumming traditions, as Jenkins arguably presupposes. Rather, the Africanisms in the drum lines of these black colleges must be viewed as an African American appropriation of a Western musical tradition that they have domesticated or indigenized with their stylistic nuances. According to James McLead, a well-informed band director, this innovative indigenization process started in the late 1970s when a few West African dance-drumming ensembles were already established. Further, newer African drumming traditions in the diaspora could have partly influenced this process. Admittedly, drum lines in black colleges deserve a critical study. However, the absence of emblematic phenomena pertaining to Africa and African America is indeed a protracted one that merits interpretation.

Pervasive prevailing intellectual philosophies, zeitgeist, worldviews, and other discursive landscapes of any given historical period in the life experiences of a people partly shape what is studied in the academy. James Campbell has observed the extent to which European and American academies had neglected the study of African history for centuries (2006: 228). As a result, Campbell notes that American university course offerings delayed or completely denied generations of African American intellectuals the knowledge and learning experiences they yearned to have about their ancestral homeland. Campbell cites Du Bois as saying, "When I was a boy in school there was no reference in my courses or textbooks to the History of Africa," and that Du Bois further remembered, "nor did Africa feature in any of the daily newspapers that he read religiously." Yet the deliberate exclusion of Africa from programs at Harvard and the University of Berlin, as Campbell notes, did not affect only African Americans and Africans. It left a void in the scope of knowledge acquired from such universities even by well-respected European and American thinkers, and as Campbell argues, the "neglect of African history [in such universities] had the force of a philosophical proposition: Africa, in Hegel's famous dictum, was land without history, a place that had contributed nothing to human civilizations." Although a multitude of scholars, including a body of Africanists, have debunked Hegel's dictum that was generated by the German's deductive reasoning rather than inductive and empirical evidence, he is not to blame completely. For, had African history been taught in those universities, such polemic assertions might not have occurred in the first place, and this great thinker might not have exposed his ignorance in that specific area.

But thanks go to Cheikh Anta Diop, the Senegalese scholar whose work has yielded a new historiography of Africa. In writing on "Diopian historiography," Molefi Kete Asante acknowledges that "He [Diop] established conclusively that the ancient Egyptians were black-skinned Africans and that the origin of civilization must be traced to the Nile River" (Asante 2007: 118). Similarly, the "Black Kingdoms of the Nile," Disc 1 of Henry Louis Gates's *Wonders of the African World* video, corroborates Diop's position as Gates bases his conclusions on the study of the Nubia, who are black (Gates 2000).

However, given the continued representation of Africa stigmatized by some as a "dark continent" full of "heathens," who should fully blame the American academy when writers did not paint a picture that would motivate and inspire the study of anything relating to Africa? The perceptual norms with which Westerners compared themselves to Africa and Africans, with stark differentiations between the civilized and the primitive, or the enlightened and the savage, constituted an ideological veil that hindered any early consideration of studying phenomena relating to Africa in the academy. In her contextualized and multi-paradigmatic study of jazz in the late 1950s and early 1960s, Monson (2007) has, for example, explicitly discussed the centrality of interplay among any kind of practice, social structures and systems, as well as overarching discourse necessary for a deeper understanding of jazz's situated role during the civil rights movement and Africa's liberation cause of that era. Monson's synchronic study spans only a decade. And yet, the parallel to be drawn here is that in a diachronic survey of centuries' absence of phenomena on Africa in the American academy, only major changes in the prejudices and predilections held about Africa can predict a probable embrace of studying Africa and Africans in American universities.

Another presumption that Westerners held against Africans was that they were not as knowledgeable as other people. This mentality of intellectual or rational supremacy and superiority of one race over the other extended even to African Americans. But James Campbell observes that Franz Boas, for example, "In a germinal 1894 essay, 'Human Faculty as Determined by Race,' denied that African Americans were a 'lower type of humans,' . . . arguing that observed differences in accomplishment were best explained, not by biology, but in terms of social and cultural factors. . . . Boas [thus] challenged [and debunked] prevailing ideas of fixed racial inheritance—the so-called natural limits of the racial mind" (Campbell 2006: 193). The preceding resonates with the kind of prejudices that had to be corrected through partial efforts of researchers—here, anthropologists, whose major preoccupation had been the study and sharing of findings about the "other."

Taking after anthropologists, ethnomusicological research methodology until in recent decades also had privileged the other. Accordingly, American and European ethnomusicologists concentrated on studying the other through various field research projects that last years, during which music culture, other forms of behavior, and languages of the researched were acquired. Ethnomusicologists predicated their studies of the other on the need to cover other musical traditions and types (world music) beyond notated Western art music, which had been the preoccupation of other caliber of musicologists. Although sharing research findings about the other was not without its attendant prejudices—at times evident in comparative terms including "the primitive," "exotic music," "savage," and "illiterate"—both anthropologists and ethnomusicologists have gradually refined their descriptive terminology and attitudes with greater sensitivity, perhaps after recognizing the "nobility" in the cultures of the so-called "savages," the musicality of the hitherto "primitive" men, or the ingenuity in the creativity of "barbarous" musicians.[11] Thus conducting research and sharing only through written reports are no longer satisfying enough for most ethnomusicologists. Rather, participant observation and learning to perform musical instruments and to dance within frameworks of mentor-and-student relationships have opened new worlds of understanding and appreciation of the other's music for many foreign researchers. Accordingly, sharing thenceforth includes performances that researchers have learned during field studies.

Today, it is very revealing to see how far some ethnomusicologists have come in acknowledging the richness in local knowledge of the other, as partly suggested in the titles of books including John Blacking's *How Musical Is Man*, an assertion reached after the author encountered Venda music; Ruth Stone's *Let the Inside Be Sweet* on the Kpelle of Liberia; Tim Rice's *May It Feel Your Soul* on Bulgarian music; and Jacqueline DjeDje's *Touching the Spirits* on Fulbe, Huasa, and Dagbamba fiddle music. These changing landscapes and attitudes of American researchers have yielded unprecedented representation of the other with a fairer, more balanced, and positive reflexivity in which both the researched and the researcher are regarded as equally rational beings. This personal appraisal in no way suggests a completely satisfactory representation of African music in the academy. Yet, although we still have a long way to go, it is important to acknowledge the long way that we have traveled thus far.

In tracing the pivotal changes from 1954 to 1967 that culminated in the ascendancy of world-consciousness and world-mindedness during post–World War II America, Teresa Volk (1998) acknowledges the advisory roles that Charles Seeger, David McAllister, Mantle Hood, Elizabeth May, Kwabena Nketia, William Malm, and other key ethnomusicologists played in providing direction for multiculturalism in music education in America. Additionally, however, she also thematizes factors including the civil rights movement, black power and nationalism, desegregation of schools, roles of professional associations, international conferences, and symposia, and the quest for global peace and understanding as important change-effecting initiatives. Yet, newer challenges of intensified study of Africa in the American academy are emerging, especially the sonic mass media that plays a dual role (both positive and negative) in the context of globalization.

As an African, I will be the first to admit the problems with which my continent is confronted and the challenges that need strategic addressing. Poverty, disease, wars, genocide, and, in some cases, lack of integrity of leadership and governance are plaguing Africa's progress. Nevertheless, Africa has a great history of civilizations, Africans are as knowledgeable as other people of the world, and African music genres are compellingly very rich. It is therefore very disconcerting to observe that the American media mainly portrays negative images about Africa as though nothing strikingly good remains in that part of the world. In a casual conversation with a reputable African American ethnomusicologist regarding the lack of interest in Africa shown by the younger generation of African Americans, we both agreed that the media has played a major role in this perception. The media has taken over the stigmatization discussed earlier in this chapter. The American youth who depend on the media to assist them in imagining places they do not know tend to believe the representations they are offered, thereby being discouraged from exploring and pursuing possibilities of visiting or learning more about Africa. Several students and researchers who have visited Africa have discovered something special about the people of that continent, far beyond what the media continues to portray.

In the context of the subject of this book, West African drumming and dance is an aspect of Africa's sublime creative and expressive art that is available to American students. In the following chapters I discuss the implications of this genre in its multiple ramifications for various caliber of people. Accordingly, absence has partly given way to the presence of West African drumming and dance, specifically in the American academy, where the proliferation of West African dance drumming in our universities and other colleges is gaining ascendancy and currency, and thus gradually becoming an engaging theme for discussion in the classroom, conferences, but as audiences' source of affect in concert auditoria.

2

SELECTED UNIVERSITY ENSEMBLES

History, Resources, Repertoire, Teaching, Learning, Performance(s), and Reception

This chapter provides narratives on the West African dance drumming programs at University of California at Los Angeles (UCLA), Wesleyan University (Middletown, Connecticut), University of California at Berkeley, York University (Toronto), University of Toronto, University of Pittsburgh, Tufts University (Medford, Massachusetts), Massachusetts Institute of Technology (MIT), University of Mississippi (Ole Miss, Oxford, Mississippi), and Binghamton University, New York. But before discussing these selected institutions I visited as part of my ethnographic study, I provide information regarding other colleges that have African dance drumming ensembles, year founded, founding and current directors, and countries from which ensembles' frequently performed genres and repertoires originate. This information, which was gleaned from responses from many members of the African Music Section of SEM, is contained in Table 1.

UNIVERSITY OF CALIFORNIA AT LOS ANGELES (UCLA)

Each time I listen to or read narratives about the beginnings of West African drumming and dance at UCLA related by trusted informants, I sense the joy of initiative, accomplishment, recollection of the pleasant past, and participation in a historic venture—both for the early stages and the sustenance of the ensemble. This feeling was most intense when I visited Los Angeles and had separate revealing conversations with Jacqueline DjeDje and Kobla Ladzekpo. DjeDje is a UCLA alumna who still had vivid memories of her teachers, colleagues, and the prevailing academic terrain. She also is a former

Table 1: Data on African Music and Dance Ensembles in North American Universities and Other Colleges

Academic Institution	Ensemble or Course Name	Year Founded	Founding Director	Current [2011] Director	Genres by Country	Credit
University of California at Los Angeles (UCLA)	West African Music and Dance [Ensemble]	1964	Robert Ayitee, Robert Bonsu	Kobla Ladzekpo	Ghana, Togo, Benin	Yes
Columbia University, New York		1964	Kobla Ladzekpo		Ghana	Yes
Wesleyan University, Middletown, CT	West African Drumming and Dance [Ensemble]	1968	Abraham Adzinya	Abraham Adzinya	Ghana	Yes
University of California, Berkeley	African Music and Dance [Ensemble]	1973	Christopher K. Ladzekpo	C. K. Ladzekpo	Ghana, Togo, Benin	Yes
University of Toronto, Canada	West African Drumming and Dance [Ensemble]	1974	Russell Hartenberger	Kwasi Dunyo	Ghana	Yes
Tufts University, Medford, MA	Kiniwe African Music and Dance [Ensemble]	1979	David Locke	Nani Agbeli	Ghana	Yes
Oberlin Conservatory of Music	Oberlin Mandinka [Ensemble]	1977	Roderic Knight	Roderic Knight till 2006	Gambia, Mali (Jaliyaa)	Yes
York University, Toronto, Canada	West African Drumming and Dance [Ensemble]	2000	Robert Simms	Kwasi Dunyo, Anna Melnikoff, L. Graves, I. Akrong	Ghana, Mali, Guinea, Burkina Faso	Yes
University of Pittsburgh, PA	West African Music and Dance Ensemble	1983	Willie Anku	Charles Lwanga	Ghana, Congo, Uganda	Yes
University of Bowling Green, OH	Afro-Caribbean [Ensemble]	1990	Steven Cornelius	Olman Piedra, Sidra Lawrence	Ghana, Nigeria, Cuba, Kenya, South Africa	Yes
University of St. Thomas, St. Paul, MN	African Music and Dance Ensemble	1998	Sowah Mensah	Sowah Mensah	Ghana, Benin, Congo, Senegal	No
University of Virginia, Charlottesville	UVA African Music and Dance Ensemble	1996	Michelle Kisliuk	Michelle Kisliuk	Central African Republic, Ghana, Togo	Yes
Wabash College, Crawfordsville, IN	Wamidan World Music [Ensemble]	2000	James Makubuya	James Makubuya	Uganda, Kenya, Ghana, South Africa	No
Vanderbilt University, Nashville, TN	Sankofa African Performing Ensemble	2000	Greg Barz	Kwame Ahima	Ghana	Yes
Indiana University, Bloomington, IN	African Music and Dance Ensemble	2004	Sleasby Matiwre	Bernard Woma	Ghana, Zimbabwe, Benin	Yes
University of Rochester, NY	West African Drumming Ensemble	2011	Fana Bangoura	Fana Bangoura	Guinea	Yes
University of Alberta, Canada	West African Music Ensemble	1999	Michael Frishkopf	Robert Kpogo	Ghana	Yes

Figure 2.1 Schoenberg Music Building, UCLA, home of the first West African music and dance ensemble in a North American university. [Photo by George Dor, July 2007]

African music ensemble member, an African American who did her fieldwork in Ghana, became a UCLA faculty member, and was the chair of the Department of Ethnomusicology when I interviewed her. How cannot such a consultant be patriotic about her alma mater? Similarly, Ladzekpo had also taught at UCLA as an indigenous Ghanaian master/mother drummer for more than three decades.

Other memorable moments that concern the ensemble include the Africa Meets North America Symposium held in October 2009 at UCLA. It offered participants the opportunity to recollect, celebrate, and revitalize the agency and collaborations of Mantle Hood and Kwabena Nketia, as well as of Klaus Wachsmann, who invigorated the "building of bridges" between Africa and the so-called West at UCLA. Of those three, Nketia, blessed with longevity, was the only one present at the symposium. I personally considered it very symbolic that my paper presentation at AMNA on this very book project took place in the Gamelan Room,[1] and especially when at a stage I had to point at the green-painted *Atsimewu*[2] that Togbui Kobla Ladzekpo helped Mantle Hood acquire in 1963 from Ghana. Some audience members even stood up to have a better glimpse at this historic instrument as Ladzekpo said a few words to legitimize the data I shared.

Figure 2.2 Kobla and Beatrice Ladzekpo in *Kente* and leaning on the *Atsimewu*. [Photo from Ladzekpos]

UCLA houses about a dozen world music ensembles, since 1964 including the West African dance drumming ensemble. Ladzekpo and other informants confirm that West African drumming was introduced at Columbia University in the same year. Though private establishments, Asadata Dafora Horton's 1943 African Academy of Arts and Research, and the Olatunji Center for African Culture, which he founded in New York about 1960, were the most notable institutions for the teaching and learning of West African dance drumming that predate the inception of the genre at UCLA (Charry 2005: 9; Olatunji 2005: 151). However, the introduction of African drumming and dance into a recognized public American university was a product of the agency of ethnomusicologists and Ghanaian drummers. Recalling the formative stages of this campus tradition at UCLA, however, one has to pay tribute to Robert Anane Ayitee and Robert Osei Bonsu, the first two master drummers who gave instructions in Ewe and Asante dance drumming, respectively. According to Schrag and DjeDje, Kwasi Badu, Hood's drum teacher in Ghana, replaced Ayitee and Bonsu in 1969, and Ladzekpo took over in 1976.

Given the cultural background of the previous and current directors of UCLA's ensemble, the repertoire has been primarily Akan and Ewe, as evident in the drums I saw when DjeDje led me into the Gamelan Room in 2007 and during my return to UCLA in 2009. Akan instruments suggest dances including *Kete*, *Fontonfrom*, *Adowa*, and *Sekyi*, while Ewe dances including *Agbadza*, *Gahu*, *Atsiagbekor*, and *Adzogbo*, to mention a few, have been taught, learned, and performed over the years. Yet as exemplified in the performances of the ensemble during AMNA and a track of UCLA's West African Music Ensemble's current DVD, some of the old Ewe dances taught by Ladzekpo such as the Adzogbo, originated from among the Beninese Ewe.

Figure 2.3 Yeko Ladzekpo, Kobla's daughter and understudy on the *Atsimewu*. [Photo from Yeko Ladzekpo]

Thus such dances invoke broader historical, transnational, and geo-cultural symbols for the Ewe of West Africa. Evidence from the same DVD reveals two kinds of collaborations in which the ensemble director teamed up with students to choreograph a combined piece "Agahu," inspired by airplanes—a symbiosis of the Gahu dance with another dance from the Caribbean. Further, Sulley, a Dagbon musician and former master drummer of the Ghana Dance Ensemble, featured as a guest artist in this concert, doing a solo dance and then performing the *Damba Takai* dance of the Dagbamba of Northern Ghana, which he had taught the students. The following is an excerpt from my 2007 interview with DjeDje regarding the repertoire of the ensemble under Ladzekpo.

GD: What kind of dances? Primarily Ewe, or did he teach dances from other parts of West Africa?
JD: The course is called "Music and Dance of Ghana." So, it is primarily dances from Ghana. But when he performs, his ensemble, he focuses on the music of West Africa. In addition to Ewe, he does something from Nigeria, something from Benin, and some traditions from

Figure 2.4 Class session with Kobla Ladzekpo in UCLA's Gamelan Room. [Photo by John Price and Ethan Fox, October 2012]

Northern Ghana, particularly the Dagbamba. So he gives them a broad experience in drumming and dancing. Originally, it was his wife, Beatrice, who was also a member of the early Ghana Dance Ensemble. She came here, participated, and worked with him. But more recently, he now has his daughter who is a good dancer, so she now assists him.

GD: Was there ever any East African element of drumming or music at UCLA?

JD: Well, taking advantage of our students, whatever they could share with us. Actually there was a performer of Yoruba *dundun* music, a student by the name of Tunji Vidal, from Yorubaland, and now a professor at Ife University, and so when he was here he used to teach those who were interested in *dundun* drumming. The same can be said for James Makubuya. He was here for several years working on his Ph.D., and he was an outstanding performer. We had a course that was offered so that he could teach students interested in the music and dance of East Africa.

Like many other African ensembles, UCLA's regular performances include end-of-semester concerts. The 500-capacity auditorium is reportedly always full during performances by the West African music ensemble. Two

Figure 2.5 The 1963 *Atsimewu* that Kobla Ladzekpo helped Mantle Hood acquire. [Photo by John Price and Ethan Fox, October 2012]

observations emerged from this trend of reception and patronage of this and other world music ensembles. First, Mantle Hood's dream of the ensembles partly serving the immediate cultural communities has been realized and sustained. Second, the enthusiasm of aficionados during West African dance drumming concerts poses the question of whether reception should play a role in deciding what the priorities of music departments should be in this era of globalization. As a tradition, UCLA's world music ensembles take advantage of the spring weather and give outdoor performances dubbed Spring Festival, which creates a different flavor and avenue for intensified interactions among students, staff, and faculty. The West African ensemble has featured in performances during the African Year, which DjeDje initiated with the intent of creating increased awareness of African music at UCLA and beyond. Also, the ensemble always performs during conferences hosted by or at UCLA. As would be expected of such a unique campus ensemble, the ensemble has featured during other campus events, as well as off-campus events at which they have been invited to perform.

During my 2009 visit to UCLA, I attended a class session of the West African music and dance ensemble. That class consisted of about twenty students; Kobla Ladzekpo, the director, was playing more of a supervisory role because his daughter Yeko was doing the teaching. I was not surprised because I have heard about her deputized role already. Rather, it made me appreciate the flexibility that Ladzekpo attached to gendered musical roles—a woman teaching African drums and playing lead-drumming role. DjeDje had every reason to praise Yeko on merit for her talent and efforts. Moreover, DjeDje recollected how Kwasi Badu did not allow female students to drum in his early 1970s UCLA ensemble, as he rigidly adhered to the Akan tradition.

JD: I was primarily interested in Ashanti music because here at UCLA, we had a man by the name Kwesi Badu, who taught drumming and dance, and that was all [Akan ethnic dances] we did.
GD: So you learned to drum?
JD: No, I should say during that time, women did not drum!
GD: Okay!
JD: Because we were told that that was not what women were supposed to do. However, there was one lady who was part of our class, and she insisted that she should learn to drum and he allowed her to learn to drum. But the majority of us women only played the rattle and danced. But we sort of accepted that because we felt that was the way it was done. So that was what I did at the Masters level. (Interview, July 2007)

But for more than three decades, female students now learn to play all the supporting instruments of the ensemble including drums, although they may primarily dance and not drum during major performances.

West African drumming was well integrated into the programs at UCLA. DjeDje shared: "When you are a graduate student, I think you must have at least two years of performance. When you are at the undergraduate level, you have to have at least four years of performance in one ensemble every quarter" (DjeDje, interview, July 2007). Certainly, students have several performance options to choose from, and as DjeDje introduced me to the Gamelan Room, she said:

We have a Javanese gamelan, we also have some instruments from Cambodia. We have instruments from India, instruments from Thailand, instruments from Latin America. And we have experts teaching all these instruments, including sitar and tabla from India. The whole

Figure 2.6 Jacqueline Cogdell DjeDje and George Dor at UCLA. [Photo from George Dor, July 2007]

idea of bi-musicality, that is what Mantle Hood was all about; to put it to practice rather than only theory, you have to have master musicians to teach it. This is our African music section, even though we call it Gamelan room, we have instruments from everywhere, Afro-Cuban instruments, which are here, that is the other reason why we are looking for more space. We have twelve different world music ensembles that are offered. That does not include the jazz ensemble. (Interview, July 2007)

Yet, the novelty that UCLA has many world music ensembles comes with its challenges. From my personal observations, the main challenge for UCLA's African ensemble, perhaps like for those of other world music ensembles, is the difficulty of expansion. The Gamelan Room serves a dozen ensembles with the same space responsible for housing different instruments. I presume space may be a problem assuming UCLA intends to expand its West African dance-drumming program. Also, the use of the same space means distribution of rehearsal time with other ensembles. The issue of time becomes compounded and crucial when one remembers that UCLA operates within the term system rather than the semester system; since a term is shorter than a semester, less can be learned or perfected than would be the case within the longer semester span. Notwithstanding these personal observations, I commend the agency of all people responsible for the sustenance of the ensemble that has meant so much to several people. The significance of this ensemble will become clearer through further discussion in subsequent chapters. It would be hoped that UCLA continues to maintain and support this ensemble as a historic first of its kind in a North American university.

WESLEYAN UNIVERSITY, MIDDLETOWN, CONNECTICUT

Wesleyan University has one of the most consistent and vibrant West African drumming and dance programs in the United States. Although Abraham Adzinya is the most important player in Wesleyan's African ensemble since 1968, when he first taught there as a visiting performer and instructor, I have been unable to interview him, to put it subtly. Accordingly, information on Wesleyan in this discussion has been based on my separate interviews with Eric Charry and Samuel Nyamuame, the Abraham Adzinya Tribute Concert CD (which Charry gave me), complementary information from David Locke and Russell Hartenberger, who both are Wesleyan alumni, and my personal observations of the roles of Wesleyan alumni percussionists and dancers who participated in the concert organized by SEM's African Music Section during the 53rd Annual Conference of the Society for Ethnomusicology, held in 2008 in Middletown and hosted by Wesleyan University. Eric Charry, the key consultant for this section, became a member of the music faculty in 1998, chair of the music department from 2001 to 2004, and although he joined the faculty about two decades after the inception of the African drumming and dance program, he shared much about the history of the West African dance drumming program. Additionally, as an Africanist Charry had taught some Mande music, the focal area of his research. He formed the Mande ensemble in which various students comprised the djembe group, *balofon* group, a few other students learned to play the kora, and others still the guitar in domesticated Guinean and Malian stylistic veins (Interview, December 2007). However, his ensemble was short-lived, and as Charry explained, his intent to form a Mande ensemble was not to compete with the well-established Ghanaian dance drumming ensemble but to create awareness of other West African musical genres there.

According to Charry, David McAlester and Richard Winslow were the brains behind the establishment of the music program at Wesleyan in the 1960s. A distinction was drawn between Western music and experimental music as the two focuses of the program. The experimental component was

Figure 2.7 Abraham Adzinya and Samuel Elikem Nyamuame, directors of the West African Music and Dance Ensemble after fall concert, December 2007. [Photo by George Dor]

intended to help composition students explore new sonic resources and effects. By the early 1970s, the department housed Indonesian gamelan, a jazz ensemble, and other ensembles playing music from China, Japan, India, and the Caribbean. Charry locates the continuity of the West African drumming and dance ensemble in what he describes as a "small school with a big music program." He notes that it is one of the older ethnomusicology programs after UCLA and the University of Washington, Seattle, and that it has produced both American and international graduates.[3] Specifically, Freeman Donkor, a dancer, later joined Adzinya to make the Ghanaian dance drumming even stronger.

Factors that made the Wesleyan West African drumming program unique include the fact that, while with most university African ensembles the same director teaches both drumming and dance, and the sustenance of the ensemble is solely within the music department, the dance department of Wesleyan has cross-listed courses on West African dance drumming and was responsible for the employment of Freeman Donkor, who collaborated with Abraham Adzinya. So dance was a core part of the program. It must be stated that the dance program by itself is well developed with non-Western genres from Indonesia and China, in addition to the Ghanaian. Accordingly, one person teaches drumming while the other dance. When Donkor died, Helen Mensah was hired to replace him, and Mensah had given instructions for about a decade until her retirement in 2008.

Figure 2.8 Some Akan, Ewe, and Dagbon musical instruments in storage. [Photo by George Dor, December 2007]

The West African dance drumming program traditionally attracts a huge student enrollment with music and dance majors as well as non-majors normally participating in the preliminary course. For the masters and doctoral programs in ethnomusicology, two semesters of different non-Western performance courses are required. Some students are attracted to Wesleyan because of the performance component of the program, and some take gamelan and African drumming for three years. Anyone writing a thesis on an African, Caribbean, or Latin American theme would like to remain in the African ensemble, because Adzinya, according to Charry, teaches both the artistic and the cultural elements of drumming. He teaches three levels of the course, two courses per semester. Both Samuel Nyamuame and Charry confirm that the beginning level has an enrollment limit of thirty-five, but always has a long waiting list. Hence the administration recognizes that it is a popular course in terms of numbers. While the intermediate may have an average of fifteen students, the advanced level of the course may consist of about five serious students, some who end up going to Ghana on study-abroad programs.

During end-of-semester concerts, intermediate and advanced students mainly do the drumming; however, all participants perform dances meant for their courses and contribute to singing, clapping, or other organizational

Figure 2.9 Elikem Nyamuame with some of the Ghanaian drums. [Photo by George Dor, December 2007]

aspects of the performance. Concert tickets for the 425 seats are normally sold out. The concert usually lasts two hours, at times without an intermission, and one thing that fascinates people who know the amount of work involved in both the preparation toward the concert and the concert itself is the physical fitness of all the instructors, even some as old as sixty. The repertoire is primarily Ghanaian dances from the various ethnic groups including the Akan, Ewe, Ga, and Dagbomba. It may be helpful to say that all Adzinya, Donkor, and Mensah were members of the Ghana National Dance Ensemble, and thus replicated the model acquired from Ghana in the Wesleyan African ensemble's repertoire. The concert I attended and the drums I saw featured the normal canons of Akan, Ewe, Dagbamba, and Ga dances.

There seems to be some dances that are always taught while a few set of dances are rotated so as to ensure that some variety in concert programs is achieved. For example, Gahu, the Anlo Ewe social dance, is one of the favorites at Wesleyan, performed normally as the concert program's finale that draws participation from the audience when they are invited to the stage to dance. While continuity in a program is a positive thing and new participating students will find their dances quite fresh, faculty and staff who work at the institution for decades may become familiar with the normal concert

Figure 2.10 Eric Charry interviewed by George Dor, December 2007. [Photo from George Dor]

items that are likely not to motivate them if newer dances are not featured. Admittedly, newer choreographies of the same dance or new and gorgeous costumes may add refreshing dynamics to the repeat of the same dances performed during previous concerts. Normally, visiting artists inject a sense of anxiety in audiences. However, parents, family, and friends of students have unflinching support for their parties during performances. Although the replacement of Adzinya by Nyamuame during the former's sabbatical leave offered the program new dances and choreography that enthused long serving faculty and staff, Adzinya's permanent position as an adjunct faculty is very appreciated by many for the development of the program. For elsewhere, programs of some schools depend on visiting professors, whereby artists come and go.

In spite of the great Ghanaian drumming and dance program at Wesleyan, Charry wishes other West African dance drumming traditions were taught at Wesleyan, including, of course, his area, Mande. The Ghanaian drumming in the American academy has become a hegemonic tradition. Was it simply an issue of language of communication, or the agency of Ghanaian ethnomusicologists or master drummers, or where American researchers first conducted their fieldwork? Is the technique of djembe hand drumming more challenging than kpanlogo hand drumming, for example? Perhaps working together in a Ghanaian ensemble of multiple drums and each percussionist contributing to the composite interlocking and polyrhythmic structure is more attractive to people when they experience their communality through creativity. These are some of the questions I will be addressing in chapter 6.

Nevertheless, Charry spoke highly of the drumming program at Wesleyan, as he thinks it serves as the entry point to learning about Africa for most students by "initiating students into an African experience." Students committed and genuinely devoted to the West African drumming course continue and develop the experience into integral aspects of their future careers as performers, teachers, composers, and/or researchers. In chapter 6 I will discuss the role of the presence of West African drumming on our university campuses in the conduct of research on African rhythm, drumming, and related themes, and the extent to which dissertations, and in some cases other scholarly works, had their foundations or inspirations in drumming courses. These theses include those by Hewitt Pantaleoni, Russell Hartenberger, David Locke, and Royal Hartigan. The best overview of West African dance drumming at Wesleyan under Adzinya is the befitting concert that his students organized to honor, celebrate, and acknowledge his impact and influence in an indelible way.

UNIVERSITY OF CALIFORNIA, BERKELEY (UC)

An overarching theme and attitude that I noticed during my two interviews at Berkeley in July 2007 is what I may call "a chain of gratitude." During my interview with Professor Emeritus Olly Wilson, I thanked him for his role in founding the West African drumming and dance program at Berkeley. His response was that I should rather thank Christopher K. Ladzekpo (CK), who agreed to begin the program in the first place. Wilson also added that he remained indebted to the Guggenheim Foundation for the fellowship that made his field travel to Ghana possible. In any case, I reminded this accomplished but humble personality that it was his choice to go to Ghana, and his idea to begin the program as well as his followup initiatives to bring CK to Berkeley that cannot escape notice and commendation.

As I interviewed CK later and similarly thanked him for his role in founding, sustaining and growing the program, he also told me that I should rather thank Professor Wilson for the reasons I have stated earlier. Yet, CK extended his response and further remarked that he did not deserve any

Figure 2.11 Prof. Emeritus Olly Wilson, during an interview session at his home. [Photo by George Dor, July 2007]

gratitude as an Ewe master drummer. Rather, his ancestors who instituted the rich Ewe musical practices are those who deserve to be acknowledged. Admittedly, CK was, like Wilson, being modest, yet his drawing attention to the musicality and ingenuity of the usually forgotten and "unsung heroes" of musical creativity was indeed an important and ineluctable fact. The following excerpt is CK's dictum on the respect that indigenous custodians of orally transmitted music traditions in Africa merit. "I am not the innovator. I am just a messenger, a carrier of wisdom that is not my creation. A creation of my ancestors, and if there is any glorification, it does not belong to me. It belongs to the culture" (Interview, July 2007).

I responded to CK: "You are right, but you are also part of the culture, a conduit responsible for the perpetuation of that traditional wisdom or knowledge. One day, you will also become an ancestor who would have to then be respected as somebody who carried on the tradition of previous ancestors. But I understand what you mean, first and foremost" (Interview, July 2007).

What this "chain of gratitude" suggests is the interaction between the agency of different calibers of people who are normally responsible for the establishment of any single program or academic institutional ensemble. Yet if genealogical consciousness informed Wilson's decision to go to Africa, it was his positive experiences during the fellowship that motivated him in deciding to arrange that a portion of the musical seed would be planted at Berkeley upon his return. These positive impressions include 1) the model represented in the Institute of African Studies, whereby competent indigenous drummers and dancers are drawn from various ethnic groups to form the national dance ensemble; 2) travels he made with the group to festivals and other performances that partly enabled identification of new membership recruits for the ensemble; and 3) the artistic proficiency of the performers that could win the appeal of both national and international audiences. As Wilson recalled in an interview:

> You know I am a scholar, I am a composer, I can play some drum, but I knew to be a good drummer, you've got to focus on that, and I knew I was nowhere near that. So I said what we really need to do is to get somebody who is really good to come to the United States, and to teach there, and somebody who is an excellent teacher and somebody who has the kind of foresight and has a great repertoire. Because you see, a lot of musicians stay at one place [ethnic locale] and perform there, and they will not understand the music of the North [Ghana], or they would not understand the music of the West [Ghana], music of the Fante or music from various places. So . . . I looked around and I watched people, and I said to myself that CK Ladzekpo was the one. This young guy was really extraordinary, he knows them all[4] and he learns, and he understands and plays in the style of the various cultures. So I talked to CK and said: CK, I don't know how I was going to do this, having been an Assistant Professor for just a year before coming to Africa. But I said it would be a great addition if you would like to come to Berkeley. I don't know how to do it, but I am going to see if I could do it. So he said "I would like to come." So I came back and began to use all the persuasive powers that I had, to try to convince, first the department, but more importantly the dean of the college for source of funding for such a position, which was not a traditional one. (Interview, July 2007)

CK indeed confirmed Wilson's unflinching consistency by narrating: "When he returned to UC Berkeley, he made the university to hire me. So I came down here in 1973." In addition to CK's indebtedness to Wilson

Figure 2.12 Christopher Ladzekpo and George Dor. [Photo from George Dor, July 2007]

was CK's tribute to "Professor Denis, Chair of the Music Department, and somebody with a lot of vision, but unfortunately died shortly after I came. It looked like all of a sudden my program had become an orphan." And after I said a word of pity, CK further explained: "A program can become an orphan if those who actually brought that vision are no longer around. But luckily, Professor Wilson was . . . always there for me and he did his best to keep the program afloat" (Interview, July 2007).

For almost four decades, Berkeley has offered two levels of West African drumming and dance to students. The repertoire has been primarily Anlo Ewe dances, and as evident from postings on CK's personal website, he prefers teaching some of the older forms of Ewe dances. He occasionally teaches popular dances from other ethnic groups of Ghana. CK has a teaching philosophy that blends traditionalism with flexibilities that draw on newer approaches as dictated by contexts, a subject I will discuss in chapter 3. He is also careful to draw a distinction between dances that he teaches as closely as possible to the traditional village style, on the one hand, and those that have been choreographed with a touch of modernity for stage performances, on the other. This is another theme I will discuss in a subsequent chapter. His enculturation from Anyako, an Anlo Ewe town, and coming from the Ladzekpo musical family of drummers and singers is an asset.

Although I met several of CK's past students, who spoke very positively of his efficiency as a good teacher just as Professor Wilson did, one would have wished that Berkeley continued to have an Africanist ethnomusicologist whose courses support and complement the African ensemble. Examples abound with UCLA, Wesleyan, Pittsburgh, and Tufts. However, this absence may discourage prospective students who may be looking for mentors in African music scholarship before enrolling. And although Berkeley has a vibrant West African drumming and dance program, its complementary function in the music program rather serves world music, performance, and general music. The students regularly perform at the end of semester concerts and other performances that are university-related.

Both Wilson and CK mentioned the importance of the professional group that the latter formed off-campus and to serve other means. The group's membership includes some of the best previous and current dancers and percussionists who use the group to consolidate their professional training as future directors and art administrators. Beyond further practice, members also have the opportunity to make more money from performances, especially during the summer when the student ensemble is not around. The multiracial demographics of Berkeley, Oakland, and San Francisco provide the bulk of audiences for performances. In fact, such professional groups are not peculiar to CK. Kobla Ladzekpo in Los Angeles, Gideon Alorwoyie in Dallas, and David Locke in Boston all have such professional ensembles.

CK is a great organizer with entrepreneurial abilities that he demonstrates in organizing summer music and dance festivals at both national and international levels. He solicits grants for major projects that at times involve bringing African national dance ensembles to San Francisco. These projects confirm his commitment to stay connected with the kinds of troupes that nurtured his professionalism with a touch of modernity, from which he continues to draw. My later discussion of the models from Africa that are represented in the American academy will include Christopher Ladzekpo's perspectives. My observation of the absence of a permanent Africanist ethnomusicologist does not nullify the numerous benefits of West African drumming and dance on the American student, which I will discuss in chapter 4.

YORK UNIVERSITY, TORONTO, CANADA

My field trip to Toronto in January 2010 turned out to be one of the most revealing, even though I initially had to overcome all odds to embark on that trip. In addition to interviews, I had the opportunity to observe class sessions in Toronto, which was not possible with the preceding schools that I

Figure 2.13 Packed carved Ghanaian hand drums in a classroom at York University. [Photo by George Dor, January 2010]

visited during the summer. As such, my comments regarding classes or teaching should not be misconstrued to suggest any unfairness to the wonderful teachers in the other institutions. According to Robert Simms, the ethnomusicologist, he started the African music ensemble at York in 2000. Prior to this time, however, sporadic summer workshops in West African drumming were conducted in the 1990s before Simms joined the faculty. Today, York University has one of the most vibrant and dynamic West African drumming and dance programs in North America. Factors that make the York program unique include 1) the number and kind of dances represented, 2) number and levels of course sections offered, 3) classroom space and number of instruments that serve as partial pedagogical tools and enablers, 4) competence of instructors as well as the quality of instruction that I observed, 5) path-finding agency of ethnomusicologists and/or administrators, 6) dialogism between Toronto's multicultural demographic makeup and culture-related courses, and 7) appeal of the music genres and student patronage.

York University teaches more dances from West Africa than any other university I visited. York has four instructors, although I was able to observe and interview only two of them. Thus while Kwasi Dunyo, the coordinator of the West African drumming and dance program in 2010, teaches primarily dances from Ghana with Ewe concentration, Anna Melnikoff teaches Mande drumming that includes djembe and dundun drums. Larry Graves also gives

Figure 2.14 Kwasi Dunyo interacting with a student during a class, Performing Arts Building, York University. [Photo by George Dor, January 2010]

instruction in Ghanaian drumming, and Isaac Akrong, a doctoral candidate from Ghana, teaches Ghanaian dance drumming while venturing into other West African dances. While both Larry Graves and Isaac Akrong were away in Ghana during my visit, and as such I could not visit their classes, Kwasi Dunyo and course listings confirm that Graves and Akrong have their own classes. Evidence from interviews, and as further confirmed by course listings, shows that four levels of West African Ensemble are given in Ghanaian dances and Mande dance drumming, respectively. Since each level lasts a year, a student may choose to take classes in the same ensemble (Ghanaian or Mande) for multiple semesters and years (Interview with Kwasi Dunyo, January 2010). During my class observations of West African drumming at York, I noted that Kwasi Dunyo taught two sections of the same level, as did Anna Melnikoff in her Mande drumming class. Besides ensemble dance drumming, private lessons are given to individual students in smaller studios, and both Melnikoff and Dunyo gave such lessons when I was at York. Admittedly, such an impressive enrollment will constitute a source of partial funds that support the program.

One thing that immediately caught my attention the moment I entered the classroom in which Kwasi Dunyo was about to teach was the number of

Figure 2.15 Anna Melnikoff teaching *djembe* parts as she provides the steady beats on the *dundun* drum—Mande drumming at York. [Photo by George Dor, January 2010]

musical instruments. I was very impressed with the about forty multipurpose, medium-sized Ghanaian carved drums that were packed in the corner of the very spacious classroom. And when the students arrived and began to perfect the Gahu dance that they had started to learn, each of the thirty students had a *gankogui* (bell) to himself or herself, and more than fifteen bells were still not in use. Similarly, when it was time to change over to the *axatse* (rattle), there were more than enough instruments for the students. In like manner, Melnikoff has enough djembe and dundun drums for her students as well. While I will discuss the advantages of the quantity of drums under pedagogy, it can readily be observed that it favors the maximization of class time and heightened student involvement more than rotation of only one or two bells, rattles, or a drum among several waiting students. After mastery of individual ensemble parts, creative teachers then lead their students to another level that involves coordination as a polyrhythmic ensemble.

What makes the parallel lessons in West African drumming possible at York is partly the availability of classroom space and rooms for the storage of musical instruments. Some of the multipurpose classrooms are spacious enough to accommodate drums and leave enough space for dancing in any formations that the instructors choose to teach. The Performing

Figure 2.16 Anna Melnikoff's Mande drumming class plays in multi-parts: *djembe* part by right row (seated), *dunduba* and *kenkeni* parts by left row (standing). [Photo by George Dor, January 2010]

Arts Building at York is a new facility, and Robert Simms explained to me the relief it has served the program because in the past space was a major challenge for such classes at York. I know most administrators can relate to the challenges and management of classroom and storage space for musical instruments.

Availability of instruments and space alone will not lead to a vibrant program. It does not take long to recognize the competence of Dunyo and Melnikoff as patient teachers, especially when one observes their classes. One can sense an expression of having fun, experiencing communality, seriousness of purpose, and classroom discipline blended in a balanced manner by the teachers. Credit must then go to the path-finding agency of administrators and the previous program coordinator whose initiatives yielded the identification and hiring of experts in West African dance drumming whose competence were not based on their Ph.D.s but rather on their cultural knowledge. Kwasi Dunyo, for example, is an Anlo Ewe who has been contracted by the Canadian government to teach West African music in Toronto schools. As I will discuss next, he is also the sole dance-drumming instructor at the University of Toronto. He teaches in several Toronto schools, and his experience teaching students at various levels is reflected in his passion, strategies, and confidence in the capabilities of all his students. Melnikoff shares indigenous knowledge that she had gained from being understudy of some of the most reputable Mande drummers in Africa, a subject I will return to in a subsequent chapter.

One theme that I will discuss in detail in chapter 6 is the importance of situating student ensembles within their respective demographic landscapes, of which Toronto is a classic example. During my field visit, many referred to Toronto as the "UN" in Canada because of the plurality of its international residents, leading to a long tradition of interculturalism that characterizes the cultural life of that city. This mosaic of cultures is perceived by state and federal government as a beauty; hence, cultural policies and partial support—financial and personnel—are in place to perpetuate such multiculturalism, even extending to culture-related courses that universities offer. Membership of the dance drumming classes I observed included students from various cultural backgrounds: Americans, Africans, Asians, Europeans, all caught up in the groove, synergies, and appeal of the West African dance drumming genres that they were engagingly learning.

In the same light of promoting national cultures in Toronto, the academic community of York organizes an annual African Festival during which groups both on and off campus perform dance-drumming genres that attract mass participation. Simms considers the lack of a very spacious performance auditorium as part of the Performing Arts Building as both a disadvantage and advantage. As a disadvantage, students cannot present their end of semester performances to hundreds of fans in a concert format, as is the case with several other universities. The advantage is that the lack of such a space has led to performances that rather resonate with typical African communal interactive spirit in which the academic community is encouraged to join in the dances, resulting in an atmosphere that may differ from that of a regular concert.

Importantly, however, one should not isolate West African dance drumming at York completely from the huge world music program that has both ensemble and individual instructions in more than a dozen cultures of the world. At York, the dance department has its own African dance instructor, who teaches drumming, movement, and dance-related theory or topical courses including Anthropology of African Dance. Modesto Amegago, a Ghanaian Ewe who holds a doctoral degree in dance, gave separate dance classes. This represents a different model from what pertains at Wesleyan, where dance and music departments team up to support the same program. I present my findings not with the purpose of passing any value judgments on any of the programs, for I understand the meaning of the Ewe saying that everyone has to "kill the snake with the stick in his hands." These are models that I share for those who may be planning to begin West African drumming and dance in their institutions in the near future. However, I am positive that those institutions that have ensembles will understand that there are different stages of development of programs that come with their attendant infrastructural and systemic constraints and enablers as well.

UNIVERSITY OF TORONTO, CANADA

Russell Hartenberger, dean of the faculty of music at the University of Toronto, introduced the teaching of West African drumming shortly after he was hired in 1974. He recalled that Tim Rice, now at UCLA, was the only other ethnomusicologist at that time, when there were no non-Western performance ensembles and classes. At the formative stage of what would develop into the first world music ensemble at the university, Hartenberger drew on his Wesleyan and Ghanaian training in West African drumming to start instruction in drumming, without dancing, only to percussion students. It initially was an extracurricular and non-credit-earning activity, so the group sometimes met on weekends. But the interest shown by faculty and students in response to the ensemble's casual performances, at times in the lobby during lunch breaks, led to its formalization into a course, which still involved only drumming. It became quite popular and other music students who were not percussionists joined the class. Further, after Rice left Jim Kippen, a tabla drummer, replaced him and, together with his wife Annette Sanger, an ethnomusicologist who specialized in Balinese gamelan, founded two other world music ensembles (Interview, January 2010).

As a second major development of the West African ensemble specifically, Hartenberger later invited Cathy Armstrong, one of his students who had visited Ghana to study dance, to add the teaching of dance/movement and singing components that contributed further to the popularity of the class. After Hartenberger stopped directing the program, Joseph Ashong, a talented Akan drummer and dancer, expanded the program as he became the main instructor, teaching predominantly Ghanaian ethnic dances. Hartenberger recollected how different Ashong's dances were from the Ewe ones that he himself had taught.

Other cultural activities in the city indirectly informed the development of the West African drum ensemble. For example, when Bob Becker,

Figure 2.17 Dean Russell Hartenberger, founder and first instructor of the West African drumming ensemble at the University of Toronto. [Photo by George Dor, January 2010]

Hartenberger's mate at Wesleyan, moved to Toronto, that city's cultural landscape encouraged him to found the Flaming Donos, an African drum ensemble. It comprised talented percussionists who rehearsed on Saturdays and gave several memorable concerts. Given their unflinching pursuit of excellence, the group on a number of occasions brought established master drummers to visit and coach them and also to perform as guest artists. Hartenberger remembers the visits of Abraham Adzinya, their teacher, and Godwin Agbeli, the Ewe master drummer who was then teaching at the University of Florida. Elsewhere in this book I discuss the reciprocal reinforcement that university ensembles and such vibrant performing groups in a city of a university provide each other, be it in Los Angeles, Boston, Berkeley–San Francisco, or Dallas.

Yet, it was Kwasi Dunyo, the gifted instructor whom I met, and who also teaches at York and several other schools in Toronto, who took over and developed the program exponentially into an incredibly popular and enviable one, as partially evident in the two classes I observed, the space and instrumental resources he showed me, and more telling, the compliments from Dean Hartenberger. As of January 2010, the University of Toronto offers two courses, beginners' and advanced levels. While one of the two beginner-level classes is open to all College of Liberal Arts students, the second class is for music students. Kwasi Dunyo is the only instructor for the program. As did his predecessors, he focuses on a repertoire of Ghanaian ethnic dances. As

Figure 2.18 Kwasi Dunyo instructing a class at the University of Toronto. All students play the same hand drum part. [Photo by George Dor, January 2010]

such, Mande drumming courses are not given at the University of Toronto, a feature that seems to be the norm in most of the universities I visited in the United States. Like classes I observed at York, the students of the service class were racially diverse, capturing the internationality of Toronto that I have mentioned earlier.

The University of Toronto houses an even larger variety of Ghanaian drums including Ewe, Akan, Ga, and some Dagbon drums. I inspected two storage rooms full of drums, and during the two lessons that I observed, there were enough hand drums, bells, and rattles that about twenty-five students played simultaneously. The longevity and continuity of the program, and the support of the dean who is a percussionist, may partly explain the substantial number of the instruments. Dunyo recounts the numerous Ghanaian dances he has taught at the University of Toronto to include *Kete, Adowa, Sekyi* (Akan dances), *Nagla, Bambaya* (Northern), *Atrikpui, Agbadza, Atisagbekor, Kenka, Tokui, Gota, Gahu, Borborbor, Zigi* (Ewe), *Kpanlogo, Kpatsa,* and *Fume fume* (Ga-Adamgbe). Dunyo is generally satisfied with the quantity and quality of costumes that University of Toronto has acquired for the ensemble. Like Wesleyan, costuming is really a challenge for instructors, especially given the number of students that take the classes.

Figure 2.19 Dunyo's class divides into multi-parts, drummers, bell and rattle players (standing). [Photo by George Dor, January 2010]

University of Toronto also has a spacious rehearsal room Where Dunyo gave the two classes I observed. As in many rehearsal halls, the golden rule of removing footwear was observed, and it was easy to notice and appreciate the cordial class atmosphere within which each of the two-hour classes occurred. "Create an environment of happiness so that students will be willing to come to class," Dunyo observes. Although I will return to Dunyo's teaching approach in a subsequent chapter, I will mention here that he considers appreciation and enjoyment of dance drumming as a magnetic act that must flow pragmatically, through actions and different modes of communication, from the teacher to students, and then to audiences. Bell and rattle players, for example, never sit down in his classes; they stand, alternating their foot stamps to outline and correspond to the pulse of the music, an act that also externalizes their learned perception of the dance. Hence, what sustains students' interest is the teacher's patience, flexibility, and accommodating nature; the varied activities in which every student is expected to master the required drumming, dancing, and singing components of the course; and how students are led to enjoy what they are performing, as well as the interaction among the students themselves—a rewarding pedagogical sight.

72 SELECTED UNIVERSITY ENSEMBLES

Figure 2.20 Time for dancing with instruments put aside. Dunyo leads as the students watch, listen, and imitate. [Photo by George Dor, January 2010]

As in many other universities, midterm and end-of-semester performances are integral to course grades. However, several other memorable performances—especially by the advanced class or a select few to represent the university—provide additional source of motivation. In response to my question about the most memorable performance Dunyo's UFT African ensemble has given, he recalled an event they had with other groups during winter in Quebec in which they had to perform in the snow. It was so cold that drummers of the group, according to him, had to play some of their drums with their gloves on, and dancers had to wear their costumes on top of multiple layers and they danced with all their energy to stay warm, a climatic reason that compelled some to dance their best ever.

The growth of the West African ensemble must partly be situated within the broader support it (like other world music ensembles) enjoys from the music faculty, the dean, and the larger university administration. Based on the entire faculty's understanding of the ways in which world music broadens the cultural and intellectual horizons of students, Hartenberger informed me that all first-year music students are required to take a class in one of the world music ensembles, and West African dance drumming remains a favorite choice. Also, it is important to reiterate the multiculturalism of Toronto, a theme I have discussed under York, and how such demographics, and government support to maintain the cultural diversity, nourishes world music ensembles.

Today, the University of Toronto boasts of a body of world music ensembles, including *taiko* drumming, Korean drumming, steel drums, and Georgian vocal music. However, West African dance-drumming, gamelan, and taiko drumming have remained the cornerstones of the world music program. According to the dean, there is high demand for another course section requested by the social sciences. However, its feasibility depends on other modalities including logistics. In any case, it is Dunyo's wish that more classes could be offered in the future, as is the case at York, and that theory courses on the music of Africa could be taught to provide complementary understanding of the music cultures represented by the dance drumming program.

UNIVERSITY OF PITTSBURGH (PITT)

William Oscar Anku founded Pitt's African Music Ensemble in 1983 and directed it until 1988. While pursuing his graduate study in ethnomusicology at the University of Pittsburgh, he introduced Ghanaian dance drumming to students. Although J. H. K. Kwabena Nketia was by then the main Africanist ethnomusicologist at Pitt as the Mellon Professor of Music, he concentrated on teaching theory-based courses and research work, leaving the African ensemble to the initiative of Anku, his student. This preoccupation with the teaching of drumming to students inspired both Anku's masters and doctoral theses on African dance drumming rhythms (see Dor 2010: 110–123). By teaching this course as part of his graduate fellowship, Anku has set the precedent for a practice and a unique model pertaining to the future direction of the African music and dance ensemble at Pitt. Like Anku, most subsequent directors of the African music dance ensemble at Pitt have been graduate ethnomusicology students from Africa. This practice constitutes an antithesis to most of the other institutions discussed here, where the director is a full faculty member. Hence other student directors include Damien Pwono from Congo: August 1988–December 1990; Anicet Mundundu from Congo: January 1991–December 1996; Sylvia Nannyonga-Tamusuza from Uganda: January 1997–December 1999, July 2000–April 2001; J. S. Kofi Gbolonyo from Ghana: May 2005–May 2009; and Charles Lwanga from Uganda: since September 2009.

74 SELECTED UNIVERSITY ENSEMBLES

Figure 2.21 Akin Euba (seated), Agatha Ozah, Kwabena Nketia, Anicet Mundundu (middle row), Eric Beeko, George Dor, Kofi Gbolonyo, Willie Anku (back row). [Photo from George Dor, taken at AMNA at UCLA, October 2009]

Comparatively, the cultural and professional backgrounds of Pitt ensemble directors come with attendant advantages as well as disadvantages. The preceding data show that directors' nationalities include Ghana, Congo, and Uganda, or to use names of sub-regions, western, central, and eastern Africa. Accordingly, the repertoires they have taught over the years are dances from different African countries. Such changes every two or three years in genres that the ensemble performs provide a source of freshness and novelty, perhaps more than at institutions in which the same genres are taught and performed under the same director for about three or two decades. The immediate university cultural community will have cause to be excited about a new director from another African country with diverse music cultural experiences.

Notwithstanding, there is the probability that some of the students may not be as virtuosic as the accomplished directors in other institutions. As such, performance standards of the ensemble may fluctuate and be commensurate with the director's abilities. Admittedly, I have discussed the humble beginnings of some ensembles by their initiators and can therefore observe such standards may compare with those of the not-very-accomplished graduate directors. Yet the difference is that most of these initiators often relinquish their ensembles to competent drummers and dancers who take their programs to higher levels. However, the Pitt situation and practice depends on probability of recurrence. Luckily, most of Pitt's ensemble directors have been very able performers who maximize their performance and teaching skills from semester to semester. Their cultural backgrounds as fully or partly enculturated Africans, and their academic training as ethnomusicologists, shape how they direct their ensembles.

While one celebrates diversity in genres that new directors may bring, the lack of continuity in terms of repertoire is somewhat a challenge. After a director completes his graduate program and leaves, or he/she goes to African for a semester or two to conduct fieldwork, the Africanist professor and the chair of department always have the challenge of getting a replacement. The replacement may mean a total discontinuity in the repertoire of the previous director. In cases where directorship changes hands, the same musical instruments and costumes that have been previously used become irrelevant for the newly introduced genres. As can be seen and would be expected from the list of central and eastern Africans who directed the Pitt African ensemble after Willie Anku, the Ewe drums that the university acquired and used in 1983 to 1988 were no longer in use. I vividly remember how John Chernoff, who lives in Pittsburgh and had conducted research on Ewe drumming, encouraged music students and faculty to revitalize these Ewe drums as he led us to play *Gahu* and *Agbekor*. At that time Mundundu was teaching the regular credit-earning African Ensemble and what Chernoff led was just for fun. Weintraub, a faculty member who had done some Ewe drumming under C. K. Ladzekpo at Berkeley, was part of this team. On my part, I participated out of nostalgia and my general love for dance drumming. Yet Pascal Younge resurrected the Ewe genres and the use of those instruments when he was the part-time instructor of the ensemble from 2001–2002. Kofi Gbolonyo further canonized those Ewe drums and genres when he became the ensemble director in 2005–2009 and raised the performance level of the group to a semi-professional one. Luckily, Charles Lwange has once more resurrected the Baganda dance drumming traditions including the drums that Nannyonga-Tamusuza originally acquired for the University of Pittsburgh in 1997.

Active and long-serving members of the ensemble who have learned to perform specific genres under an immediate previous director become invaluable assets for the ensemble regarding continuity. For example, Charles Lwanga had performed under Kofi Gbolonyo and learned Ewe dances before becoming the next director. Accordingly, he could rehearse the Ewe dances

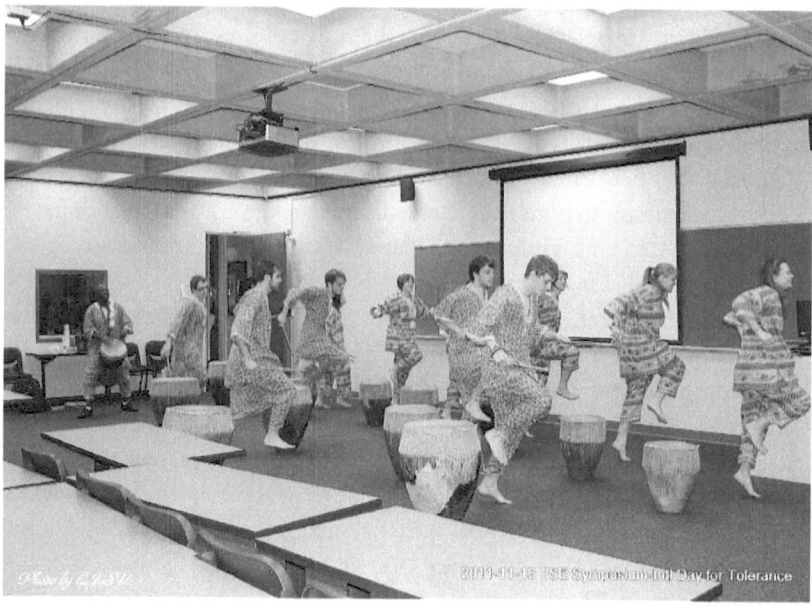

Figure 2.22 Pitt African Music and Dance Ensemble directed by Charles Lwanga features Ugandan dances. [Photo from Charles Lwanga, 2012]

along with the East African genres that he had resurrected or introduced. Similarly, because Agatha Ozah was a member of Gbolonyo's ensemble, she was able to hold the fort by teaching it for a semester when Gbolonyo went to Ghana to conduct his dissertation fieldwork. Furthermore, Gbolonyo had told me how gifted student members of the ensemble remained loyal to it and continued not for the sake of earning credits. Such members, both drummers and dancers, offer the needed continuity as they could facilitate the teaching and learning of dances they know to newer student participants.

The inception and sustenance of the Pitt African Music and Dance Ensemble can partly be attributed to the strong African music program established by Kwabena Nketia and later Akin Euba, who were Andrew Mellon Professors of Music. These world-renowned native African music scholars drew graduate students from Africa into the ethnomusicology and composition programs at the University of Pittsburgh. Also, the activities of the gamelan ensemble and the general ethnomusicology program mean that the African music ensemble is not an isolated case in the department. Furthermore, the international demography of Pittsburgh, which includes African Americans and Africans, and the university's departments including Africana Studies, African Studies, International Studies, and other programs and courses of international fervor support the saliency of the African Music Ensemble. Additionally, the proximity of Morgantown to Pittsburgh facilitated Pascal Younge's ability to commute to Pitt to instruct when there was no African graduate student capable of directing the ensemble in 2001 and 2002. It also enabled collaboration among University of West Virginia and Pitt ensemble members in joint performances.

A constant interaction exists between the directors' multiple music-related activities, including performance, teaching, and academic work and training as aspiring ethnomusicologists. Directing the African ensemble sustains student instructors' interests in genres that later become the themes or focuses of their dissertation studies. Anku, Mudundu, and Nannyonga-Tamusuza are classic cases. Another example in which directing the ensemble has reinforced other activities of the instructor is Kofi Gbolonyo's use of African drumming and dance for presentations on the Carl Orff method of teaching. Hence the intersection of world music, music education, and ethnomusicology is at play here, an interdisciplinary enterprise that has become almost synonymous with Gbolonyo.

Personally, I have been part of several African dance-drumming activities while a student at Pitt. These included performing with Pascal Younge, playing supporting drums and some lead singing during a performance, and playing supporting drums for Sylvia Nannyonga-Tamusuza when she directed and taught Baganda genres including *Baksimba*. As the music director of the Community of Reconciliation Church, Pittsburgh, I taught some Ewe drumming to my church members during the summer of 2000. But the most memorable activity was when Akin Euba himself directed the ensemble in 2000. Beyond playing as a non-credit-earning member, I had to fill in for him whenever he traveled. He introduced the playing of *atenteben*, a Ghanaian flute, to his students. Consistent with Euba's strong liking for experimentation, he taught the students to drum through simplified notation for non- music majors. He wanted to prove that music that is traditionally oral can be taught through notation and that those who are not music majors can be taught to read music that is written with their capabilities in mind. It is appropriate to mention that the Andrew Mellon Tuition Fellowship supports African ethnomusicology students who direct the African music and dance ensemble as well.

TUFTS UNIVERSITY, MEDFORD, MASSACHUSETTS ("KINIWE")

David Locke founded Tufts's West African drumming and dance ensemble in 1979 and has instructed it as an Africanist ethnomusicologist, both scholar and performer. But before I share details of his training—both schooling and ethnographic experiences—it is important to mention that his position as a tenured faculty and chair of the Tufts music department from 1993–2000 facilitated support for and growth of the African ensemble. Also, Locke formed an off-campus cultural troupe called the Agbekor Drum and Dance Society in Boston from 1979–96. This group and the student ensemble reciprocally reinforced each other—while the professional group partly consisted of several former members of Tufts's student ensemble, the community-based ensemble participated jointly with the campus ensembles in some events.

David Locke's story of becoming a lead drummer and instructor of these ensembles is revealing and worth sharing. He pursued his undergraduate education at Wesleyan University, because the well-established ethnomusicology program there attracted him. Consistent with his love for other world cultures, Locke listened a great deal to a variety of world music genres held at the good university library, and eventually became interested in anthropology and the world music program, which laid the foundations for him in the process of becoming a performing artist. At this early stage, Locke did not consider himself a musician because he did not major in music, never played in a symphony orchestra, nor was he a member of the jazz band—activities that typify serious music students. Luckily, however, his mother was a piano teacher and his father a music lover. Accordingly, he took some basic music lessons. Such a formative musical background could have been deemed a disadvantage, but Locke thought it positively provided him with a greater initial openness to different kinds of cultures than "those who are heavily schooled in Western music."

At first, Locke played in the gamelan, the only world music ensemble available when he got to Wesleyan. However, through the aid of listening to several recordings, African music appealed to him most. He thus approached David McAlester for direction, who recommended that Locke go to Columbia University. He did so in 1969 and studied Ewe drumming under Alfred Ladzekpo, the master drummer, although Kobla was also around. Locke's academic African music teacher was Nicholas England, who concentrated on teaching him notation of African music. Upon his return to Wesleyan, Abraham Adzinya, a former member of the Ghana National Dance Ensemble, came to Wesleyan at the recommendation of Professors Kwabena Nketia and

Figure 2.23 David Locke directs the Tufts "Kiniwe" Ensemble in a concert as they play a piece on the *gungong* drums of the Dagbon of Northern Ghana. [Photo by Tufts University Photography]

Mawere Opoku. Adzinya founded the African drum ensemble at Wesleyan and Locke joined and participated in it for two years. Locke was satisfied that Adzinya provided both practical training and theoretical explanation of the genres he taught.

When Locke returned to Wesleyan in 1972 to pursue his doctorate, he was assigned the duty of assisting Freeman Donkor—the Ghanaian dancer and artist-in-residence—to teach African music and dance at Woodrow Wilson High School. This project, which Locke enjoyed very much, was made possible through a federal grant.

If the preceding experiences of Locke at Columbia and Wesleyan provided the foundations for his Africanist career, then, it was his two-year stay in Ghana from 1975 to 1977, where and when he conducted his field research, that consolidated his training as a lead drummer. While in Ghana, Locke was affiliated with the University of Ghana and under Kwabena Nketia as the supervisor of his fieldwork. So his work involved classes in African music theory, lessons in performance, and ethnographic work. While he had discussions on notation of African rhythm with Nketia, he understudied Godwin Agbeli, Abubakari Lunna, and Gideon Alorwoyie, accomplished Ghanaian master drummers. Locke recalls how the active music scene in Accra introduced him to Ewe musicians and his subsequent love for Ewe dance

Figure 2.24 Perry and Marty Granoff Music Center, home of two Ghanaian ethnic dance-drumming traditions. [Photo by George Dor, July 2007]

drumming. His first teacher was Godwin Agbeli, who was then working for the Arts Council of Ghana. Not only was Agbeli a master drummer of the Folkloric Dance Company of the Arts Council, but he also was responsible for training NGOs and students in drumming and dance. Locke traveled from Legon to the Arts Center, in downtown Accra, to take drumming lessons from Agbeli, and recalls how he enjoyed the Saturday shows at the center, figuratively called Anansekrom ("the village of Ananse, the trickster in Ghanaian folktales"). Agbeli introduced Locke to Abubakari Lunna, from whom the American would learn to perform Dagbamba musical genres and learn about this Northern Ghanaian ethnic group. Locke was aware of the existence of the Ghana National Dance Ensemble at the University of Ghana, and when the government of Ghana was compelled by the International Monetary Fund's conditionalities under its "Structural Adjustment Program" to dissolve one of the national dance ensembles, only the Legon ensemble was kept. Gideon Alorwoyie of the Ghana National Dance Ensemble was the third master drummer and second Ewe drummer who taught Locke drumming while in Ghana.

Locke studied Agbekor, an Anlo Ewe war dance genre, for his dissertation field research and elected to spend brief periodic visits to towns and villages

Figure 2.25 David Locke, founding director of Tufts's Kiniwe Ensemble. [Photo by Tufts University Photography]

to conduct interviews rather than long-term field stays in a single village. He also privileged the Anya Agbekor group in Accra, an urbanized welfare and musical group, and then traveled to Anyako for what he calls "first existence" version of the genre, or what some may call the "village rendition." After Locke returned to Wesleyan and completed his dissertation in 1978, he relocated to Boston, where he did part-time teaching for six years before securing the job at Tufts.

In chapter 3 I will discuss Locke's preference for teaching a limited number of dances in a semester and the extent to which he advocates interplay between scholarship and teaching. Locke has maintained great relationships between himself and his teachers, bonds that have yielded mutual benefits. On a number of occasions he has invited each of his three Ghanaian mentors to Tufts for brief but rewarding workshops on and performances of the genres the students were learning. These virtuosic encultured performers brought their knowledge to Boston to validate, reaffirm, and reinforce Locke's efforts, and returned home with honoraria that they could not have earned if they had remained in Ghana. In an interview I had with Gideon Alorwoyie, he told me that Locke was very supportive of Alorwoyie's North Texas job search.

Locke continues to collaborate with his former teachers in a number of projects, be it a video recording of Gahu dance by him and Agbeli, or the more recent *Agbadza* project between him and Alorwoyie. Locke's love for his teachers was exemplified in his actions when Abubakari Lunna died in 2008. He organized a fundraiser concert at Tufts to celebrate his mentor's life and to raise money to assist Lunna's family. Locke traveled to Ghana to be part of the final rites. It was then appropriate that Diane Thram[5] used Lunna's photo for the cover of the *African Music Journal* (vol. 8 no. 3, 2009), in which this custodian of Dagbamba traditional knowledge was playing the *lunga*.[6] More telling is the extent to which Locke has shared the perspectives of his teachers in Titon's world music textbook (2009: 76–91)[7] and other publications. An enduring model that Locke introduced was the planting of a performance society within an urban setting, thus pulling musicians and dancers from the larger Boston area together to make music. His spirit of collaboration was evident in the key role players of the Agbekor Society as well, with Agbeli co-leading the group and Alorwoyie now assuming master drummer role during more recent performances[8]

In July 2007 I observed a workshop that Locke and Alorwoyie collaboratively organized for percussionists in the Boston area. After three afternoons of Agbadza drumming, participants put up an evening concert, and all these activities took place in the Perry and Marty Granoff Center, which houses the Ewe and Dagbon drums as well as instruments of Tuft's gamelan ensemble. He continues to influence many of his students, some of whom are directing ensembles in colleges. Also, he has arranged study-abroad exchange programs for his students to travel to Ghana and study drumming and dance from reputable indigenous practitioners. Currently, Nani Agbeli, the son of Godwin Agbeli, leads the Kiniwe Ensemble as an artist-in-residence. I consider it a great honor to African music that Tufts University would give its African Music Ensemble one of its two Andrew Mellon Grants. Here too, Locke's advocacy for the African ensemble and his position as a previous chair played a key role.

What a lesson for other institutions regarding what could be a priority for a particular university!

MASSACHUSETTS INSTITUTE OF TECHNOLOGY (MIT)

MIT's African Ensemble is an important and unique model representing a tradition from Senegal, a Francophone country, thereby offering a contrast to the predominance of Ghanaian genres taught and performed in North American universities. MIT does *Sabar* drumming, which originally belongs

Figure 2.26 Lamine Toure, co-director of MIT's Sabar Ensemble, leads a performance. [Photo by Patricia Tang]

to the Wolof, another added dimension to the Mande musical traditions that most American students tend to be more familiar with. According to Patricia Tang, the founder and co-director of MIT's *Sabar* ensemble, she started the group as a non-curricular activity in 2001, soon after she was hired as an Africanist ethnomusicologist. Today, Tang directs the ensemble with Lamine Toure, a Wolof griot. It is intriguing to know how an Asian became interested in African music in the first place.

(Before discussing the *Sabar* ensemble, the focus of this segment, I would like to acknowledge that James Makubuya gave lessons in playing of East African musical instruments at MIT in the 1990s as the Africanist that preceded Tang at this institution. In the table at the beginning of this chapter, one could see how Makubuya has formed a similar ensemble at Wabash College in Indiana, where he had moved to after teaching at MIT.)

Patricia Tang first got interested in African music when pursuing her undergraduate studies at Brown University, which has a powerful West African dance drumming ensemble. Directed by Obeng, the ensemble played Ewe and other Ghanaian ethnic dances. Tang took advantage of this dance drumming class and participated in it. She sustained her interest and performance

Figure 2.27 Patricia Tang, founding director, MIT Sabar Ensemble. [Photo by George Dor, November 2010]

of Ewe music when she gained admission into graduate school at Harvard in 1993 by spending time with David Locke at Tufts. Tang joined the Agbekor Society troupe that Locke founded and collaborated with Godwin Agbeli as the native master drummer of the group. Although Tang gained much cultural and artistic insight from the Agbekor group, her interest shifted to the music of Senegal after taking some theory courses in African music and attending some Senegalese performances at the larger Boston area. After her coursework, Tang traveled to Senegal and conducted field research there for a year in 1997–98, focusing on Wolof griots that specialized in Sabar drumming. Learning to perform on Sabar drums was part of Tang's research activities and have culminated in writing her doctoral dissertation and ultimately her first book on this tradition, *Masters of the Sabar: Wolof Griots Percussionists of Senegal*. When Tang returned to Harvard, she started a small drumming group (Interview, November 2010).

At MIT, Tang formed the ensemble she named Ramba; shortly after, Lamine Toure, who comes from a family of musicians with whom Tang studied in Senegal, came to the United States and began to assist her formally with the group. As a native African musician, Lamine Toure has tremendously contributed to the growth of the ensemble. According to Tang, the students really enjoy working with him, and he became an artist in residence at MIT, co-directing the ensemble she founded. Together they have transformed it into a credit-earning class that has an enrollment of about forty students, and the course is available for students from all departments as an elective. Lamine Toure has now moved to an adjunct teaching position, and Tang further disclosed: "Just last year Lamine won a campus-wide award as the best teacher of the university. That is unusual because that award normally goes to a professor. That shows how the students appreciate working with him." Lamine Toure's success story was partly possible because of Tang, especially when the linguistic factor has been a major constraint for native Africans from French-speaking countries in giving instruction in American universities. Tang initially had to assist as a mediator between Lamine and the students to ensure effective verbal communication. Now Toure is more comfortable with the English language and Tang's role is more in administrative aspects of the ensemble.

Although I will return to the extent to which linguistic challenges reflect in the relatively small representation of ethnic dances from French-speaking African countries, my discussion of university ensembles thus far in this chapter provides ample evidence of this phenomenon. According to Tang, only two Sabar ensembles exist in North American universities; the other is Arizona State's African ensemble, founded and directed by Mark Sunkett, an African American ethnomusicologist and percussionist who received his doctorate from the University of Pittsburgh. Like Tang, Sunkett conducted his ethnographic research in Senegal and similarly wrote a book on a drumming tradition (1993). However, he was a professional percussionist before going to Africa and teaches in a percussion department [sic] of his university. Earlier, in my discussion of West African dance drumming at York University, I covered Mande drumming with keen interest, and although I was unable to get to Gainesville, I have mentioned the University of Florida as another institution that offers classes partly on Mande drumming. Tang informed me that Harvard also has a native djembe instructor from Mali. It is for this reason that one has to be excited about the growth of non-Ghanaian drumming traditions, although the predominance of Ewe, Akan, and Dagbon traditions do not constitute any problems for Tang at all.

Like all the other credit-earning ensembles, MIT's Sabar ensemble stages end-of-semester concerts, and also performs annually during African Students Association events as well as other campus multicultural and international activities. MIT, as Tang observes, is a multicultural university with several Asian and African students. MIT students serve as the core of the ensemble's aficionados, although some patrons come from Boston and its immediate cultural sub-region. Out of the ensemble's several off-campus performances, a memorable one for Tang, was a festival that David Locke organized at Tufts University in which four university African ensembles in the broader Boston region (Trinity College, Tufts, MIT, and Binghamton) came together and shared their drumming, dancing, and singing through workshops given by each group as well as performances during an evening concert. The event was very collegial and the communality and camaraderie were exceptional and without the spirit of unhealthy competition.

Another experience that Tang shared was the trip to Senegal she and Lamine organized for members of the ensemble. Tang noted, "Besides learning about the music cultural tradition that the students have been taught about, they had the opportunity to perform at major festivals." To both teachers, it was an exciting experience presenting their students to their Wolof communities, who were stunned at the level at which American students could perform on Sabar drums. The positive impressions about the students' performances were legitimizing for both the students and their teachers. For, although the students had confidence and trust in their native teacher, it was rewarding in many ways when indigenous people confirmed the authenticity of what they were learning.

Eric Charry, Kwasi Dunyo, Kobla Ladzekpo, Robert Simms, David Locke, Russell Hartenberger, Olly Wilson, and other administrators and ensemble directors have all stressed the importance of West African dance drumming's function to generate and sustain interest in American students in Africa until they one day visit there. MIT ensemble members originally had to raise their own monies for the trip, which was not even organized as a study-abroad program. In spite of the sacrifices of Patricia Tang and Lamine Toure—including using their own instruments to begin the drumming program at MIT—they are very grateful to the administration, especially the music department, for its support, and to other grant foundations that have provided partial funding for the ensemble's sustenance. Tang is very positive about continued support from the music department and the larger university as they anticipate expanding the program with more instruments and costumes. But the most important awareness is what students derive from their participation in the ensemble. While I intend to discuss other aspects of my interview with Tang, I hope all readers will read about how the humble beginnings of several university African dance drumming ensembles have today developed into expansive programs. This, I believe is the hope for MIT's ensemble, which is older than that of University of Mississippi's, the next and my own group.

UNIVERSITY OF MISSISSIPPI (OLE MISS) AFRICAN DRUM DANCE ENSEMBLE (OMADDE)

Mississippians, like many African ethnic groups, are famous for storytelling traditions. And given my background as an African in Mississippi, I would like to present my discussion of the Ole Miss African Drum Dance Ensemble (OMADDE) through the discursive genre of a narrative. As can be recalled, a phrase often interjected by a participating audience member during a typical Ghanaian storytelling setting is "I was there when something happened." Immediately when this formulaic statement is heard, the main narrator pauses his/her narration and allows the audience member to interject a catchy song or a dance movement to propel the idea in the tale. Such a moment heightens and stirs up the imagination of the audience. However, in the case of the African drum and dance ensemble at the University of Mississippi, "I was [really] there," and as such, my narrative is not fictional. Also, the insights and contributions of key players in the ensemble's growth that I may cite will resonate another African storytelling practice in which anybody can contribute to the narration in a number of ways (Agawu 1995; Dor, 2006). Now comes my story.

Before coming to the University of Mississippi in 2001, I was well informed about two things. First, I had read about how African drumming was not encouraged during the period of slavery in the United States of America. Second, I knew that a number of American universities had African drum and dance ensembles that I could use as models to suggest the formation of such an ensemble during my interview prior to my probable appointment. Yet while preparing for the job interview and exploring the possible themes I could lecture on, Elizabeth Payne, the former director of the then McDonnell-Barksdale Honors College (now Sally McDonnell Barksdale Honors College), suggested that I talk about African drums and drumming, a topic she thought would be engaging to the students. Although I ended up not lecturing on African drums, I brought along some Ghanaian Ewe drums that I used in my teaching and lecture demonstration. I was really amazed at the musicality of Professor Ricky Burkhead and his percussion students; their rhythmic sensibilities left an enduring and impressive image on my mind, leading to my resolve to found an ensemble, contingent upon getting the job.

Consistent with my ambitious drive and determination to establish an African drum and dance ensemble, I applied for the Partners and Associates Grant, an internal source, during the 2001–2002 (my first academic) year at the University of Mississippi. However, the reply to my application was one

Figure 2.28 OMADDE, at 2011 Black History Month Concert in Nutt Auditorium, performs *Tokoe*, a Ga-Adangbe (Ghana) puberty dance-drumming genre. [Photo by Don Cole, University of Mississippi]

of those "we regret" responses. Yet persistence normally pays off. Accordingly, when the opportunity came for me to lead a team of Honors College faculty to Ghana[9] on a study tour aimed at exploring international collaborations, I requested Elizabeth Payne pledge some money toward the purchase of some drums from Ghana. She did, and during that visit in the summer of 2002 I started the negotiations with Amoh, an assistant instructor of the Ghana National Dance Ensemble (now [2010] the director of the National Theatre), to help me with the purchase of the instruments as I returned to Ole Miss.

The process of acquisition was pretty involving, to say the least. But my thanks to Steve Brown (former chair of the Department of Music[10]) and John Samonds, then assistant director (now associate dean) of the Honors College, for their hard work and support. It was a time when Douglas Sullivan-Gonzalez had then taken over from Payne as the dean of the Honors College, and as such, it was Samonds and Dianne Daniels-Smith, the administrative secretary, who after mediating with the two heads (Honors and Music) were responsible for the process of shipping, after the Music Department provided supplementary funds for shipping.

Eventually, the drums were delivered at the Honors College in April 2003. But after deliberation on where the drums should be kept, it was decided

Figure 2.29 YOCONA 2008 Children's Festival on Ole Miss Grove, OMADDE on the stage and kids having fun. [Photo by University of Mississippi Communications Photography]

that Meek Hall, the former location of the Department of Music, was the ideal place since our rehearsals and future performances were going to be in Meek Auditorium. It was good that I decided to share my small office at Meek Hall with the fifteen drums, because there was something spiritual about the experience I had each time I opened my office and saw those precious and carefully crafted carved drums. Also, I remember about twenty university faculty and staff visiting my office at Meek to see the new drums and maybe to celebrate the beginnings of the new cultural strides we were about to make at the university. Those visits were a revelation to me about the extent to which Americans appreciate aesthetic beauty of artifacts, even if they are from different parts of the world.

Yet the news of the acquisition needed to be broken to the larger academic and cultural community. Accordingly, I invited Dr. Steve Brown, Dr. John Samonds, and Professor Ricky Burkhead, the main percussion instructor at the university, to join me as we took photographs with the instruments. The professional photographer who froze this moment of joy and anxiety was Kevin Bain of UM Brand Photography. His frozen images remind me of the formulaic phrase "I was there."

Figure 2.30 Four faculty percussionists, with an administrator and two student members of OMADDE. [Photo from George Dor, March 2010]

The acquisition of this fifteen-piece set of carved Ghanaian drums by the University of Mississippi in 2003 received exciting news media coverage. The publication of articles written by Diedra Jackson[11] on these drums seem to suggest some degree of symbolism that these instruments represent to individuals, the university, and the larger cultural community of Mississippi. While UM News desk story #3204 on these drums, including an imposing photo of the tallest drum of the set (*Atsimewu*), was published on the university web site, *Black Issues in Higher Education* (6/19/03) reported the acquisition of these drums under "Noteworthy News." The Jackson *Clarion Ledger* (5/29/03), *2003 Ole Miss Rebels* (11/1/03), *Daily Mississippian*, and *Oxfordtown* also carried stories on the acquisition.

But how and when did the university first hear the sound of the drums in a performance, and who was instrumental in this formative stage of what we now call the Ole Miss African Drum and Dance Ensemble? Since most African drum and dance ensembles begin and depend on the availability of capable percussionists, I discussed the possibility of teaching Ricky Burkhead's percussion students a dance that we could do during one of his concerts. He embraced the idea and we raised a team of great musicians and I taught them to play Gahu, a Southern Ewe social dance. Although played without dancing, that performance went very well. I remember that many

Figure 2.31 OMADDE performs "Liberate the World," a commemorative highlife piece, during Ghana50 Concert at the Gertrude Ford Center, University of Mississippi, March 6, 2007. [Photo by University of Mississippi Communications Photography]

university professors attended this concert. Professor Ron Venon, associate dean of the College of Liberal Arts and director of the university orchestra, was particularly impressed with the sonorities of the drums, especially the largest, Atsimewu, and came to admire the instruments up close after the performance.

Around the same time that the news about the acquisition spread, I was invited to serve on a university committee charged with the responsibility of planning the first International Conference on Racial Reconciliation as an extension of the "Open Doors" ceremony, intended to publicly proclaim the university's commitment to inclusiveness and fostering of diversity. This conference was the brainchild of the William Winter Institute for Racial Reconciliation, whose director, Dr. Susan Glisson, chaired our planning meetings. The committee agreed that a performing group be invited to grace the celebratory component of the conference. But after the planning committee considered a few groups with their accompanying performance fees that were deemed too high for the conference budget, Susan Glisson came up with an alternative idea, which really resonated with one of my dreams behind the acquisition of the drums. To paraphrase her, she asked the committee why not encourage George (myself) to get some of our students to learn a dance and perform on our new drums during the conference. She readily won the support of the committee, but remembering that the feasibility of such a great idea depended on the answer to the final question that the committee threw to me: "George, can you do it?" As I answered yes, we could all imagine the wisdom in asking students of diverse ethnic backgrounds performing an African dance for the "Open Doors."

I assembled a group of six dancers (three girls and three boys) and six percussionists (including myself) and we prepared the Anlo Ewe Gahu dance that we performed at the "Open Doors" ceremony held in the forecourt of the Lyceum. Dance drumming at the University of Mississippi for the first time was historic indeed.

The ensemble continues to grow with new sets of costumes, instruments, and symbolic performances that I will discuss in subsequent chapters. For now I want to acknowledge the contributions of Gideon Alorwoyie, Kofi Gbolonyo, and Samuel Nyamuame, ensemble directors that paid working visits that have taken OMADDE to higher artistic levels. Also, the commitment of Ricky Burkhead, percussion professor, and David Carlisle, now the principal percussionist of the Memphis Symphony Orchestra, as two regular pillars of OMADDE and the willingness to expand their knowledge and to collaborate with me as the director, is a source of strength for the group. Yet, the African students, especially Nigerians, who formed the core of the ensemble's membership over the years, have made a phenomenal impact that I will discuss later. More recently, Bob Damm, a percussionist and professor at Mississippi State, and I have mutually benefited from each other's collaborative performances on the campuses of the two major state universities. In addition to the continued support the ensemble receives from Dr. Charles Gates, the music department's chair, as well as from other university offices and administrators, the participation of my family (wife, two sons, and daughter) out of love for me and the dance drumming genre, has partly sustained the Ole Miss African Drum and Dance Ensemble in a special way. This explains the reasons for which I partly dedicate this book to my family in Oxford, Mississippi.

BINGHAMTON UNIVERSITY, NEW YORK ("NUKPORFE")

According to James Burns, the founding director and teacher of West African dance drumming at Binghamton University in Binghamton, New York, the ensemble began in spring 2006 with a drum class that he taught

Figure 2.32 James Burns directs Binghamton University's Nukporfe Ensemble as they perform the Anlo Ewe *Agbekor* dance. [Photo by Binghamton University Photography]

under the auspices of the Departments of Music and Africana Studies. At the end of spring 2006, Burns approached the Theatre-Dance Department about creating some African dance classes, which they agreed to sponsor. As a result, the university, per Burns's advice, hired Pierrette Aboadji from the Ghana Dance Ensemble, Legon, who came that fall to teach beginning and advanced African Dance courses in the Departments of Africana Studies and Theatre-Dance. "Together we [Burns and Aboadji] inaugurated the Nukporfe 'Seeing is Believing' African Dance Drumming Ensemble in the fall of 2006. In fall 2011, Aboadji had to go back to Ghana, and the dance classes have continued with her senior student, BU graduate Marcel March."

So James Burns, who is a faculty member of the Institute of African Studies, has used his agency in selling the salience of West African dance drumming to cognate departments for which the genre and courses are highly interdisciplinary. As such, Binghamton represents another model whereby three departments rather than only music (or in a few cases, music and dance) recognize the relevance and resonance of West African drumming to their fields. Four classes—1) African Dance Beginning, 2) African Dance Advanced, 3) African Music Ensemble, and 4) African Performance Ensemble—are cross-listed with Theatre Dance, Africana Studies and Music Departments. Accordingly, dancing (movement) and singing of songs are the main activities of the dance classes, while drumming and singing are the focus of the African music class. Yet, to reflect the genre's African conceptual realism, the instructors integrate all these components of the arts at the ensemble level.

Figure 2.33 James Burns, director of Nukporfe, Binghamton University, and George Dor. [Photo from George Dor, October 2007]

Regarding the selection of members of the Nukporfe group, whether BU alumni, faculty, or staff and others from the larger cultural community may be considered, or if is it strictly for current students, Burns explains as follows. Like the orchestra and all other music performance courses, students have to pass an audition for the class part of Nukporfe. As such, students who have already taken one of the dance or drum courses, or have a background in African music (BU has many Ghanaian and Nigerian students), have the advantage of gaining membership into Nukporfe. In addition, alumni and community members are allowed to sit in, and about five to ten of them come regularly. Also, many students who cannot overload with more credits just come for the love of the music, especially given that class numbers are so high, with an average of forty dance students in each class, and twenty to thirty drummers.

Concerning the African dances that the BU ensemble performs and students of other classes learn regularly, and whether any reasons account for these preferences, Burns explains that given Aboadji's Ewe heritage, and his own research into Ewe drumming, "we have chosen to specialize in the Ewe dances, including the choreographed pieces of slow and fast *Agbekor*, Togo

Atsia, *Sohoun*, and *Gahu*, as well as the community dances *Agbadza*, *Kinka*, and *Borborbor/Akpese*. We also do *Kpanlogo*, *Kpatsa*, and *Sikyi*, and have done *Adowa*." As can be seen, Burns's ethnographic work has informed the repertoire of the preceding multiple Ewe dances. However, Aboadji's experiences and influence as a former member of the Ghana Dance Ensemble partly favored the performance of a few other Ghanaian ethnic (Ga and Akan) dance genres.

All music and dance classes perform for the "Mid-Day Series" each semester. Each class does the dance/music it has learned, including songs that are taught concurrently in the dance and drum classes, while performance ensemble Nukporfe fills in the rest by doing their own dances and providing extra dancers and musicians for the other classes. Nukporfe performs two times each semester on campus, and two to four times a semester off campus. Nukporfe, BU's African Drum and Dance Ensemble, has collaborated with the Binghamton choral groups, the university chorus, Harpur Chorale, and the women's chorus. Nukporfe's other engaging and interesting collaborations include with BU string faculty and graduate students for the original concert *Africanaise*, which featured arrangements of Bach's music for drums and string quartet. The concert also featured an original composition by James Burns for Ewe drums and strings, with original dance choreography. The ensemble regularly goes to Cornell University to give workshops and performances there, and the group has been to Princeton and Tufts University to perform. In the community, the ensemble performs for festivals, events, and for schools.

But beyond factors of vitality and appeal of the dance drumming classes, and the cross-listing of classes, other reasons for good student patronage depend on their ethnic backgrounds, their levels of world-mindedness, multiculturalism, and the internationalism that characterizes the demographics of New York. Burns informs that: "We have a solid base of Ghanaian, Nigerian, and African diaspora [African American and Caribbean] students, as well as a large number of Chinese/Korean students. We also have many Latino, Jewish, and Caucasian students" (Interview, October 2008). The New York metropolitan demography is extremely important, as the classes are able to draw on Ghanaian and other West African students and community members to bring the cultural experience of Ghana to the other students. "It also gives our group an edge in the music and dance, because many of the students have grown up around it," Burns observes.

In answering my question, "How important is the ensemble to the university, and how do you know?" Burns replies:

Nukporfe [the ensemble] has done a lot for the University—performing at the State Capitol and for visiting dignitaries, and have been featured extensively in the local news, television, and other media. Through such performances the ensemble has gradually won support within the university, and it has brought a great deal of positive attention to BU within the larger community. As a result, our visibility at the level of the president and provost as well as dean is very high. Incidentally, the university hired a professional photographer to shoot some publicity photos, and our group was among them, so I regularly see us on magazines, brochures, posters, and an 8 x 10 framed photograph in the dean's office! They have acknowledged their support by keeping the dance-drumming program going during cutbacks, even after we learned that it was allegedly slated for cancellation. The administration has pledged to create a full-time position in African dance for the fall of 2013. This would allow us to hire a dance teacher from Ghana full time. (Interview, October, 2012)

Burns further details that "The costumes and instruments have been purchased by the university, but all of the financial support came from the dean, and not from my individual departments. Africana does not have much money, and Music is already committed to sponsoring its major ensembles, so I have had to fight at the higher levels to get support." I appreciate Burns's empathy for the financial obligations of the departments that host the African dance drumming courses. I am positive that with time they will also show their support in other ways in addition to the provision of space and administration of the courses.

It is easy to sense how passionate Burns is in sharing the positive developments regarding the growth in the BU African dance drumming program. My reading of the preceding quotation includes Burns's expressions of (1) his personal joy of fulfillment, (2) explicit gratitude to the dean's office, and (3) sharing such a great story with me, a friend and colleague with shared interests. However, in chapter 5 I will discuss in detail why I am convinced that beyond visibility, fame, and personal accomplishment, an overarching reason explains BU dean's office lending such unflinching support for Nukporfe. Admittedly, the Ghanaian Ewe say *Detsivivi yehea zikpui* (It is the sumptuous soup that draws the stool), and nobody will take anything away from acknowledging the deserved accomplishments of Nukporfe. But after interviewing Professor Glenn Hopkins, dean of the University of Mississippi's College of Liberal Arts, I have a fuller understanding that what largely motivates such support is university administrators' awareness of the extent to which a world music ensemble is partially fulfilling broader college ideals and values that enrich the lives of an academic community.

3

PEDAGOGICAL APPROACHES OF DANCE DRUMMING INSTRUCTORS

West African drumming and dance instructors and ensemble directors are an indispensable group of key players in this process and presence of a genre, a group I also call implementers. To facilitate understanding or appreciation of their agency as instructors and performers, I will classify them into groups before proceeding to their teaching approaches. Ensemble directors in North American universities can be subcategorized under (a) former master drummers of the Ghana National Dance Ensemble, or other west African national dance troupes; (b) Ghanaians or other West Africans who have pursued or are pursuing their doctoral or masters degrees in American universities; and (c) Americans who have conducted ethnomusicological field research on a west African drumming tradition. Kobla Ladzekpo, Abraham Adzinya, Alfred Ladzekpo, Christopher K. Ladzekpo, Godwin Agbeli, and Togbui Ameanyo II (alias Gideon Alorwoyie) belong to the first category, which draws heavily on the models of West African dance troupes in terms of multiple national dances they teach and perform. The second group consists of teaching fellows or assistants, and some who later become professors in American universities; William Amoako, Willie Anku, and Pascal Younge belong here. David Locke, James Burns, and Patricia Tang have studied drumming and dance through apprenticeship in West Africa during their field research, and belong in the third category. Ensemble directors from this group tend to focus on the musical genre or the ethnic group(s) they studied. As Locke explains, he prefers the *habǫbǫ* or group model, because this typical village model enables his research to inform his pedagogy and permit him to teach to his strength, for it also allows for specialization (Interview, July 2007). More recently, an emerging group of ensemble directors are outstanding former student drummers, who eventually go to Africa to experience the contextual realities of the dances and to study with various master drummers.

EXAMINATION OF TERMINOLOGY FOR LABELING THE DRUM ENSEMBLE DIRECTOR

Differing preferences of the appropriate names used in qualifying drum ensemble directors and instructors in the American academy exist in relevant discourse. The discussion of these semantic options necessitates drawing retrospectively on clues from the original West African traditions that ensemble directors represent in the diaspora, as well as having cognizance of the categories of ensemble directors I have delineated earlier. While the expression "master drummer" has been the most common usage and reference, some Africanists think that this qualifier has a Western semantic baggage and root, similar to a master musician or a maestro. Some critics may even contend the preferential use of master drummer, like "master of ceremony," betrays the male hegemony in literary discourse on several world cultures. Yet, since most African drummers are men, I hope extremists will not infer the overly stated and preconceived notion of African male chauvinism as the point at play here. Rather, Meki Nzewi, for example, favors "mother drummer" over master drummer, because he maintains that mother drummer is more African-centered (Nzewi 2009). And yet, David Locke advocates the use of "lead drummer" to reflect the musical role that such a musician plays during performance (Interview, July 2007).

I support the use of all three labels—"master drummer," "mother drummer," and "lead drummer"—for a critical examination of these descriptive phrases reveals nuances that implicate and emphasize related but different phenomena pertaining to the caliber of drummer in question. Accordingly, the choice of label should depend on the specific context being evoked. In my opinion, "master drummer" signifies an attained degree of competence, outstanding exhibition of compelling knowledge of a drumming tradition, and a designation of a virtuosic class that the aesthetic evaluators of the carriers of a given culture may confer on a particular drummer. Beyond a demonstrated outstanding level of proficiency in his art of drumming, a master drummer, in some cases, may be regarded as a living repository of his cultural knowledge (Nketia 1963; Euba 1990; Locke 2009: 87–91). He is well informed of the history of his people and should be ready to recall a praise-name or perform a praise-poetry of a ruler if such a drummer is associated with a court tradition. A master drummer, for appropriate contextual performance, must also know names and histories of clans, villages, and towns of the sub-region. Kwasi Dunyo thinks a master drummer must also demonstrate command over a vast repertoire of ethnic dances that he could convincingly perform and teach. Hence an Anlo Ewe master drummer must know and distinguish the drum motives of Atrikpui from Agbadza, Atisagbekor or Kenka from Gahu, and so forth. Further, formulaic sequences of dances characteristic of the ritual ceremonies or idiosyncratic dances, rhythmic motives, and/or "drum languages" (Agawu 1995: 5–6) necessary to invoke the presence of a specific deity are acquired and specialized forms of knowledge that partly define master drummers who operate within indigenous religious contexts. However, master drummers of many social dances, though artistically competent, may not require the same kind of cultural knowledge as those associated with the courts and religious institutions. Additionally, special ritual ceremonies may be performed by some master drummers for spirits of deities and ancestor master drummers to come and inhabit and bless their art; give them direction, retentive memory, and creative acumen; and protect them from evil people and spirits. Among some ethnic groups, including the Dagbon, Akan, Yoruba, Wolof, Mande, and Ewe, "master drummer" commands recognition as belonging to a respectable social rank or status. Here, a master drummer qualifies to be designated as a lead drummer as well, especially when playing that role during performance, or as a mother drummer, who generates or recreates drum music according to acceptable cultural, artistic, and creative practices of his drumming tradition.

Meki Nzewi, one of the leading advocates for foregrounding indigenous African perspectives in African music research, thinks mother drummer best translates the indigenous African conception, as specifically evidenced in Igbo culture (Nzewi 2009). Similarly, in an interview I had with Kobla Ladzekpo, he explained and drew my attention to the meanings of two Anlo Ewe words, *azaguno̱* and *wuno̱*, that partially corroborate Nzewi's position on the use of mother drummer (October 2009). *Azagu*, according to Kobla Ladzekpo, is a F*o̱*n word for drum, thus a synonym to *wu*. *No̱*, the suffix to both *azagu* and *wu*, means mother. It follows that each of these two words, *azaguno̱* and *wuno̱*, literally translates as "mother of drum" or "drum mother." Yet the etymology of *azaguno* and *wuno* calls for the understanding of the ways in which two domains of Ewe culture can be merged or implicated in a usage. Here, aspects of musical creativity and concepts from the family, specifically the mother's role, are inextricably indexed. Considering the leadership roles the ensemble's director plays during performance, Kobla Ladzekpo, for example, referenced familial roles of the mother as somebody who does most of the talking and frequently directs the kids as a source domain of a conceptual metaphor that *azaguno* suggests. Kofi Gbolonyo has also provided insights on this Ewe word (Gbolonyo 2009: 1364–136).

As one is about to settle for mother drummer as a better term that may be used to replace master drummer, as in Nzewi's terms, Ladzekpo further observes the terms *azaguno* or *wuno* do not designate the master drummer alone. All recognized drummers within a given ensemble qualify to be called *azagunowo* or *wunowo*, with the suffix *wo* indicating the plural forms of those terms. This clarification corrects the erroneous notion carried by younger Ewe that *azaguno* means an outstanding master drummer. Additionally, Ladzekpo reminds me of how during performances the Anlo Ewe can call for invigorated drumming by shouting "*Azagu! Azagu! Azagu!*" (Drum! Drum! Drum!), and all of a sudden, the drummers would be spurred on to step up their creative intensity and vitality. Nevertheless, the suffix *ga*, which means great, needs to be added to *azaguno*ˆ; thus, *azagunoga* (the great drummer) evokes the aura of a mother or master drummer.

Later in our discussion of the meaning of *azaguno*, I provided my personal understanding of the word *nǫ*, and I thought my take was quite convincing to both Kobla and his wife, Beatrice, just as their insights opened new windows of understanding for me. Drawing on my background as another Ewe, I suggested the generative properties of a mother carried in the suffix *nǫ*. Just as a mother gives birth to a child, and an Ewe mother could be called *vinǫ*, Kwasinǫ, or Georgenǫ (mother of a child or children, Kwasi's mother, or George's mother), the drummer is also conceived as somebody who gives birth to drum music. Not only in terms of generating drum genres, but a drummer also always engages in a degree of re-composition using well-known resources and procedures during creative contexts (Anku 2007: 5), as well as allowing his artistic individuality to manifest during his improvisation on and transformation of rhythmic motives.[1]

One lesson the preceding Ewe construction of gender offers is that gender formations do not always match the biologically determined sex of people. Biologically, a mother of children is a female. Yet, the mother of drum music or of songs may be male. Furthermore, when a male practitioner of a cultural activity is deemed by the Ewe as obsessed, preoccupied with, or consumed by his cultural or social roles, he can be considered as being married to that endeavor. Thus, a man can become the wife of songs as a composer-poet, *heno* or *hesino* [*he*: song, *si*: wife, *nǫ*: mother], or even in the domain of religion, a traditional priest may be known as the wife of a particular deity, *husino*. Hence, the biological, generative, and behavioral are implicated in my preceding discussion of *nǫ* or mother.

Yet, Kwasi Dunyo's take on the semantics of *azagonǫ* provides another interesting perspective. He translates *nǫ* as an act of inhabitation, dwelling, or embodiment. He explains drumming in Anlo conception, wherein song is viewed as a spirit that can embody someone, making that person's body the place of residence or perpetual abode of the spirit of drumming (Interview, January 2010). This version is equally convincing.

The label "lead drummer," David Locke's preferred qualifier, is more role-determined. In coordination with lead singers and dancers, the lead drummer provides cues that dictate changes in dance movements and interacts with other percussionists as to when to begin and end a piece, when to have dialogue with supporting drums, when to have waiting moments so as to thin out the texture and density of drumming, and when to resume drumming to invigorate the performance.[2] While the expression "lead drummer" may be contextually specific, designating the act of leading a performance of a piece, it may be an appropriate term to apply to those drummers who may not possess all the accolades associated with master or mother drummers. Accordingly, a director of a university ensemble, who can teach various aspects of drumming and dance but admits his lack of cultural knowledge of the ethnic group he represents, may best be called a lead drummer. Similarly, an African who directs a university ensemble in America but cannot perform lead drummer roles in his village or city, or cannot be called a master drummer back home, may best be referred to as a lead drummer. This designation is not to demean the leadership roles of such directors, who may be famous for other kinds of music in their home countries or may be established scholars of African music. Rather, such differentiations will affirm our respect for African traditional knowledge and their custodians, recognition of rank, status, virtuosity, proficiency, and competence by indigenous African evaluative processes and standards. Finally, distinguishing between these three terms contextually affords selective clarity as to whether one is evoking conferred titles, creative processes, and/or performance roles. And in the same way as exceptionally talented Ewe song makers can be described by multiple labels—composer, poet, and lead singer—a virtuosic drummer may qualify to be designated as a master, mother, and lead drummer.

PEDAGOGICAL APPROACHES OF WEST AFRICAN DRUMMING AND DANCE INSTRUCTORS

After I presented a paper on this book project at a symposium on the music of Africa and its diaspora, a young male student approached me and wanted to know my position on the different pedagogical approaches that were used in teaching West African drumming and dance at three different schools he attended. According to him, he took drumming at a university in which the focus was on a single genre and the pedagogical approach was mainly rote, more African in nature with little or no use of Western notation to facilitate the learning process. Contrarily, his experiences in the second school was the antithesis of the first in terms of multiple dance genres they learned to perform, and the extent to which the instructor frequently encouraged the deployment of Western notation in transmitting West African drumming. However, the student's experiences in the third school seem to be a blend of partial learning procedures from the first and second institutions. Whereas his third teacher offered fewer dances as his course content and repertoire than in the second school, his pedagogical approach was really African because he was a traditionalist. Thus, the student's question was, "Which approach do you think is the best?"

Cautious not to implicate or betray any of the three teachers, I framed my answer in a way the student could appreciate something specific from each of his drumming and dance courses. I reminded him of the importance of the cultural and historical consciousness of each of these instructors, and the number of dances they each know and could teach with confidence. Also, the objectives of each drumming and dance course—whether the courses are designed for first-time drummers and dancers, introductory, intermediate, or advanced course, whether or not the course is intended for music majors or minors, or if any student across the board could take it—have implications for pedagogical methods. Further, teachers have different teaching philosophies that may inform their teaching and learning procedures and tools. The preceding and other variables make it unfair to declare one pedagogical approach as completely better than the other. I thought I sealed my effort to convince this promising student by reminding him that all newly designed courses go through a stringent evaluative process prior to their approval, and the confidence such a process provides all students is the ability of any approved course meeting desirable learning goals commensurate with broader academic program objectives.

My conversation with this student simply echoes a long-standing debate that may never have a conclusive resolution. I present insights of my consultants as they answered my questions on their approaches to teaching drumming, dance, and songs. In each case, several minutes of conversation revealed a recurring theme as the most important for a particular instructor, and these are the areas I highlight, hoping they will constitute an immense source of wisdom for future teachers and students.

RECIPROCITY OF WEST AFRICAN DRUMMING AND DANCE IN PEDAGOGICAL CONTEXTS

The seemingly inextricable nexus between African music and dance has been explicitly thematized in numerous critical discourses on the performing arts of Africa. These texts include Jones (1959), Nketia (1966; 1974), Nzewi (1971), Knight (1974), Sunkett (1995), Wesh-Asante (1996), Agawu (2003), Green (2004), and Hill (2011). Specifically pertaining to drumming and dance are perspectives from Jones (1959), which Agawu (2003: 94) revitalizes and advocates for a deeper understanding of metrical frameworks of specific dance-drumming genres. Between Jones and Agawu was Pantaleoni (1972), who also contributed to the discussion on the symbiotic analysis of drumming and dance. Coincidentally, Kobla Ladzekpo, a highly respected Anlo Ewe drummer and a major source of the data that informed Pantaleoni's work on this subject matter, had remained very consistent in his advocacy for the interplay between drumming and dance. The following excerpt is from a distilled version of my October 2009 interview with him at his home in a suburb of Los Angeles on the topic.

Beginning with a reminder of the name of the course he teaches at UCLA—"Music and Dance of West Africa"—Kobla Ladzekpo emphatically asserts: "Don't take the dancing away from the drumming. Just play the drums without singing and dancing and it is dry. People will not enjoy it. You have to put them all together. They are like twins. You can't separate them" (Interview, October 2009). As a traditionalist, he then situates this symbiosis between drumming and dance by citing pragmatic examples from (1) Akan cultural practices, (2) transformative development of his former colleague ensemble members of the Ghana National Dance Troupe, and (3) the case evidence of his daughter who assists him as an understudy.

In Akan *Adowa*, for example, dancers make specific gestures, some symbolic, according to what the Atumpan player is directing them to do. The most visible and audible motive is the turn, which is both played and danced. Knowing the meaning of drum motives and drum languages so that a dancer could respond with the appropriate matching and desirable behaviors is a testimony of an informed cultural bearer. When teaching his students, Kobla Ladzekpo occasionally tells his students about relevant phenomenological truths of specific cultures. Further, before a community installs somebody as their chief among the Akan of Ghana, they have to educate him about drum languages so he recognizes text-bound appellations and rhythms that invite other symbolic responses and behavior from him. For, according to Kobla

Ladzekpo, if state drummers play a drum motive or a praise name and the chief does not respond or is not responding as tradition demands, drummers can insult such traditional rulers through playing other text-laden phrases on their drums, if they choose to do so. This is drummers' privilege that can be used against any chief or even kings without it being viewed as a disrespectful act against authority. It is one of the reasons prospective chiefs are taught how to dance, and here follows Ladzekpo's vivid reminiscence exemplifies the practice.

> Yah, this recollection was about the late Asantehene [sic],[3] who was a lawyer. Before he was enstooled, I had the privilege to be at the Institute of African Studies, University of Ghana, at that time, so they [kingmakers] sent him to Job 600,[4] where Mawere Opoku[5] taught him how to respond to drum languages associated with the Asante royalty. Professor Opoku was assisted by his sister [sic],[6] who was also a great dancer. (Interview, October 2009)

In response to my question on what advice he has for younger directors of West African drumming and dance, Ladzekpo reiterated the need to present drumming and dance as two facets of the same art form. However, he now uses another anecdote on the artistic strengths of the pioneering members of the Ghana National Dance Troupe, which he remembered comprised six men and six female artists. He named the men as Sackyefio, Doudou, Adinku, Klottey, and Mensah, whereas Patience Kwakwa, E. Tamakloe, L. Harrison, Beatrice Addo, and Edna Mensah [sic] were the females. Yet the most important point Ladzekpo made using this list was how initially most of the male artists were only excellent dancers and not versatile drummers, and how he used to advise them to learn to become drummers, because that added knowledge could help them become future ensemble directors on their own. As some of them came to the United States of America and formed their own ensembles, they then realized the pragmatic wisdom in Ladzekpo's advice to them. Luckily, learning to play the leading/master/mother drum as a dancer is easier than for a newcomer to the art. Dancers will normally begin to remember the drum rhythmic motives and patterns as well as cues to which they have responded for years as they transfer those aurally and visually configured images and structures onto the drums.

Yet Kobla Ladzekpo brings his point even closer to home as he recalls his daughter's process of enculturation as an archetypical testimony of the reciprocity of drumming and dance, a reliable pedagogical approach. Although

I heard from DjeDje about Yeko as a girl who regularly assists her dad, the story about how it all started is very revealing. Perhaps an innate musicality, it was Beatrice, Yeko's mother, who started the process of exposure. As a dance instructor, Beatrice would take Yeko along to her dance classes as the father did the lead drumming, not knowing that the girl was critically observing her mother and her students. During a special performance at California College of the Arts, Beatrice recalls how the six-year-old Yeko decided to claim part of the performance space for herself as she danced beautifully to the admiration and amazement of the audience, almost stealing the show from the formal and original dancers. Since then, Kobla and Beatrice, after witnessing public affirmation of their daughter's promising artistic talent and capabilities, never relented in training her in dance and later drumming. Kobla thus compared her daughter's process of learning to drum to those of his ensemble colleagues discussed earlier. He observes his daughter learned most of her drumming as a dancer, and uses the following conceptual analogy to clarify the relationship: "It is question and answer. Somebody asks you a question, you must know the answer. The drum plays a pattern, you know where to turn as a dancer. So when you go to the drum, you try to reproduce it. That was how she learned it herself. I just affirm how she drums with little guidance" (Interview, October 2009).

Awareness of one's ethnic or ancestral background coded in negative pride and utopian claim to automatic knowledge by virtue of identity, according to Beatrice, have in many students affected the extent to which they could have mastered specific West African dances. Rather, the key to good execution of West African dance is willingness to learn, listen to one's teacher, and at times be ready to relearn some movements according to the acceptable aesthetics of a specific culture from which a dance originates and is part. Sometimes this process may require undoing the different dance baggage students bring along from other cultures; the aesthetics for West African dance is completely different from that for ballet, and aesthetic nuances may exist between dances from two different ethnic groups of the same African nation. However, persistent spirit and desire to know the right thing eventually pays off for students irrespective of their ethnic backgrounds.

Granting the commonplace knowledge that the performing arts of Africa are inextricably integrated, and while most teachers would like such an awareness of this realism to inform their teaching of dance drumming, I have discussed cases in which only drumming had been taught by percussionists without movement. Also, given the structural constraints imposed by certain universities that seek separate development in African dance drumming under their individual departmental auspices, a few instructors, including David Locke, had to teach dance and drumming components separately for the departments under which they are subsumed, before bringing them together for performances. James Burns does the same at Binghamton University. This practice is a complete antithesis to what pertains in several other universities that house the West African ensemble in the music department and considers the course first and foremost as belonging to the music department although it may be cross-listed with dance and reflects a typical Western epistemological tradition in which departmental autonomy triumphs over the ontological and phenomenological attributes of the art forms being taught in the classroom, thereby resonating the prescriptive and circumscriptive dictates of systems on agency and practice.

In spite of the diversity in traditional African music genres, one overarching commonality among ethnic traditions resides in their perception of the performing arts as integrated. In addition to Kobla Ladzekpo's position on this theme, Hill (2011) draws on djembe drumming and dance of the Mande to similarly advocate the reciprocity between drumming and dance. Specifically, Hill's article corroborates the position on the symbiotic approach to teaching West African drumming and dance. While the oral and aural aspects of instruction of dance drumming have been stressed in many writings, Hill additionally emphasizes the visual dimension of learning to perform African dance. Thus, his list and discussion of rich video recordings on "The Dancing Djembe" by renowned performers is intended to provide a guide for learners and teachers to access these invaluable visual instructional aids. Hill also discusses the learning procedures of imitation, with the use of vocables to simulate important drum motives in what he calls "drumming with the mouth" as a strategy of memorizing. Similarly, matching memorized drum motives with corresponding dance movements facilitates the articulation of the synthesis of the related arts that emerges from the coordinated application of oral, aural, and visual senses central to the fullest cognition of African dance drumming.

FAVORED ORAL-AURAL TRANSMISSION AS "AUTHENTIC" PEDAGOGICAL APPROACH OF REPRESENTATION?

Gideon Alorwoyie, Kobla Ladzekpo, Kwasi Dunyo, and other dance-drumming instructors advocate pedagogical approaches that are as close as possible to those used by the indigenous cultural bearers in transmitting the art. As can be seen, this category of teachers are all master drummers who first and foremost consider themselves custodians and perpetuators of their cultures. Accordingly, they teach wholly by rote with no writing in teaching drumming, movement, or singing. For drumming, they privilege the oral tradition in which vocalization of rhythmic configurations serve as a mnemonic device to which the learner has to listen attentively (Wade 2004: 16–19). One must be careful not to generalize and say the use of vocables in teaching reflects a total authentic way of teaching drumming. Certainly, it may be easier for a teacher who focuses on only dances from a single ethnic group to learn to transmit through such acceptable learning devices. However, it is unrealistic to imagine an instructor of dances from five different ethnic groups learning the characteristic vocables in all five different languages. At best, these instructors normally specialize in the vocables of their native ethnic groups, and create their personal learning devices for teaching other dances. Although I want to avoid overgeneralization, I hope I have suggested the desire of these instructors to be as close as possible to the traditions they represent, and where and when possible, some have partially learned from their fellow master drummers from other ethnic groups. Nevertheless, to elucidate how other aspects of oral-aural methods of teaching and learning are equally important, I share a portion of my interview with Kwasi Dunyo regarding his teaching approach and what has worked for him in his classes:

- Creating the learning environment where students feel happy and relaxed, "though balancing such atmospheres with discipline or insisting they do the right thing at the right time, is the first classroom requirement."
- "A problem of a student in your class is not really his or hers. It is the teacher's." The teacher has to watch the student to determine whether the problem is from the hand technique, incorrect rhythmic perception, manner of holding the instrument or positioning of the instrument, or learning attitudes including retention level of individual students.
- The teacher must be mindful of the differences between fast and slow learners and identify such categories of students in each class.
- Discourage intimidating behavior from fast learners toward their classmates.
- Teacher must also encourage slow learners and let them know the confidence he or she has in them, because it can be very frustrating for

slow learners when they are struggling with something others spend little time in grasping.

Dunyo tells didactic stories he has originally made to teach life lessons to his class. For example, rather than simply making a factual statement "Do not give up, keep on trying," he will present his class a narrative as follows:

> Try and Success are twins, and while Try is a boy, Success is a girl. Whereas Try has so much of energy and he is very strong, Success is very beautiful and humble. Try loves his sister so much that he does not allow anybody to see or worry her unless one passes through him. As such, people need to knock very hard at Try's door persistently if they yearn to see his sister. And although Try is a strong boy, he easily gets tired, and will eventually open the door to the one who keeps on knocking for him/her to see Success, his sister. (Interview, January 2010)

The message and lesson for the class, especially slow learners, is "Never stop trying, never stop knocking at the door of Success. Face it, else the devil is waiting and watching so that if you give up, he will take over, and the devil's name is Failure. Nobody wants to see that face, so students must keep on knocking the door of Try until they succeed." The advantage of such brief narratives, I think, is that students can remember the story better than a single sentence expressing the same idea.

Another aspect of his teaching approach is breaking down the piece into units to facilitate comprehension and later putting them together. For Dunyo, as almost all drumming teachers, the bell part, called time line, is the first thing to teach. As discussed earlier, students must be inspired and taught to enjoy what they are performing in order to induce a positive affect and response from audiences.

Native teachers of drumming alone do not use the oral-aural approach of transmitting West African drumming. In the desire to honor the traditions that they have learned but also because they found the new approaches fascinating and effective, both Anna Melnikoff (York) and Patricia Tang (MIT) teach their classes as they were taught,. Accordingly, even when Lamine Toure joined Tang to co-direct the MIT Sabar ensemble, Tang encouraged Toure to stick to the rote method of teaching, which she describes as follows. Lamine Toure provides preliminary instructions on technique for about two weeks. Sabar drumming involves a combination of hand and stick techniques. So, the teacher first teaches different strokes—the three different hand strokes and many more stick strokes. The next stage is teaching the *bak* [*sic*], pre-composed musical phrases that form the bulk of the repertoire. While some of these are lexically meaningful as translatable proverbs and other wise sayings, some of them are simply abstract vocables. He teaches the students to learn to speak them in Wolof, as a drum language, before they later transfer these motives onto the drums. Given the understanding that students are also to learn about other domains of the culture, Toure spends time explaining the meanings of these proverbs as well as how they are situated within the Wolof culture to the students. He teaches these phrases by ear: he says them and the students imitate him; he plays and the students copy him. Hence, attentive listening, speaking, and watching provide the congenial atmosphere necessary for a rewarding learning experience.

As may be expected of sub-Saharan ensemble drumming, Sabar drumming involves different parts within the polyrhythmic matrix. Toure ensures every student learns to pay each part. Normally the bulk of the ensemble plays the basic part, while a few members play complementary parts resulting in a composite structure. Another interesting stage of a performance is the time for solos, which demands intense improvisation from member to member, permitting everybody to express his or her individuality in creative terms (Tang, Interview, November 2010).

In her response to my question on how the students respond to the oral-aural pedagogical approach, Tang observes:

> American students are spoiled by the written tradition, so when I am there they will ask me to write in Wolof what the phrases are and what they mean. Lamin's pedagogical approach is to help the students internalize as they learn aurally. Because we find out that the moment I start writing on the board, they all start to lose focus on the drumming. However, we record some of the performances on the Blackboard [software] so that students can listen and practice on their own. Although there is little fear that the student may practice the wrong way, it gives them the advantage of being actively engaged in the learning process as they practice before coming to class. (Interview, November 2010)

Melnikoff's approach is similar, and she also emphasizes students' mastery of good technique. She uses descriptive words like "melody," or "bass" for drum parts when teaching. Such terms reflect the ways in which contemporary native teachers conceive the structure of the drum genre in relation to their knowledge of parallel terms that would have been normally used for vocal genres.

DEBATE ON REPERTOIRE: THE OPTION OF MULTIPLE OR LIMITED DANCES

The practice of teaching multiple dances to a particular university ensemble or ensemble director's habit of changing a set of dances after a number of semesters, on the one hand, and the specialization of an instructor or school in one or two (limited) dances, on the other hand, have far-reaching pedagogical implications that my consultants shared, and in some cases defended. The most common practice in the universities I have discussed so far is the learning and performance of multiple ethnic dance-drumming genres normally selected from different regions of the same country. This practice can be called the dance ensemble or dance troupe model, which has been crystallized by the many former Ghana National Dance Ensemble's master drummers and leading dancers who have made phenomenal contributions to the strong presence of the genre in the American academy. It has become so popular that even other directors who were not in the National Dance Ensemble have replicated this model that regularly features Ewe, Akan, Dagbamba, and Ga dances within the same semester.

Some North American instructors who had traveled to Africa to conduct field research and/or learn to perform one or two dance-drumming genres from a reputable indigenous virtuoso tend to specialize in only one or two dances they know very well and could teach to their students. This category of teachers includes David Locke, who teaches a dance per semester either from Anlo Ewe or Dagbon cultures; Patricia Tang of MIT, who focuses on Sabar drumming of the Wolof of Senegal; and Anna Melnikoff, who teaches Mande drumming at York. While Locke and Tang are ethnomusicologists and have conducted field research on their chosen dance traditions, Melnikoff, according to Robert Simms, was hired by York because she earned her knowledge as a performer and teacher of djembe drumming studying with great master drummers in Guinea and Burkina Faso.

James Burns, who also conducted his research on the Anlo Ewe and teaches dance drumming at Binghamton, takes a mixed approach by performing multiple northern and southern Ewe dances. Certainly, the assistance he later received from Pierrette Aboadji, a Ghanaian dancer, complemented his efforts and facilitated the teaching and performance of multiple dances including Akan and Ga genres.

While some may simply explain the practice of specializing in one or two dances as an indirect result or betrayal of lack of knowledge in multiple dances, David Locke has revealed how this choice has deeper implications for a healthy interplay between research and pedagogy. While Locke agrees he is comfortable with teaching what he knows best to his students, he asserts he could have learned more Ghanaian dances if he had wanted to use the dance troupe model. As a Wesleyan graduate he has experience performing other Ghanaian dances; and while he was in Ghana and working with Godwin Agbeli, he played other Ghanaian dances beyond those he critically studied, both artistically and scholarly.

But what is the pedagogical debate implicated in the two models? For the dance troupe or dance ensemble model, one or two teachers instruct American students in multiple dances from a country. Here, the drum instructor is trusted as an omniscient perpetuator of multiple dances. The Ghana National Dance Ensemble, for example, was formed with the intent of promoting interethnic integration, thereby leading to the construction of national identity through the representation of diverse regional dances. Some of the finest drummers and dancers were recruited from the country's various regions and experts from each ethnic group were encouraged to teach their idiosyncratic dances—drumming, movement, and songs—to group members originally from other regions. This practice of sharing broadened the scope of repertoire and performance skills of each member of the national ensemble. Accordingly, former members of the Ghana National Dance Ensemble teaching in North American universities have an appreciable degree of competence in multiple dances they can teach with confidence. Also, an original objective of the ensemble was to mirror the representation of a nation during a single performance. As such, featuring as many as possible dances from a country within a two-hour performance would have satisfied audiences and national cultural officers in this process of identity mediation. In North America, one certainly expects a different set of meanings to be constructed by audiences during the performances of these re-contextualized genres. However, the plurality of dances tend to offer broader university cultural communities enduring affects engendered by a variety of dances—drum rhythms, movements, songs, and costumes—during a single performance. Also, in cases where West African dance drumming is used as a tool and site for educating the audience and performers about the diversity in ethnic cultures of Africa, a single performance that privileges the dance troupe model may offer such insights.

Contrarily, Locke criticizes the preceding model and advocates the teaching of limited dances for a number of reasons. First, Locke considers West

African dance-drumming pieces as works of sublime artistic expression composed and performed by virtuosic native musicians. Perhaps influenced by a Wesleyan approach of what he calls the "classical conservatory model," which according to Locke emphasizes the study and performance of artworks, he consolidated his conviction that the indigenous people with whom he had studied view their creations in that light. Hence, the study and performance of repertory, according to Locke, must be done to reflect ethnographic realities. To him, the model of multiple dances parallels the performance of "excerpts," and does not allow for the rendition of the entirety of a work, and as he observes:

> It does not get deeply into the artistic nuances of the dances. And to me it sends the wrong message about what African performing arts culture is, because the works that groups do are very deep and rich, and they contain many drum compositions. My scholarly work is telling me that this performance of excerpts is a distortion of the ethnographic reality in Africa, and it was a big thing for me to try to integrate my scholarly work with teaching, and to bring my ethnographic understanding that I have partly gained from my study of ethnomusicology to inform my pedagogical approach. I integrate the practical conservatory model with the academic study even in my teaching. (Interview, July 2007)

As can be seen from the above dicta, a university teacher's research and teaching approaches and philosophies must reinforce each other. Further, in order to provide students with profound insights on genres, Locke thinks the instructor must teach fewer things (here, dances) more comprehensively.

To further support his position, Locke uses what the Ewe call habǫbǫ or "group" model as what pertains in the village or town where a dance-drumming ensemble normally focuses on a dance genre, although it may perform another rhythm or dance for the sake of variety. For this model, the name of the genre also serves as a partial label of the group, and a classic example is the performing group Locke formed in the broader Boston area called the Agbekor Society. Accordingly, the choice of teaching a single dance throughout a semester reflects this model rather than what urban-based dance troupes do. Avorgbedor's urban ethnomusicological writings also discuss the musical and welfare dimensions of *habǫbǫwo* (groups) formed by Ewe migrant workers living in Accra (Avorgbedor 1998: 389–399).

Expatiating on his rejection of what he calls the performance of excerpts, Locke makes a case for the elaborate nature of a performance of a genre such as the *Agbekor* or *Agbadza*. As such, he opines that performances should help correct people's erroneous, simplistic, or reductionist notions about African dance drumming. He recalls that the Agbekor Society had a one-and-a-half-hour performance of the same genre the audience liked very much. His discussion of the form and structure of Agbekor covers shifts from unaccompanied to accompanied singing, singing without dancing to stages involving singing, drumming, and dancing, as well as stages of group dancing intermitted by pair dancing. Temporal shifts abound in Agbekor, including slow to fast drumming (Locke 2009: 274–287). Moreover, moments of invoking the presence of their objects of worship to bless the performance are done with no drumming and dancing. Further, the meaning of songs and understanding of changing dance movements, coupled with other contextual activities in situ, should actually make a single genre engaging. I agree with Locke that we do not always have to perform or program simply to please the audience by doing things in ways with which they are familiar. "In fact the audience I was going for was a sort of people who would enjoy steeping themselves deeply into one thing" (Interview, July 2007). By implication, the ensemble director or teacher must know his audience or challenge his audience to understand and enjoy new things more deeply.

The last scenario Locke recalled to illuminate his preference for a single dance per semester was a workshop he organized in collaboration with Gideon Alorwoyie, which I observed. Locke remembers the doubts a participant[7] initially had about how a workshop can be organized around just a single dance-drumming genre for three days. Would it be engagingly interesting enough?

> "Start with the same tempo, play the same supporting instruments?" And then the student quickly found out that a single *Agbadza* song is a world to itself; and the drumming composition was different; and although the *gankogui*, *axatse*, and *kaganu* may remain the same, when one changes the song, the *sogo* [lead drum] and *kidi* parts correspondingly change. He realized that the combination of each song with the instruments was substantially a different sound. (Interview, July 2007)

The idea of thinking that it is the same thing throughout a performance is a misrepresentation of the music, and to say the Ewe play the same type of bell rhythm, for example, is an indication of ignorance, Locke asserts.

Sustaining the interest of student participants and their audience for both limited and multiple dances is another challenge for the ensemble directors. Admittedly, there could be enough variety in a single dance genre—some of which are suites, like the Asante *Kete*—but to perform the same genre for about six semesters may not be very exciting without new costumes, input of invited artists, new songs, and new choreographies. Yet, to say which model is better than the other is similar to asking whether a survey course is better than a themed or topical seminar; both have advantages and disadvantages in terms of scope and depth. The good thing is that each course, as I suggested earlier, has passed through the rigorous process of approval and must be deemed consistent with the academic and cultural goals of a university, prior to it being taught to students.

RESPONDING TO NEW CHALLENGES WITH SOME DEGREE OF FLEXIBILITY

Regarding pedagogical approaches to teaching West African drumming, dance, and songs, some ensemble directors cling to African modes of teaching by rote and mnemonic vocables, with little or no notation for the sake of authenticity. To others whose teaching philosophies prioritize assisting the student to benefit from the learning process through multiple learning tools, some degree of notation may be used to complement oral and aural procedures. Hence, this debate on pedagogical approaches—whether to present traditional dances to audiences with little or no modifications, and programming for new contexts and yielding to dictates of modernity—remains a regular challenge for most directors.

Through my personal experience, I have noted some percussionists, who throughout their training and careers have used the written score in playing everything, feel very challenged in adjusting to the rote oral/aural procedures used in teaching West African drumming. First, most students who are not familiar with specific rhythmic motives of dances may find performing them initially difficult. Even those who may be familiar with certain rhythmic structures may still encounter problems not necessarily with how they hear these structures as the way in which they perceive them. Second, playing one's part accurately within the polyrhythmic matrix while remaining in sync within the metrical framework is often a new skill that new or first-time West African drumming students acquire and develop. Hearing the regulating pulse, the beginning of the time line structure, and entry points of all instruments in relation to the time line, while at the same time listening to cues from the lead drummer demands new modes of orientation.

Given this challenge, it makes sense that Christopher Ladzekpo makes basic conducting gestures, a regular and helpful learning procedure that helps his students externalize the pulse during drumming classes. Most drumming teachers encourage students to clap rather than to tap. For, when their hands are busy during performance, either by holding a rattle, sticks, or playing with the palm, they can still feel the pulse, hemiola, and other important orienting rhythmic patterns of the structure. However, since a student drummer's externalization of the pulse through tapping in class may lead to a performance habit that is considered un-African, most teachers discourage tapping as percussionists' learning procedure. Even in some Western music traditions, tapping during performance is considered amateurish. Nevertheless, tapping can aid dancers as a pedagogical behavior that marks the pulse although some West African dances do not always outline such recurring pulses. Further, getting used to and satisfied with playing a repetitive rhythmic structure throughout a musical piece, a practice that is based on the concept of communal creativity,[8] constitutes a new creative ethos for some students. Concentration can become a problem for even very musical students who may be carried away by bewildering rhythms from the master or lead drummer.

Third, the partial key to overcoming these initial challenges is letting go of the cultural baggage of some Euro-Americentric learning procedures, in which one's preparedness and openness to accept new ways of perception, hearing, and performance behaviors are all involved.

Some students who join ensembles egoistically demand that drum and dance instructors use pedagogic procedures with which they are already familiar. Firm teachers do not often yield to such demands but systematically control their classes, including their teaching procedures. General modes of transmission can be culture-specific. Hence, students who are patient and willing to learn, end up learning not only how to drum, dance, and sing but also how to teach those related facets of a West African dance-drumming tradition through non-American learning procedures.

This theme of disadvantages that arise from ways in which people's prejudices, preconceptions, and mannerisms of learning shape their habits resurfaced in my interviews with some directors. Such habit behaviors often become manifest when learning a cultural phenomenon from a foreign culture. David Locke, for example, considers it a blessing in disguise that he "did not originally pursue music as his major field when growing up" (Interview, July 2007). He thinks if he had done so, it could have resulted in a conservative way of learning several things through only Western procedures and prisms. He further observes he might have faced the same difficulties some of his friends face in suppressing their ethnocentrism and resistance to respecting and accepting new ways of learning foreign cultural phenomena, such as West African dance drumming.

James Burns admits he had to develop new ways of listening to West African drumming, especially as he was getting ready to start instructing. Burns thought that in hearing each instrument separately, but at the same time, the resultant or the composite polyrhythmic whole was a "challenging and an engagingly interesting experience" (Interview, October 2007). He describes acquiring this skill as a transformative process for him, and yet a prerequisite for any West African drum ensemble instructor. This vivid recollection and observation resonates in how John Blacking had to sharpen, if not adjust, his listening skills when he was appreciating the challenges of understanding the musicality of the Venda. It is unsurprising that he devotes a chapter to the importance of listening. Indeed, teaching of West African drumming, like other traditions, involves both aural and oral communicative procedures as well as oral and aural receptive abilities and skills (Wade 2004t: 16–19).

But if oral and aural procedures are crucial to teaching and learning drumming and songs, then the sense of vision is the quintessential tool for learning dance, for imitation of movements after carefully watching facilitates faster grasping of even challenging dance gestures. To curious music education and education students such approaches provide new horizons. But just within the past decade, James Burns along with his dance instructor(s) have developed a pedagogical approach that blends the oral, aural, and visual within the framework of some degree of the written tradition complementing the oral. He describes the approach and model: "We base it [the learning approach] on the experiential learning in Ghana whereby students observe and participate in group music-making. Our combination of veterans, cultural exponents, and teachers allow us to maintain a high level of musicianship that helps new students to come in hearing the music at its best" (Interview, October 2012).

As can be seen from the above excerpt, Burns emphasizes experience as a typically Ghanaian aspect of the learning process. In addition to the instruction of the main teachers, experienced members, including African members of the ensemble, facilitate new members' faster understanding of the music cultures they imbibe. In a situation where roles are well defined within an environment of mutual respect, civility, and positive communality, such a model is very helpful.

As I have already discussed, in many of the ensembles paying equal attention to all the components of the integrated arts not only reflects the African conception of a dance-drumming genre, but also sustains interest and members' joy of learning more about the cultures though creative outlets of singing, drumming, and dancing. In such a spirit, Burns's Nukporfe ensemble "also integrates singing, with a corpus of over one hundred songs [with drumming and dancing, and this practice] becomes another way that both dancers and drummers get exposed to the music through song" (Interview, October 2012).

Furthermore, flexibility in pedagogical approach aimed at assisting the students can be helpful. For example, Burns has

> over time . . . written a self-published drumming manual/song book, with two CDs of audio examples containing all of the drumming and songs. This book goes through the stages of learning Ghanaian music, from the bell and rattle, to the support drums, and finally to the response drums (the lead drum is not covered). The book covers stick and hand drum techniques, as well as basic rhythmic patterns. (Interview, October 2012)

While it may sacrifice some degree of the African oral pedagogical practices, this manual will definitely assist students to varying degrees, depending on the levels at which they comprehend the symbols in the manual. While music education students who are members of the ensemble and also interested in observing different non-Western models of learning may not have everything they expect, the songbook will help with the lyrics of the songs whose mastery could have been overwhelming for students familiar only with the written tradition. Understandably, one cannot satisfy everybody (Interview, October 2012).

Describing his teaching approach further, Locke also allows considerable flexibility as he tries to balance "writing-free and writing constraints," his coinage for the so-called "written" and "non-literate"[9] (oral) traditions. He notes the rhythmic motives and gives them to the students, although they are not supposed to use them in class. Demonstration, illustration, and emulation are the core learning activities. Locke does not discourage people from bringing paper to class, and toward the last third of each class he will ask students to relax on the floor as he goes back to review what they have covered in each class. This is a good time for students to take brief notes. Locke will then use numbers to talk about where beat 1 (the strong beat) is, and so on. At times he uses notation to explain what the rhythms are; however, he does not mix that concurrently with the practical teaching. For teaching dance, Locke has done Labanotation and thus has the ability to notate movement, and although he has handouts and books, he prefers to teach his students to use the visual imagery.

In defending his combined use of both written and rote, rather than one of them, Locke does not understand why university students cannot be allowed to use notation as a learning tool. He thinks "they are learning to be literate, to develop high cognitive skills," and he thinks that "to separate their experiences with African music from their experiences of broad cognitive training will send wrong messages. Any liberal arts college, like Tufts, must promote some continuity and consistency in how students can draw on different disciplines to develop their cognitive capabilities or capacities" (Interview, July 2007).

Here, too, barring the use of notation in a class with several music-major students may be frustrating just as would be the use of notation in a class of many non-music students. Moreover, virtuoso performers have been produced through both written and oral transmission models throughout the world. The choice is the teacher's, whether the procedures of transmission remain loyal to the indigenous practices or whether concerns of re-contextualization are extended to teaching approaches, to a large extent.

THE PROBLEM OF THE "OUTSIDER-INSIDER" BINARISMS IN THE AUTHENTICITY DEBATE

The debate about authenticity within the context of representation of West African drumming to American students has been presented with a suggested sharp contrast between indigenous African and other (mainly American) instructors, thereby invoking the age-old discourse on the "outsider-insider" differences. The problem may not reside in either side of the debate. Rather, the binarism with which this debate is normally approached has an inherent problem, and although such an approach may yield logical conclusions or simply protract the conundrum, I argue such polarized positions will prevent access to the perception of the realities of a more complicated phenomenon. At SEM 2010 in Los Angeles, the African Music Section organized a roundtable discussion session on the theme "Teaching African Music in the American Academy: Challenges and Directions." Realizing that African dance drumming is an activity of the section, the co-chairs[10] asked Kobla Ladzekpo to represent this category of teachers as a panelist. I now evoke Ladzekpo's presentation and its emergent reactions because they resonate with the authenticity debate. Characteristically, Ladzekpo asserted his philosophy of "teaching the right thing" as the ideal thing all African dance-drumming instructors must endeavor to do. But, based on opinions expressed during a previous Africanist session on the same day that resonated with the authenticity debate, as well as possible similar past experiences, David Locke could not hide his frustration with this seeming binarism he thought was inspiring and influencing people's value judgments on the teaching of West African dance drumming. He problematized the general notion that nonindigenous teachers were ostensibly being accused of lack of credibility in their work. Gideon Alorwoyie came to the defense of his former student Locke, and made other observations I will later discuss. Further, although it was not clear whether or not Ladzekpo intended his remark about teaching "the right thing" to target only non-African teachers, the fact is we all know there must be something called "the right thing," and the binarism in the debate exists.

A seemingly mediating view of the binarism may offer suggestions for those who may be reasoning along such lines. Although it is now commonplace that a body of Caucasian American Africanists, who have understudied accomplished master drummers, have attained high levels of artistic excellence and have demonstrated their capabilities as lead drummers, dancers, and teachers, some of them are very sensitive about their racial backgrounds in relation to what they teach. Considering that some may be practicing within racially charged communities, and they are aware of ways in which drums and African dances index ethnic cultural homologies and symbolic signifiers for Africans and their descendants, some white instructors are very careful about how to practice what they have acquired without offending people who may perceive even secular drums differently. Nobody situates this sensitivity to West African drumming within the context and discourse of racism more than Locke. He discusses the theme under "Factoring in Race" in the article he contributes to Solis 2004 (Locke 2004: 181–182). Also, I noted during my interviews with Locke the extent to which he is careful with this reality. Throughout this book, I keep referring to Monson's reminder of the interactions between musical practice, social structure, and discourse, and these perspectives hold true for the case at hand here. Yet, excessive caution not to offend has led to instructors of this category at times setting boundaries for themselves individually, a situation I have observed could constrain the future development of such practitioners as well as their joy of sharing what they know.

Several lead drummers who belong to this category of instructors do very well artistically even though they may not have an African's historical or cultural consciousness, in Gademer's terms (1976: 8). Furthermore, some, as epitomized by David Locke, are the greatest collaborators with their mentors. Most of them celebrate the various forms of African cultural knowledge, and consider African music as artistically intricate and complex as any other kind of music in the world. More telling, they venerate the competence of their mentors as virtuosic and do not claim equality to them in what they have learned (Locke 2004: 170–181). Therefore, I think it is important for indigenous master drummers and other Africans and their descendants to be very selective in their choice of words, even if they intend to offer legitimate suggestions to such overly sensitive non-native instructors; or put differently, African instructors also need to play their part of the sensitivity game more positively.

Admittedly, some foreign performers of West African dance drumming might assume some degree of presumptuous, inflated aura of capability that certain Africans and their descendants may want to correct, at times using undesirable reactionary approaches in registering their disapproval. Further, Africans in other situations may be responding to ethical issues including ownership of music, how informants are presented in public spheres without protecting the confidentiality of individuals or the culture, or the exploitative manner in which some field researchers fail to credit their consultants in kind or other forms of advocacy. On the other hand, some African instructors of the genre may simply be reacting to a position that conflicts with their teaching philosophies, which they have tested as effective for them. Whatever be the case, overgeneralizations or simplistic conclusions based on binarism may not promote a high probability of paying closer attention to the specificities of scenarios on a case-by-case basis.

Returning to the mediation of such possible tensions, it may be helpful for non-native teachers of the genre to desist from rushed conclusions they reach by assuming that, whenever authenticity or "correct" representation is referenced, they are the targeted subjects. First, they have to remind themselves of the competence of their respective mentors who supposedly taught them the "right thing." Second, Kobla Ladzekpo, Gideon Alorwoyie, Abraham Adzinya, Alfred Ladzekpo, Godwin Agbeli, Christopher Ladzekpo, and Kwasi Dunyo all have taught American students to play the right thing. And just a night after the heated debate on "teaching the right thing" with its emergent misconstrued or implicated binarism, during their Friday concert Kobla Ladzekpo did not play the *Atsimewu* by himself when his group ZADONU performed. Rather, the lead drummer for the dance was a former white student of his. Similarly, students of the aforementioned master drummers have on countless occasions played what may be regarded "the right thing." It follows that the advocacy of ensuring authenticity should not necessarily be inferred on the basis of the binary oppositions people carry as prejudices.

During the roundtable session under review, Alorwoyie made a great observation that there is nothing like a single "right thing," for sub-regional

Figure 3.1 Three African music and dance ensemble directors and other Africans present at African Music Section's SEM 2010 roundtable discussion. [Photo from George Dor, November 2010]

or even town-to-town stylistic variants exist of the same dance genre. As he framed it, "Anyako[11] *Agbadza* is stylistically different from Afiadenyigba[12] *Agbadza*," notwithstanding the overarching broader similarities. Hence, awareness of such subtle nuances should inform the way we pass value judgments on what may be deemed "the right thing." Similarly, Locke (2004: 171) discusses such stylistic differences as they pertain to the performance of Damba/Takai by and among the Dagbamba of Ghana.

The preceding considerations do not nullify the truth that "the real thing" exists, and misrepresentation is still a problem. Moreover, as Alorwoyie reiterated and I think Ladzekpo implied in video examples he played during the presentation, what may not be acceptable and thus deemed inauthentic also abounds in Africa where some incompetent people are teaching drumming and dance in Accra, Dakar, or Conakry, for example. Returning to North America however, Kwasi Dunyo related to me how he had to challenge a fellow African for misrepresenting a dance that he taught and performed. The source of this problem is that only a few master drummers can be very versatile with authoritative knowledge of dances from multiple ethnic groups or different regions of the same country. Thus, for somebody who had not had the experience as a master drummer in a national dance troupe, or if adding

Figure 3.2 Gideon Alorwoyie from Anlo Afiadenyigba, and Kobla Ladzekpo from Anyako—two reputable master drummers in the American academy. [Photo by George Dor, November 2010]

the role of lead drumming to a previous role of a dancer, one needs to learn dances from fellow drummers who are experts of their ethnic traditions.

The drum circles tradition is another area of concern to West African dance-drumming instructors in terms of authenticity. Samuel Nyamuame, Anna Melnikoff, and Kwasi Dunyo have lamented about the state of drum circles in North America, especially when one thinks about the anything-goes mentality with which they perform. However, participants are being misled into believing what they are playing is authentically African. Frankly, the current perpetuators of the drum circles tradition need not be blamed fully. As Charry (2005: 14–17) notes, Babatunde Olatunji joined the drum circle movement in the 1960s not with the objective of playing "the right thing" in the African sense on those drums. Rather, drum circles were originally promoted to encourage inclusive participation in which world harmony and peace were sought through communal drumming. At times, drum circle practices have totally lost the polyrhythmic structure typical of Sub-Saharan African dance drumming. Instead, drum circles tend to outline the same rhythm as if they belong to a Japanese taiko ensemble, although they play mostly on djembe and conga drums. To avoid overgeneralization, some of today's taiko ensembles include some degree of polyrhythmic structures in some of their pieces. As can be seen, the sources of playing what may be deemed inauthentic are diverse, thus rendering untenable the common binarism between "they" and "we" in this case.

But as Dunyo has rightly observed, it is difficult to say so blatantly when more informed people are convinced that somebody is not teaching or performing the right thing. And rather than telling his students about such misrepresentations, Dunyo has chosen to play his part well and then organize study-abroad programs for students to go to Ghana and discover for themselves the authentic thing within the village cultural setting. To him, this experience—in which students do drumming and dancing for weeks, and attend performances during ceremonies—provides the needed affirmation of what instructors back in North America have done right or wrong. Kobla Ladzekpo has made a similar observation, and throughout this book I have reported informants' opinions on the importance of traveling to Africa to experience music genres within their original contexts.

FURTHER PERSPECTIVES ON PEDAGOGICAL APPROACHES

The responses of student ensemble participants to my survey questions regarding the teaching approaches of their instructors pointed out two things. First, students recognized differences between the instructional habitus of their African dance-drumming teachers and those of other teachers. Second, almost all respondents do not see these newer approaches of teaching as an impediment to understanding what was being imparted to them by their respective African teachers. Also, my conversations with ensemble directors and administrators reveal that the nature, levels, objectives and goals, and participants of West African dance drumming are diverse. And as I have explained elsewhere, classes are available to all students; a blend of music and non-music students participate in the same course, the most common practice in schools that do not have multiple levels of the course or the norm with introductory or beginners' classes. Courses only for music students exist at the University of Toronto, for example. UCLA, York, and the advanced class at Wesleyan emphasize the performance aspects of such courses. In addition, York gives studio lessons in drumming to individual students. Furthermore, expectations of undergraduate or graduate music students specializing in performance, theory/composition, music education, or ethnomusicology may differ regarding what they desire to derive from a West African dance drumming class. The foregoing variables should naturally attract different teaching strategies and pedagogic considerations deemed appropriate for the differences identified above. Accordingly, to suggest the use of one and the same preferential approach for teaching these different types of dance-drumming classes would be problematic. When David Locke speaks of "African teachers" (2004: 174–175), it is unclear whether he is referring only to teachers who have remained on the continent or if he includes those teaching in the North American academy for decades.

Although Locke notes differences between American and African preferred methods of teaching, it will be unrealistic to presume that the habitus of African teachers in the United States will not adjust to the preferred classroom climates. I have noticed with keen interest the adjustments African teachers have made to various types of American academy systems' regulations. Ricardo Trimillos discusses in relation to native teachers: "The [native] teacher may use elements of traditional instructions that are different from but that nevertheless do not challenge basic American notions of teaching and learning." And as Trimillos reminds about restrictions, "However, not all traditional teaching practices are acceptable in a university setting; some run counter to American practice" (2004: 39).

Admittedly, scholars of phenomenological hermeneutics including Martin Heidegger, Hans-Georg Gademer, and Paul Ricoeur have argued the reflexive power of cultural and historical consciousness in the formation of people's cultural behaviors. Such determinants leave indelible traits on cultural patterns that distinguish a native teacher from outsider practitioners or from foreign ethnomusicologists. However, Pierre Bordieux (1977) has suggested that habit behaviors respond to new landscapes in which people find themselves and correspondingly undergo some degree of modification. Thus, speaking about African teachers who have taught courses in American universities for four, three, or two decades as though they rigidly operate with only their original African instructional strategies without any changes may sound prejudicial.

After presenting perspectives from my informants on their teaching approaches, thereby privileging an inductive methodology based on ethnographic data, I now close this chapter with a few critical responses to the insights that seasoned ethnomusicologists have contributed in *Performing Ethnomusicology: Teaching and Representation in World Music Ensembles*, edited by Ted Solis. This book resonates with the theme and issues discussed thus far in this chapter, and I have already cited and partially engaged ideas from one or two essays. First, I would like to begin with David Locke's essay, the only one on West African drumming, and which reverberates directly with the present book. Although I have found Locke's essay insightful and engaging in a number of ways, I struggle with some of the binarisms and generalizations he makes because they are at variance with my research findings and experiences. For example: "Keenly aware of how little exposure to African drumming the students have had, I favor filling class time with music making by the whole group. African teachers often have students play one by one or in small groups. They use competition and pride as motivations and know that in performance situations students will need to execute under pressure" (2004: 174).

I have already discussed the pedagogical approaches of a number of African teachers in this chapter. While the student surveys and other conversations have shown substantial gratitude to their teachers for the knowledge and experiences imparted, one cannot attribute all their successes to the dictates of their new working environments. Like Locke, I think all African teachers are equally aware of the "little [or no] exposure" of their students to West African dance drumming. From the few classes I have observed and information regarding teaching approaches from instructors and students, all African teachers do not teach rigidly and totally the same way. Indeed, they come from objective cultures, and yet they have individualities that define their personhood. For example, I have mentioned how I observed three two-hour classes, one in York and two at University of Toronto, taught by Kwasi Dunyo. There was no single instance in which he asked a student to play by him/herself. In one of the classes, after all the students played bells, they all moved on to rattles, then to the first hand drum, and finally to the second hand drum which has a different rhythm. These concurrent shifts by all students to the same type of instrument lasted about forty minutes before the instructor divided the class into four groups of about five or six students on each of the Zigi[13] ensemble instruments. At this stage the class is divided into groups in order to play as an ensemble. The class then had a brief break after which the teacher changed the activity to teaching the dance (movement) for about thirty minutes before concluding the class with learning of songs. The class ended with satisfaction and fun expressed in the students' countenance and demeanor.

The class discussed here does not look any different from the picture that Locke's own preferred approach paints. Even those African teachers who may ask students to play one by one or as groups may be motivated by convincing reasons other rather than competition and pride—rather, the intent to help each individual get the various instrumental parts, which when done within the right atmosphere may not be frustrating as Locke suggests.

In several other university courses that may be completely new to students, such as modern languages, classes are often divided into groups for a number of interactive activities that the teacher supervises. I presume competition is not the underlying reason for such group work in those classrooms. I argue that African teachers of dance drumming will, under normal circumstances, ask students to play individually only after spending enough time collectively on a specific instrumental part. Further, Locke's preferred practice, of allowing more performance during class time before later coming back to attend to individual parts or problems, may have its advantages. Yet it should not be done at the expense of helping the student understand the basics of drumming, which may be unduly deferred to another class day. Admittedly, group participation and lack of frustration in students are desirable. However, relearning wrongly perceived and played parts may be a pedagogic concern and challenge as well. Spending time on at least the time line, the pulse, and basic perceptual norms may be foundational to any West African drumming class. At times, students may serve as better judges in ascertaining whether or not native Africans are excellent teachers. My interview with Patricia Tang presents a classic example of how Lamine Toure, a Senegalese *Sabar* drumming instructor, won MIT's campuswide best teacher award (Interview, November 2010).

Ricardo Trimillos's article "Subject, Object, and the Ethnomusicology Ensemble: The Ethnomusicological 'We' and 'Them'" (2004:23–52) resonates with the theme under discussion here. The strength of this lead essay of the book, I think, is the author's experience and interpretation of the subject matter. However, if his observations, categories, and other insights apply fully to the world music traditions he analyzes, they do not fully capture the complexities, multiple spaces, and the currency of the world music landscape as suggested by the practice of West African drumming and dance. I have already problematized the binarism suggested in the article's title, and while his discussion of the issue of authenticity is very persuasive, a multilayered interpretive framework could have better encompassed the context at hand.

I offer the following excerpt as an example: "The ethnomusicologist brings several pedagogical strengths to a study group [ensemble]. His learning experience, as cultural outsider, more closely approximates that of a student" (2004: 35). While I do not want to diminish what ethnomusicologists bring to the ensemble, I am cautious about generalizations. First, the academic backgrounds of African native teachers of drumming are not all the same. Today, not all ethnomusicologists who are ensemble instructors are "cultural outsider[s]." Understandably, Trimillos is talking about ensemble instructors, so I would not use Kwabena Nketia as somebody who studied his own African cultures. Rather, one can name William Amoako, Willie Anku, and more recently, Stephen Kofi Gbolonyo, who all received doctorate degrees in ethnomusicology from the University of Pittsburgh, and have all taught as ensemble directors of various North American universities. Abraham Adzinya, who is a native instructor, received his masters from Wesleyan. Furthermore, Pascal Younge, who received his doctorate from West Virginia in music education, remains one of the best instructors of West African drumming in the American academy. Similarly, I hope there are Indonesians now directing a gamelan ensemble who have received a masters or doctorate degree in ethnomusicology. The author's categories therefore are not inclusive and reflective of current trends in the world music enterprise in our universities.

While I agree that any further academic training an ensemble instructor pursues is an added pedagogical asset, we should not think as though we are still in the 1960s. Each time we discuss the subject matter of "outsider" and "insider," we need to be more critical and mindful of what is happening now in the academy, else our discourse may in part suffer from anachronisms. Imagine discussing field methodology and still using texts that completely consider every ethnomusicologist as a cultural outsider and their informants as the only insiders. Meanwhile several Africans, Asians, Europeans, and Americans are studying their own music cultures as ethnomusicologists. Hopefully, newer texts on fieldwork methodology will take such changes into account.

My final observation addresses whether all trained ethnomusicologists fully recognize and celebrate the worth of the processes involved in acquiring the traditional knowledge that native teachers bring to the pedagogical settings in our classrooms. My critical engagement was stirred after reading "For the ethnomusicologist teacher [of a world music ensemble], authority is not a matter of cultural entitlement.... His authority devolves from a process of acquiring it, which contrasts with the authority of the native teacher as one 'who culturally knows.' The ethnomusicologist's authority is earned rather than inherited" (2004: 42). The terms and concepts including "cultural entitlement" "culturally knows," and "inherited culture" deserve critical examination. Although the point the author makes is clear, one must not downplay the agency required in the processes of transmission that shape a master drummer, or a virtuosic *kora* player, for example. A master drummer does not simply inherit his cultural tradition. Truly, he grows up in it, and yet he has to undergo training, understudying established musicians. As such, native teachers also have to earn their authority, even those believed to have received their musicality partly through divine intervention. As such, two sons of a Mande *jali* or a Dagbamba *lunna* may innately have the potential of becoming virtuosic bearers of their cultural knowledge. However, if only a son of a *jali* or a *lunna* undergoes the required apprenticeship while the other brothers do not pursue the same vocation, then only those who nurture their inherited talents stand the chance of earning the accolades of music specialists of their respective cultures in the future. Accordingly, specific practices define the processes of making somebody a master drummer among the Dagbon, for example. Additionally, the learning situation and intent inferred by Locke may be different from a normal American classroom context. In any case, one cannot forget the role of other prescriptive factors including limited time that a field researcher may have at his/her disposal to learn to perform before returning to the United States, and the manner in which such pressures may factor into how the foreign ethnomusicologist views his/her native teachers' teaching approaches.

During my July 2007 interview with Locke, he discussed the differences and similarities between the teaching approaches of his native dance-drumming teachers, withholding their names for ethical reasons. He noted the extent to which teachers from cultural communities where musical transmission involves apprenticeship tend to be more explicit in teaching and learning situations because of acquired institutionalized practices of teaching. On the other hand, Locke observes ethnic cultures that do not practice pseudo-professional apprenticeship, but rather depend on general and broader enculturation from multiple artists of a village or town, tend to be more implicit when teaching. Additionally, Locke notes the impact of contemporary approaches of teaching in African universities, for example, on some instructors. The preceding discussion by Locke suggests differences in the African teachers he had experience with or observed. One wonders why then he chose to generalize and rather sound unanimist,[14] because Melnikoff's mentor's pedagogical approach, for example, was a blend of Mande and French perspectives.

The debate on representation may never be over or won by any school of thought. Its realities continue to inform what we teach in a number of ways, but what we want to represent according to the goals of our teaching philosophies, course objectives, and several contextual specificities of our world music ensembles are central to the debate. While teachers from the various categories can learn from one another, collaborate, and aspire to do their best for their students with strategies that work for them, they may, like

Anne Rasmussen, at times want to say, "I have also grown confident of my own version of the tradition" (2004: 226). She does not make this dictum out of disrespect for the tradition(s) she represents as an ethnomusicologist performer. Rather, native teachers need to help build the confidence in their colleagues who are non-native ensemble instructors. Reciprocally, American ethnomusicologists need to acknowledge and appreciate the contributions of native teachers to our larger music programs.

Given the nature of what we as teachers know (dance drumming genres), our knowledge of the students we instruct (both music and non–music majors), the location of our classrooms, and how we situate what we do within other cultural frameworks, various concepts or paradigms may be suggested as hermeneutic paradigms for West African dance drumming. Some may appropriately call this campus subculture an "invented tradition," as Michelle Kisliuk and Kelly Gross view their University of Virginia African Ensemble. However, in spite of the freedom people have to reinvent an African tradition in America, what are the desirable limits and stylistic consequences for the creative modifications of original performance practices?

I want to end with the favorite "coffee and milk" metaphor. Some choose to drink their coffee dark, without milk or cream. Others like it with milk or cream, and as we all know, the quantity of milk we add changes not only the color but also the taste and strength of the original coffee. Logic will teach us that if one adds more milk than the amount of coffee, the drink dilutes completely into a milk drink, and coffee then becomes the flavor. Metaphorically, the dark coffee is the West African dance drumming as performed within its African indigenous locale, and the added milk is what the respective teachers add to the coffee as dictated by various considerations. It is then left to us individually to decide whether we want our drink to be considered as coffee or milk.

4

THE IMPACT OF WEST AFRICAN DRUMMING AND DANCE ON THE PARTICIPATING STUDENT

Students are the primary target beneficiaries of West African drumming programs. In addition to Mantle Hood's multi-musicality, other ends that the course or participation in ensemble offers include the acquisition of pre-compositional resources, team skills, new performance skills and perspectives, relational avenues, professional career development, and practical understanding of theoretical concepts associated with Sub-Saharan African drumming. DjeDje recalls how UCLA granted students' request to make drumming an end or a performance subject (Interview, July 2007). Most students who take courses in West African drumming and dance are primarily motivated by their desire to learn about another culture and the opportunity to improve their musical skills and creativity. But beyond that, the majority participate in West African drumming and dance, whether as a course or an ensemble, primarily because of the fun they have in it. It will be difficult to attend a performance or view a video of performances by most of these student ensembles without acknowledging that they really enjoy what they do. The ensembles have become expressive outlets for youth, student, or campus cultures. Although slightly different from other university African ensembles, the youthful exuberance and energy that Kwasi Ampene's University of Colorado's Highlife Ensemble emits, for example, is irresistibly electrifying. In several cases West African drumming and dance classes are moments of learning and having fun concurrently, as exemplified in Kwasi Dunyo's classes that I observed at York University and University of Toronto (January 2010).

I now provide further and detailed discussion of these multiple meanings that students construct from participation in West African drumming and dance. It is important to note that while some of the effects discussed under these themes may apply to all student participants, some are predetermined by students' specific cultural and academic backgrounds, programs, and interests. This chapter is primarily based on a survey I conducted among students, interviews I had with present and previous members of various university African ensembles, my conversations with relevant administrators and ensemble directors, as well as my observation of classes and performances.

MULTI-MUSICALITY

The cultural relativity that began in the 1960s not only fostered the ethnographer's awareness of the particularities of each culture in the world but also marked the beginning of a new era characterized by an upsurge in people's appreciation of and respect for the cultures they studied. Accordingly, intellectual philosophies about studying the "other" also took a new turn, and learning to perform musical genres aimed at deepening researchers' understanding of cultures reached a higher level of engagement. Thus beyond scanty participant-observation sessions on the field, some ethnomusicologists chose to become preoccupied with learning to play instruments of various ensembles as an integral component of their field research activities.

As part of the cultural relativity concept, every culture can speak of its own musicality in terms of artistic demands and aesthetic values and valuations that partly define its music. It follows that Mantle Hood acquired a second musicality after learning to play gamelan instruments. In an effort to add West African musicality to the Euro-American and Indonesian, he became caught up in research on Ghanaian drumming, an endeavor that yielded the famous film on the *Atumpan* speech surrogates. It was Mantle Hood's practical and pragmatic hands-on experience of these cultures that gave him the conviction that his students would become better musicians by learning to play music from at least a different culture, which led to the bi- or multi-musicality concept.

Yet, more telling was Mantle Hood's love for his students, his willingness to share his field "souvenirs" and to enable others to share experiences with numerous students who might not have gotten the funding necessary to travel to these field sites on their own, prior to becoming doctoral candidates. Hood arranged for competent carriers of various world music cultures—instructors of ensembles and accomplished scholars indigenous to the cultures represented—to come to UCLA as transmitters of authentic sets of musicality to the students. To DjeDje, however, it was the proposal that Hood wrote in order to explain his larger world music project and to win the university administration's support, which demanded a clear statement of purpose and objectives, that provided a written defense of the bi-musicality concept. Most of us must be familiar with questions from provosts, academic vice chancellors, and deans demanding specifics on how a particular project could help the students. To argue that students would become more musical was, in my opinion, a convincing and persuasive argument that gave Hood the much-needed institutional nod.

Although a body of ethnomusicologists, who have comprehensively studied another music culture foreign to their own, may be described as becoming bi-musical, it is John Blacking's provocative book's name that readily rings a bell whenever the term or concept of musicality is referenced. In scripting his book *How Musical Is Man*, he predicated his certainty about the musicality of man on and only after studying the Venda of South Africa, allowing the musical capabilities of this African ethnic group to inform and reinforce his foreknowledge about the extent of musicality within European music cultures. Here, experiences and awareness of another musicality gave birth to ideas that brewed in Blacking's mind, culminating in an influential book. It may not be an exaggeration to posit that most students who learn to perform music from another culture partially answer this Blacking question after challenging themselves in taking courses intended to broaden or sharpen their musicality.

Bi- or multi-musicality is an added asset in any musician's career, be it in creative and/or scholarly enterprises. The following is an excerpt from an interview I had with Professor Emeritus Olly Wilson, and although the former Berkeley professor was simply recalling his experiences, his insights validate the importance of knowledge of another music culture beyond the Western, especially in the academy, and in this specific case, the quintessential symbolism of African music to an African American composer and scholar.

> In 1971 I received the Guggenheim fellowship, which allowed me to choose wherever I wanted to go, and at that point I had longed to study African American music, and I realized earlier on that while I knew a lot experientially about African American music, and even though I have studied in great American universities throughout my life—from Washington University, University of St. Louis, University of Illinois, to University of Iowa—there was never a course besides Western European music. To study music in a serious way was to study European music, which of course reflected a profound cultural bias. I had to be in university at a time that cultural change was part of the social fabric in this country, and I participated in that. The whole idea of challenging

the status quo was part of my growing up and then I looked at what the university offered and I found myself very fortunate to have had an excellent education. But it was limited, because it did not discuss anything beyond Western European music. I felt very good and pleased about what I learned there. But I also felt a big hole in my education. (Interview, July 2007)

As Wilson further explained, his fellowship experiences in Ghana provided him not only with new pre-compositional resources but also creative ideas whose origins were rooted in African religious and other cultural systems. Discussing his original compositions at the Africa Meets North America symposium held in October 2009 at UCLA, it was revealing to listen to the manner in which Wilson used his skillful selection of orchestral timbres combined with West African rhythmic and other sonic materials to invoke the imaginary power of Ogun, the Yoruba divinity (*orisha*) of thunder and fire. Furthermore, he reiterated the extent to which his fellowship time in Africa had informed his deeper understanding of African American music.

In spring 2008 I received an email from a colleague ethnomusicologist who sought my opinion regarding a question that one of his West African drumming and dance students asked him. This student wanted to know whether or not African students also struggle when learning to play Western instruments such as the piano, violin, or trumpet. This question presupposes how this American student may be finding it challenging to learn the African musical instrument in which he was being instructed. Further, the question concerns musicality and bi-musicality. But to answer this question fairly, one must be careful about generalizations that may not acknowledge the varied degrees of musical talents noticeable among different individuals everywhere. Hence an American with a higher degree of musical sensibility may learn a West African drumming piece at a faster pace than another American student who is less musical. Similarly, not only do some Africans struggle more than others when learning to play Western musical instruments, but these differences in performance and learning capabilities are also apparent when Africans are learning to play African drums. In other words, all American students do not struggle when learning to play West African drums, and in the same vein, all Africans do not struggle when learning to play the piano, for example. Admittedly however, through the apparatuses of foreign trade, colonialism, and Christianity, Western music has been an integral part of Africa's newer music idioms for more than one and a half centuries. Because church, school, military bands, popular music, and radio and television disseminated a variety of Euro-American musical genres, any African child becomes conversant with Western musical idioms when growing up. West African drumming cannot be said to be ubiquitous for the past one hundred years in North America. Hence the African seems to have an advantage of greater familiarity and exposure to Western musical instruments than the American to West African instruments, in general terms.

At the university level, most music programs in Africa are bi-musical—Western and African. Considering that Europeans who established some of the older academic institutions also dictated the contents, structures, and systems of formal education, programs in these institutions were initially modeled along Western lines. However, rejecting the purely Western-oriented music curricula found in most African universities, several African governments have made calculated efforts to ensure the presence of strong indigenous components to their programs. Yet the pursuit of balanced bi-musical programs is an ongoing challenge and process for cultural and educational policy makers and implementers in some African countries, as Akrofi and Flolu have observed for Ghana and South Africa (2007: 143–157). Here too, one must be careful about generalizations, for African music is offered in a few American universities with a greater level of vibrancy than may be the case in some African universities.

DEVELOPMENT OF CAREER AND PROFESSIONAL GOALS

The pursuit of unwavering intent and consistent participation by serious and gifted students in West African drumming and dance classes and/or ensembles has produced future lead drummers and instructors. Partial credit goes to a host of seasoned instructors including Kobla Ladzekpo, Abraham Adzinya, Christopher Ladzekpo, Gideon Alorwoyie, Kwasi Dunyo, Pascal Younge, David Locke, and Russell Hartenberger, who in our various conversations have expressed their pride in respective former students who have matured into professionals. After playing leading artistic roles in their ensembles, and having concretized their interest in West African drumming and dance, many such outstanding students end up embarking on study tours to African countries, mostly Ghana, Senegal, Guinea, or Mali, either through study abroad programs organized by universities or personally arranged trips that may last from a summer's stay to a year or two understudying prominent cultural bearers, including master drummers. While in Africa, these prospective lead drummers experience the dance-drumming genres within their original cultural contexts by attending festivals, life-cycle events, other ritual ceremonies, state—ethnic and modern nation—functions that include cultural performances. By traveling around an African country, the student gains a pragmatic understanding and experience of the diversity that characterizes the culture of a single modern nation-state. Also, they have the chance to take further drumming and dance lessons from seasoned performers, expanding the scope of repertoire, taking on more lead drumming responsibilities, and gaining alternative pedagogical insights, especially for curious and open-minded students. As Professor Kobla Ladzekpo and his wife Beatrice advise, West African drumming and dance instructors in America must teach their students the "right thing," so that when they one day go to Ghana, for example, to work under or listen to accomplished master drummers, both our students from the United States and drummers in Africa will affirm the authenticity of what instructors have imparted to their students here (Interview, October 2009). These students return to the United States to compete in the job market; or, after the pursuit of further programs in African music, some do not waste much time before returning to Africa for major field research.

In addition to drumming, a few American students who travel to West Africa to improve on their proficiency as lead drummers explore the related semi-professional career of learning to assemble and repair drums through years' apprenticeship. Those familiar with the degree of traditional knowledge needed for the complete process of drum making, as evident in Hood's *The Talking Drums of Ghana*, for example, will understand the difficulty of these visiting students becoming drum makers in the strictest sense of the word and its attendant culturally implicated process. Going into the forest, performing the relevant rituals before felling the *tweneboa* cedar tree, cutting the log into the desired lengths of drums, leaving the log to dry up, bringing the pieces of logs home, chipping off wood according to the desired shape, hollowing the trunk by different implements, drilling the hole for the pegs to which the drum membranes will be fastened, and finally decorating the drum shell or body with culturally symbolic artistic motives—all involve a substantial degree of expertise, cultural knowledge, and work. Even though West African drums are diverse in a number of ways including their processes of construction, to grasp the making of smaller and other drums requires a long period of training in cultural knowledge. However, after drum shells have been carved or wooden slats fastened together into resonators, as is the case of Anlo Ewe drums, a few North American students have successfully learned how to assemble these drums by affixing the accompanying hides that have been processed for them. So beyond becoming lead drummers they return home and import drum shells, membranes, pegs, and strings from West Africa for their assemblage, and repair broken drums here in the United States and Canada.

I received one of the most succinct answers to my question on the impact of West African drumming on students' professional and career goal development from Russell Hartenberger, dean of the faculty of music at the University of Toronto. Speaking from an experiential and pragmatic viewpoint, he asserts that, "It changed my life, a strong influence." Hartenberger thinks that, more than an opportunity to learn about another culture, studying West African drumming also broadens perspectives of one's own culture just as learning a foreign language helps one to understand his/her own language better. It also provides a different way of thinking about one's artistic and creative preoccupation. Hartenberger further explains:

> Given the way the profession has gone now, it is essential that you know something about African music. It has become so common an element in Western music, either in composition and performance of Western art and popular music such that a Western percussion student must know the basics of West African drumming, not only in terms of the techniques of playing the instruments, but also the rhythmic constructions, ideas about time, meter, and rhythms. It really opens your mind to different concepts and perceptions. (Interview, January 2010)

A few words about Hartenberger's partial educational and professional background will provide a deeper understanding of the preceding transformational experience that he shares. Hartenberger trained as a Western classical percussionist from a conservatory. Though with a promising future as an orchestral percussionist, he became aware of the extent to which the core of his Western-based training was "somewhat limited," and that "other types of percussion playing in the world exist." He explains his impetus to learn to play West African drums as that which arose from his percussionist's desire to expand his knowledge in the world of percussion. As such, in 1970 he decided to pursue a doctoral program in world music at Wesleyan. Although it was then still a young program, Hartenberger recollects how Bob Robert started to bring foreign and visiting artists from different parts of the world. Abraham Adzinya from Ghana, and later Freeman Donkor, a dancer, were part of a program Hartenberger describes as "very exciting." After taking lessons in drumming, performing in the African ensemble that gave concerts and demonstrations in the New England area, and the subsequent participation of other percussionists including David Locke, then an undergraduate student, and John Chernoff, a visiting graduate student from a seminary in Hartford, Hartenberger enjoyed an engaging program that exactly matched what he anticipated.

This wonderful experience had enough impact to have partly informed Hartenberger's next related decision to visit Ghana after his first year in Wesleyan. He spent the summer of 1971 in Ghana, where he experienced the drumming he was learning in its original performance contexts. But as a percussionist, his primary interest was the manner in which the various forms of Ghanaian drumming were done as he traveled around as much as he could—to Tamale, Bawku, Navrongo, all in northern Ghana, and to Kumasi in the Ashanti region, although he primarily stayed at Legon near Accra.

Incidentally, Steve Reich was the one who advised and encouraged Hartenberger to go to Ghana. Reich himself had gone there and studied drumming under Gideon Alorwoyie. When Reich returned to New York, he was in the process of writing a piece for percussion called *Drumming*, which had some connection with West African drumming. It was there and then that Hartenberger met Reich and started playing in his group, a friendship that culminated in the suggestion of going to Ghana (Interview, January 2010). As Robert Simms of York rightly observes, one of the pointers of a good West African drumming and dance program in an American academy is for participation to generate an unflinching desire in a student to visit Africa later (Interview, January 2010). However, the evidence presented here by Hartenberger and Steve Reich is their ambition to develop their professional careers as both percussionists and composers. Composers are thinking of writing music using not only African instruments but also compositional techniques and formal structures drawn from traditional African music and idiosyncrasies of the instruments that composers privilege. As some may know, Russell Hartenberger is the founder and member of Nexus, a world-renowned group of percussionist-composers, and has used ideas from Ghanaian dance drumming music for some of his compositions.

Similarly, I asked Ricky Burkhead, a professor in the department of music at the University of Mississippi, what he tells his percussion students as the major reasons for which they must take courses in West African drumming, and his answer corroborates Hartenberger's position. To Burkhead, broadening one's understanding of diverse percussive musical genres of the world by going beyond the Western canons and learning different repertoires, styles, skills, discrete structural elements, and perceptions of the music, opens a new world for students. Indeed, Burkhead is a percussionist, percussion teacher, member of the Percussion Arts Association, an African American, founder and director of the steel band, world percussion ensemble, and salsa band at Ole Miss, and owns the Fastrack Recording Studio, and can thus construct his own readings into the impact of West African dance drumming on the American student from the synthesis experience he had gained over the years. However, Burkhead considers his own participation in the Ole Miss African Drum and Dance Ensemble as a major percussionist since the inception of the group in 2003 as a pragmatic experience and story that he shares with his students. As such, some of the finest drummers of OMADDE have been his students (Interview, July 2011).

MUSIC AND DANCE AS CULTURE: UNDERSTANDING ANOTHER CULTURE

All student participants, ensemble directors, and administrators consider West African drumming and dance an engaging vehicle for learning something about another culture beyond concerns of creativity and artistic skills. It is thus consensus opinion that this motivation turns out to be the most compelling impact of West African drumming and dance on most students, especially those who are not music majors. World-mindedness and world-consciousness seem to permeate the thoughts of most participating students responding to reasons underlying their membership of ensembles. In their responses to "What best describes your foremost motivation for joining the ensemble?" the majority indicated that it was their desire "To learn about another culture."[1] As "part of humanity's expressive art forms," West African drumming and dance are "a multi-cultural activity," which "in this age of globalization" attracts voluntary student participation just like other world music genres (see Survey question 47, Appendix B).

A plethora of speculative theories and well-known methodological frameworks underpin the use of music and dance for teaching and accessing other domains of culture. These include the "music as culture" framework and debate of the 1980s (McLead and Herndon 1980; Stone 1982; Seeger 1987); Merriam's tripartite methodology of understanding music as a nexus of sound, idea, and behavior (Merriam 1964); as well as Steve Feld's writings on the iconicity of music (1982); Nketia (1974); and Agawu (2003: 97–115). It is an approach explored in many world music textbooks; Titon's archetypal emphasis on the importance and use of the "music culture" model captures this symbiotic nature of music to other domains of culture (Titon 2009).

Ensemble directors' role of representing the various African ethnic music cultures attracts a sense of sensitivity and reflexive appraisal of what and how they teach. If the ensemble director is to help the American student understand related domains of the ethnic cultures, pertinent questions include how informed these teachers are about the specific cultures, how many ethnic cultures a director can teach with genuine confidence, and what programs are put in place to enable or empower directors to research into other cultures so that upon completion they could execute their roles of representation more effectively. Administrators and ensemble directors, who respect the authenticity of the ethnic dances they teach, have raised concerns on challenges that resonate with the importance of fair presentation of African cultures to students. No wonder this concern was a major overarching theme in the essays in Solis (2004). In the next few paragraphs, I discuss the extent to which this advocacy for fair representation of West African drumming and dance in the academy remains a long-standing, legitimate concern for both indigenous African and American teachers.

Kobla Ladzekpo's assertion of "Teach the right thing" (Interview, October 2009) has implications not only for pedagogical approaches but also for respect for preserving the artistic and cultural integrity of specific traditions. "The right thing" here refers to that which is acceptable to the indigenous ethnic practitioners or custodians of drumming and dance traditions. But given that ensemble directors must first know "the right thing" before they can teach it, it is important that they take a critical look at who trains them for the job. Bragging on where a student has traveled to study West African drumming and dance becomes beneficial only when the student understudies the "right" musician. For example, Samuel Nyamuame expressed his frustration and disappointment with the ways in which even some Ghanaians at home are teaching visitors various forms of Ghanaian traditional dances (Personal Correspondence, January 2009). By traditional aesthetic standards, some self-acclaimed drummers and dancers lack the mastery of cultural knowledge necessary to "teach the right thing." Thus a word of caution and advice to those American students who travel to Africa to learn drumming and dance is that they make a judicious decision on which cultural gatekeeper to study with.

A related concern is evident in Christopher Ladzekpo's advocacy for a distinction between what he calls "traditional programming" and "contemporary programming," whether in America or Africa. He observes that most ensemble directors fail to inform their students and audiences about which of the dances of a particular program—part or whole—are representations of traditional renditions and which are contemporary creations of choreographers. Dances of the latter category are often based on ideas from indigenous dances but shaped by dictates of modernity and specifically repackaged for other contextual needs. Put differently, American students deserve to be told when certain dances are performed almost in the "village style," and not as urbanized renditions. Such clarification and explanation is important because I presume participants would like to know how certain dances are performed within their original rural, country, or suburban contexts, for example.

At the same time, information on recontextualized and modernized choreographed stylized dances can be used to explain artistic responses to new forces of change. When such distinctions are routinely made, then, ensemble directors will be using drumming and dance as sites for explicating the dialectics between traditionalism and modernity to our students and audiences. As Christopher Ladzekpo rightly observes, this blurring of taxonomy is not peculiar to North America, and perhaps has its roots in Africa, in the dance troupes that partly shaped the enculturation processes of some of the ensemble directors, who have deliberately or intuitively continued to perpetuate models that they have inherited from home. One can go further to say that this is a global phenomenon. Unless such categorizations are inherently inapplicable to newly created dances that may be dubiously described as "traditional-popular" dances, it is important as cultural educators to make the distinction as a service to both cultural communities that ensemble directors are supposed to represent and educate.

After discussing the voices of two African-born ensemble directors, I note that the concern for teaching "the right thing" and distinguishing the "authentic" village style from the ballet style of drumming and dancing are sincerely and passionately expressed by North American African drumming and dance instructors and ethnomusicologists. Before drawing on the perspectives of Robert Simms, an ethnomusicologist and former supervisor of world music ensembles at York University, I now relate the manner in which Anna Melnikoff's training as a drummer in the Mande tradition provided her with personal pragmatic experiences that speak to the very concerns that the Ladzekpos hold.

Anna Melnikoff, one of the West African drumming instructors at York University, relates her narratives as follows (Interview, January 2010). As her name suggests, she is not an African; she has a Russian father and an English mother. However, her mother worked with development agencies in sub-Saharan Africa for many years as Anna was growing up. It follows that the immediate African soundscapes, an array of African music she could listen to or performances she could observe, influenced young Melnikoff's formative enculturation. Nevertheless, she did not study or learn to play any musical instrument. But as she turned 35, and now living in Toronto, Melnikoff "had the courage to start learning to play the drum," after using the knowledge she had gained about healing and meditation as a tool that empowered her to overcome her initial scare of African drumming. Melnikoff started playing congas, and then acquired her own djembe drums as she joined drum circles, a strong culture in Toronto. She played with others "with mixed drums, and most of them did not care even to know anything about the instruments than to come together and play. Sometimes it was good, sometimes it was terrible." It is not surprising that somebody who lived in Africa and has a "deep appreciation for music" to realize that she was missing something within the drum circle context; the musicality, complexity, and structure, thought Melnikoff, were lacking, and there must be something more to it. But while it was unfortunate that there was not an expert in Mande drumming in Toronto with whom Anna could study, her interest to learn to play the drum was unflinching, so she had to find alternative means of pursuing her desires and ambitions. She first bought sound recordings of traditional music from Mali, and this move reaffirmed her conviction that there was the "real thing" to be pursued.

The second phase of Melnikoff's drumming involved her identification of a couple of great djembe drummers living in New York and Columbus, Ohio, from whom she received drumming lessons, traveling to and from Toronto. Yet, as great as these drummers were on their instruments, these lessons did not quench Melnikoff's longing for the "authentic thing," because these drummers transmitted the ballet style of drumming rather than the village style. Marked differences exist between these styles, she asserts. The ballet style was a more recent development as a cultural export intended for showing off their culture to the world and bringing some money back home, and these African drummers were successful in doing that. However, they modified the culture to some extent. This practice is not completely surprising as many ballet style drummers never grew up in the village setting, and never learned the full scope of the traditional culture and its dynamic music forms. Ballet style drummers worked simply with choreographed forms and arrangements of selected local dance motives into ballet dance movements with corresponding drumming. She admits, "One should make no mistake about how ballet style required vigorous training." However, that was not what Melnikoff had expected nor wanted, so she resolved to go to Africa, and her first destination was Senegal, for she erroneously thought that djembe was originally a Senegalese drum. Her month's pragmatic experience corrected that notion: the Senegalese drummers were more interested in teaching her *sabar* drumming (Tang 2007), and when she insisted on the djembe, she was disappointed that the Dakar lessons were the same ballet style of drumming from which she was running away.

Melnikoff was closer to realizing her dreams when, during one of her travels, she met a woman in Chicago called Lillian Frieberg who had studied in Germany for twelve years, but was then studying under a "fabulous drummer called Famoudou Konate. He was a master drummer for the Les Ballets Africains for twenty-seven years, and Famoudou is considered perhaps having the best djembe technique in the world." After Frieberg introduced Famoudou Konate to Melnikoff and referred her to him, she was ready to go to Guinea for the first time, exactly a year after the Senegal trip. For two months, Melnikoff stayed in Konate's compound in Conakry, receiving an "amazing and revealing" instruction in the "authentic village style" of drumming. The following are Anna's own words about the fulfilling study under Famoudou Konate.

> The way he teaches was the village traditional style. He grew up in the village, and even when he was in the Le Ballet Africains, he spent time going to his village back and forth and remained in touch with his roots. He has a rare sense of the importance of preserving the traditional culture, and he teaches not only to impact with only the music—melody, bass, or solo phrasing—but also the contexts, the stories in the songs, and maybe the dance movements. So if you are getting drumming education from somebody like Famoudou, an accomplished drummer, you will receive a very broad education. (Interview, January 2010)

Explaining further, Melnikoff learned other things from Famoudou that have nothing directly to do with drumming. These include concepts of respect for culture and tradition, taking care of one's physical body, invaluable lessons on morals and other values, as well as spiritual lessons. "Regrettably, ballet drummers threw such a set of information at the wayside, because they have a different agenda of simply entertaining people and promoting culture abroad or at an urban center."

Contrarily, the village drumming is informed by the purpose of helping to maintain the health of the cultural community or village. Dance drumming was done to impart a feeling of joy in everybody who participated or to synergize corporate farmers' agricultural work with dynamic rhythmic drumming. The athleticism of the dancing was a great natural workout for the body. Beyond entertainment and an expressive discourse, drumming and dancing provided life, health, and impetus for love, joy, and sharing together. Melnikoff experienced most of the preceding when she followed her teacher to his village Sagbalala in upper Guinea. Today, it is easy to understand Melnikoff's criticism of the so-called drum circle practice as well as of the ballet style, within the context of teaching drumming and dance authentically while paying attention to the holistic framework of their inextricable intersections with various domains of cultural and social life. Accordingly, Melnikoff, like the Ladzekpos, has developed the habit of teaching in a way that anecdotes, accounts, and other narratives are integral to the classroom pedagogy.

Yet, using drumming and dance to educate students on other aspects of African culture is best exemplified in the nature of course design as well as the pedagogical philosophies and approaches of ensemble directors who train as dancers—performers and scholars. Moreover, dance department preferences of teaching dance-related theoretical courses privilege the presentation of dance drumming beyond its aesthetic motivation. I now use the orientations and perspectives of Modesto Amegago, who is an Anlo Ewe–born performer, but had also studied and/or taught in the dance departments of a number of North American universities including University of British Columbia, Samuel Fraser University, York University, all in Canada, and Arizona in the United States.

Amegago comes from a family of drummers and musicians, specifically from Anloga in the Volta region of Ghana, the paramount city of the Anlo Ewe. This innate potentiality of Amegago's musicality manifested itself at an early stage, and with a nurturing environment from older musicians, Amegago was playing lead drumming role before age ten. His enculturation as a drummer and dancer saw a consistent growth and maturity even throughout the various stages of his formal education. Growing up within the Anlo Ewe culture was an asset as he gradually became a leader of performing groups and the founder of other troupes, leading to his academic training in dance at the University of Ghana (Legon), and subsequently at North American universities mentioned earlier (Interview, January 2010). I must add that all programs (dance, drama, music) offered at Legon's School of Performing Arts reflect a balance between African and Western perspectives of these arts, a condition that offers a student a deeper understanding and appreciation of his/her own culture, while at the same time receiving education on important aspects of Euro-American arts. During my conversation with him in Toronto, and focusing specifically on courses he taught at the dance department of York University, Amegago cites "African Dance and Music" at both preliminary and intermediate levels. Dance (movement), drumming, singing, and information on the cultural contexts of the various dances are the major inextricable components of the course. He ensures that the students study dance within the contexts of socialization, religion and ceremonies, occupation, politics, and funerals.

This approach is not a suppression of music into an auxiliary, through which something more important is accessed. Rather, it is consistent with the African perception of dance drumming as a discourse through which social and cultural life is experienced.

On the other hand, in our conversation regarding this project, Oforiwaa Ama Aduonum had explained to me when she would at times deliberately choreograph specific dance pieces that she would teach and perform to correct the prejudices that her American students and target audiences may be falsely carrying about Africa, Africans, or a category of women in the world. Ama Aduonum, who originally comes from Ghana but was schooled in the United States, noted the prejudices that her former schoolmates as well as her own students falsely held on different people, and she has observed the effectiveness of her choreographed dances that leave enduring images that communicated powerful messages to her audiences. People from the audience would come to her and thank her for the transformational nature of the dances or concerts, she related (Interview, October 2007).

INTERACTIVE AND RELATIONAL PERSPECTIVES

An often-taken-for-granted virtue of any group of people with a clear set of goals realizable over a given period of time is their interpersonal relationships developed through interactions. The preceding assertion applies to several contexts including classes and ensembles such as world music (theory) and African drum and dance ensemble classes. But while relationships may serve as a means to a desired end or goal, spaces of specific groups constitute sites from which the nature of their activities can reciprocally enable, engender, and/or promote relationships. Accordingly, an important impact of West African drumming and dance on student members is building of relationships.

As the instructor for the introduction to world music class and African drum and dance ensemble at the University of Mississippi, I have noted similarities as well as differences in the kinds and levels of interactions that the nature of each course/ensemble may prescribe or circumscribe. Aiming to argue that West African drumming and dance allow for a higher degree of interpersonal interaction among students than is the case with many other classes, I now discuss these levels of interaction, first in the world music class and then the drum and dance ensemble, after which I compare these relational avenues.

The first few days of class are characterized by different kinds of uncertainties in students' minds. Most students in my world music class, for example, do not know each other prior to enrollment since they come from different departments. Also, they have a vague idea about what the course entails, coupled with their speculations as to how their new teacher may relate to them. But as the weeks go by, and the teacher sets a good tone for the students to interact among themselves as well as with their teacher, the original icy atmosphere begins to melt and give way to a more relaxed one for a better interaction, at times even culminating in unforeseen great relationships. More students then begin to ask and contemplate important questions, engage relevant course materials, and share their ideas through class presentations as well as through answers that may be partly informed by their cultural consciousness. By the end of each semester, some students often end up becoming great friends.

Interaction among members of student ensembles is not peculiar to the African drum and dance ensemble. Certainly, members of jazz, symphonic, wind, steel, and marching bands/ensembles interact in similar ways. However, one must distinguish the overarching levels of interaction common to any university ensemble from those that may be idiosyncratic to a specific group. Common levels of interaction in the African drum and dance ensemble include those that happen during collective rehearsals (classes), preparations for performances, performance tours, discussions that are generated by successful performances, or mundane activities like eating together before or after performances. However, certain kinds of interactions are specifically dictated by the nature of West African dance drumming, especially when they are set into motion, enabled, and synergized by the ensemble director.

For example, the polyrhythmic nature of sub-Saharan African dance drumming is highly interactive (Nketia 1974: 125–138, 168–179; Agawu 2003: 71–96; Koetting 1970; Arom 1991; Anku 1997). The interdependence of the composite parts informs the participating percussionists' awareness about their ineluctable structural and systemic relationships. After fully grasping the perception of what I call "communal creativity" (Dor 2004), partly expressed through the orientation of the supporting instruments to the time line on the bell, or the embedded cues from lead drummers to their fellow percussionists and dancers, one can hardly complete a semester or a year's participation in a West African drum and dance ensemble without having a better understanding of mutual co-dependence, egalitarianism, or the strength of collectivism.

A substantial body of literary works in African music has covered the call-and-response form as a commonplace homology of many traditional African songs. And although the specificities that define the different ways in which this form is realized in the continent's diverse song sub-genres is yet to be fully explored, the interactions between the lead singer and the chorus are among one of the first things that the ensemble members learn. Further, the whole ensemble's spontaneous responses to catch words or phrases that lead singers, drummers, and dancers interject, or the assistant lead singer's interjected phrases that cue the chorus, all contribute to another level of interaction in this genre.

Yet, the degree of interaction becomes more conspicuous in the area of dancing. Given that various dances have their prescribed behavioral codes, it is not uncommon to find dancers touching ethically acceptable parts of their neighbors' bodies, shaking hands, and male dancers catching female dancers who jump into the hands of their male counterparts as climaxes at the end of dance pieces. Further, facial expressions and different nonverbal communicative means are deployed as kinesthetic modes of expression. American students are taught how to simulate other interactive modes and gestures in order to capture the symbolic codes that may be implied in the reproduction of specific dance motives. A classic example is Gahu, the Anlo Ewe courtship dance in which motives include holding or touching parts of the immediate dancer's body while moving mostly in a circular formation. Furthermore, I vividly recollect moments in concerts of the OMADDE during which two students—male and female dancers—take center stage and momentarily dance in pairs. Their levels of interaction, whether real or simulated, mark some of the most memorable high points in the performance. Both audiences and other ensemble members appreciate such conspicuous interactions. Loud shouts or yells from waiting dancers urge their colleagues whenever they do duo dancing in *Kpalongo* or *Bambaya*, for example, registering approval and encouragement. I can still hear echoes of "That's it," "Go for it," "Be real," "Heba, heba" (Ghanaian vocable), and a dancer's name being called, such as "Go Yawa," "Dig it Mimi," or "Annette be yourself."

Figure 4.1 Tayo, Kemi, Buki, and Yawa arriving in Clarksdale, Mississippi, for workshop. [Photo by George Dor, July 2008]

These interactions during rehearsals, especially between patient, motivating directors and their understanding, curious, and industrious student learners, lead to wonderful relationships. In my own ensemble made up of students, my family, and colleague faculty members, our continued interactions within the same ensemble for one, two, three, four or more years have concretized into a kind of a pseudo-family. African students constitute the majority of dancers of OMADDE. Mostly female Nigerian students have responded positively to my invitation to all students to join the ensemble, and after becoming members, they develop strong bonds among themselves as well as with me. As an African myself, I consider and treat these students as I do my own kids (some of whom also belong to the group). Indeed, they take me as a surrogate dad, and when their parents visit campus, whether during our concerts or their kids' graduations, they express their profound joy for the artistic avenues and interactions our ensemble enables.

I now share two short narratives to elucidate the degree of mutual relationship among OMADDE members. As stated in chapter 2, OMADDE participated in the YOCONA Folk Music Festival held in Oxford in the summer of 2008. After giving an impressive workshop on the Grove Stage of the University of Mississippi to a body of schoolchildren from Oxford, Mary

THE IMPACT OF WEST AFRICAN DRUMMING AND DANCE ON THE PARTICIPATING STUDENT 149

Figure 4.2 Lara Olatunje leads a row of dancers of Ole Miss African Drum and Dance Ensemble in their new costumes in a memorable concert. [Photo by University of Mississippi Communications Photography, March 2005]

Sloan, the key organizer of the festival, had implicated me to give a similar workshop to students in Clarksdale on the following morning ahead of our evening concert. However, considering that it was in the summer and some ensemble members left for their homes, and those still in Oxford were working, our participation in the festival took a substantial amount of sacrifice, as always. Hence raising a team to join me for the Clarksdale workshop was very difficult. But as it became evident that I was left with Yawa and Shelter, my kids, and Tayo (a Nigerian female dancer), Kemi Alabi and Buki Alabi (Nigerian dancers) decided to leave whatever they intended to do and join us, saying there was no way they could leave me to go alone.

Eventually, the group was represented by four dancers and two percussionists who gave a memorable workshop at Clarksdale High School, prior to other members of the ensemble "family" joining us for the evening concert. I was not simply grateful to these students; I was deeply moved by their sense of collectivism that we have developed over time through our symbolic interactions.

This sense of family permeates the leadership roles that Lara Olatunje, Jennifer Salu, Ameze, and Kemi Alabi played—especially ways in which they

Figure 4.3 Lara Olatunje and Yawa Dor, after Lara's commencement ceremony, University of Chicago. [Photo by George Dor]

always encouraged their colleagues to attend rehearsals regularly, for prior to fall 2011 OMADDE was not a credit-earning activity. It is such developed relationships, mutual respect, and dedication from these students that first and foremost motivate me to show and reciprocate my appreciation to them on their days of graduation. For example, I drove some nine hours to Chicago with Susan Pedigo (Lara's chemistry professor at Ole Miss) when she was graduating as a doctor of medicine from the University of Chicago in 2008. Figure 4.1 features Lara Olatunje with OMADDE in a 2005 concert in Meek Auditorium during which we showcased our new costumes from Ghana. Figure 4.2 shows Olatunje in her academic regalia and enjoying her milestone moment of joy with Yawa Dor, the girl she took as a sister at Ole Miss and who has grown into a dancer in the ensemble.

Further, and more recently, I witnessed the commencement ceremony of the School of Business Administration from which two of my dancers graduated.

But if the preceding anecdotes stemmed from nostalgia on the part of African members of the ensemble, I must emphasize that we related not in isolation from other members of the ensemble. We were well integrated and did not have to negotiate our mutual bonds with other internationals including American students, faculty, and alumni members of the group. I am very sure that most ensemble directors can relate to my narratives regarding relational outcomes of ensemble membership as my narratives bring vivid memories to the many affable directors whose perspectives I share in this discussion.

In a personal correspondence I asked John L. Price, a former student of Kobla Ladzekpo, the following question: "What do you consider as the factors that have sustained your interest in West African dance drumming all this time?" Unlike the student surveys in which I cannot reveal the identity of ensemble participants, Price has given me permission to share his response to my question because he is no longer a student, and his answer reveals how much impact the African dance drumming classes have had on him as an African American.

> The number one factor that sustains my interest in African dance and music is the connection and pride I feel whenever I participate in drumming. Let's face it in America no one is beating down your door to teach you anything about black or African culture. Growing up there was virtually no exposure to African music in my schools churches or neighborhood. Being from the inner-city and growing up in the 60s the only reference to Africa that I saw was powerful images of black people with beautiful afro's and physiques that were featured in many of the black light posters which were popular at the time. Or on the other hand, the images of starvation, struggle, and disease is what permeated the media in my youth. News of the struggles for independence that were taking place in Africa was unknown to me so not a big deal to the press here at the time. Daishikis were the standard of African dress at the time in LA so if someone was wearing one you assumed they were afro-centric or at least believed in what we called at the time, black power. So I grew up with a feeling of missing out on a big part of my culture and heritage because I had knowingly no connection to Africa at the time. I could name you two tribes from Africa, Watusi and Pygmy and struggled to name any countries except Congo and Egypt without looking at a map. Not many people will admit to it but I knew nothing of Africa and thus always strived to find out whatever I could on my own.
>
> Now let's get to the point, I met the Ladzekpo's simply by being drawn to the sound I heard as I was walking through the main building of my college. I first heard a rumbling that was constant and even, as I got closer to the source of the sound it became clear that this was something I never heard. It started making sense as I got closer and then

suddenly it stopped making sense as I got closer and I found myself at the door of Kobla and Alfred's class totally mesmerized and in awe of the sound and of their abilities as African musicians. They were better African musicians than I was a western musician I quickly realized. I knew I had something to learn from them. I still do. Think about it. Starved of anything African for the first twenty-two years of my life I found myself suddenly making a connection directly with an entire African family! I couldn't resist being around these people and this music. It felt like it was my music. I confess I've been quite spoiled by the Ladzekpos when it comes to African music. They've given me more than I ever imagined I would get out of Africa and African music. They have been my connection or my portal to Africa and eventually it is my hope they will be my guide in knowing Africa. The truth is if I ever make it to Africa or not, the Ladzekpos have given me a piece of Africa that is so precious and important to me. I no longer have a hurt or shame or indifference for being deprived of such a wonderful heritage and my desire to learn African music and make sure the opportunity to learn is there for others is what drives me to continue to assist in the growth, understanding, and spread of African music. The most important thing is that the study of this music actually increases my awareness and concern for the situation in Africa today. I no longer go about my days without being somewhat aware of the on-goings in Africa. I truly can say I love Africa and have a better relationship with people in general because of long-term exposure to African music. (Personal Correspondence, December 2012)

From the preceding discussion, one may conclude that the relational impact of West African drumming and dance on participants in the academy can be transformational. It is also transformational in other ways, including multi-musicality, professional career, and perception of global cultures. However, ensembles' rehearsal and performance spaces can serve as positive tools for reinforcing processes of integration on campuses. Depending on the racial demographics of a particular university, relationships within an ensemble can perpetuate and consolidate an existing multiculturalism of a city, such as Toronto, or sites for mediating any subtle or hidden racial, religious, or ethnic differences that students may be silently entertaining.

Although I will discuss racial dimensions of the presence of West African drumming and dance in the academy in another chapter, I recall my deliberate use of the University of Mississippi's African drum and dance ensemble

Figure 4.4 Classes can be fun, cool, and engaging: students relaxing after dancing, and before learning songs at a Dunyo class, University of Toronto. [Photo by George Dor, January 2010]

in a presentation in which I argued its potency for promoting interracial relations. The October 2003 International Conference on Racial Reconciliation held at the University of Mississippi, organized by the William Winter Institute for Racial Reconciliation, drew participants from different parts of the world including South Africa. I teamed up with Michael Cheers, a friend and professor of photography in the department of journalism, as he explored the role of images captured through photography in fostering racial reconciliation. As a prelude to our presentation titled "Freedom Is a Constant Struggle: Music and Images as Tools for Advancing Racial Reconciliation," our young OMADDE gave its second performance in the rehearsal hall of the Ford Center for the Performing Arts. I strategically taught the ensemble the Anlo Ewe Gahu dance that I have cited earlier in this chapter. Its movements involve visible physical contacts—touching of colleague dancer's body—in order to sell the message of meaningful interaction as a vehicle of intensified cross-racial relations. Dancers for the event comprised three girls and three boys: one black and two white females and one white and two black males. Similarly, percussionists consisted of two whites and four blacks. Situating our performance and levels of interaction within the 1) conference theme, 2) title of the presentation, 3) Herbert Blumer's "symbolic interactionism" interpretive paradigm that we used for the presentation, and 4) the history of Ole Miss regarding integration, the levels of interaction

Figure 4.5 OMADDE girls (Yawa Dor, Kemi Alabi, and Buki Alabi) in a groovy action as they dance the Borborbor, a Ghanaian Ewe social dance, in a campus concert. [Photo by University of Mississippi Communications Photography]

offered by the dance performance provided the audience a beautiful visual of articulated diversity leading to a new perception of Ole Miss.

The impact of participation in West African dance drumming on the student can be far-reaching, diverse, and enduring. The student's racial or ethnic background, musicality, creativity, methods of cognition, sense of collectivity, self-confidence, world-mindedness, and affective sensibilities all undergo a period of transformation. However, discussion of pedagogy in chapter 3 suggests the importance of the nature of the dance-drumming program in terms of type of dance or dances, course design and delivery, and the teacher's resourcefulness and affability toward the students in shaping the impact of courses on participants.

I urge readers to look at the student survey at the Appendix. I have shared a body of insights from the survey responses in this and other chapters. The perspectives of other consultants I have shared in this chapter were mainly their recollections, especially of when they were student participants of ensembles, and how such participation shaped their current careers.

THE IMPACT OF WEST AFRICAN DRUMMING AND DANCE ON THE PARTICIPATING STUDENT   155

Figure 4.6 ZADONU, Kobla Ladzekpo's professional group in Los Angeles. It comprises several former students of his. L to R, Back row: John Price, Andrew Grueschow, Mark Sims, Kobla Ladzekpo, Kevin O'Sullivan, Jun Reichl. Middle row: Derrick Spiva Jr., Karen Liu, Neili Sutker, Melissa Sanvicente. Bottom row: Yeko Ladzekpo-Cole, Lara Diane Rann. [Photo by John Price, SEM 2010]

5

PATH-FINDING AGENCY OF ADMINISTRATORS AND ENSEMBLE DIRECTORS

In the previous chapters I have implicitly shown that the phenomenal changes that characterized the transformation of a genre from a state of neglect to that of serious embrace in the universities cannot be attributed to happenstance or only to broad changes in cultural landscapes and policies of American universities. Certainly, collective actions by groups toward change in any social, cultural, and academic context need to be acknowledged. However, this chapter provides an explicit discussion of categories of individuals who have significantly contributed and continue to contribute in establishing the presence of West African drumming and dance in their respective universities. While I have focused on students in chapter 4 and will discuss the role of audiences in chapter 6, administrators and ensemble directors are my focus here. Of course, an inextricable connection exists between all these different players that I cover in the various chapters, as well as the shared values that underlie their participation and patronage of the genre in varied ways.

AGENCY OF ADMINISTRATORS

Agency, in sociological terms, may be defined as a deliberate or calculated action taken by an individual or group of individuals aimed at bringing about change within a normally undesirable landscape. Ethnomusicologists, music administrators, and other visionaries whose various forms of agency have resulted in the founding and sustenance of West African drumming and dance in their respective programs can be called initiators, facilitators, and enablers. For example, I mentioned in chapter 2 the extent to which the agency and collaborations of Hood and Kwabena Nketia are central to the understanding of UCLA's West African dance-drumming ensemble's history. But beyond UCLA and in the context of West African drumming in the 1960s, these facilitators include Willard Rhodes of Columbia University and later, in the 1970s, David McAllister of Wesleyan University. Subsequent initiators or perpetuators include Olly Wilson of Berkeley, David Locke of Tufts, Jacqueline DjeDje of UCLA, and Russell Hartenberger of Toronto, among others.

A category of the consultants with whom I had very engaging conversations during my fieldwork were administrators who were in some ways connected with the founding or sustenance of West African drumming and dance in their universities. I have already shared some of their rich insights and would like to distill them further in this chapter. Most of the administrators I interviewed honored the legacies of their teachers who were founding scholars of ethnomusicology programs. While DjeDje vividly recalled her personal experiences with Mantle Hood and Nketia at UCLA, Locke and Hartenberger also shared lifelong memories of Wesleyan under and/or with Roberts and McAlester. Naturally, some of the ensemble directors also shared positive memories on these path-finding ethnomusicologists for their initiatives. For example, Kobla Ladzekpo discussed his years and those of his bother Alfred at Columbia under Williard Rhodes in the later 1960s before they moved to Los Angeles. This caliber of administrators introduced West African drumming as a means of expanding existing ethnomusicology programs in their institutions. As heads of ethnomusicology programs or as chairs that were by specialization ethnomusicologists, they understood the place of world music ensembles, including West African drum-dance, within the broader ethnomusicology or music program. While Africa may not be the major research area of these initiators, some have partial vested interests; Mantle Hood and Williard Rhodes both did some fieldwork in Africa. It is also important to understand the success of these personalities within the support they received from their departments and colleges.

A second category of these leaders consists of those who were established percussionists, directors, and researchers of West African drumming and dance, prior to becoming administrators. Their unflinching commitment to the ensemble's consistent growth goes beyond concern for the expansion of the ethnomusicology program. They also share similar vested interests that stem from their artistic and academic/scholarly preoccupations. Hartenberger and Locke could not hide their support for West African drumming and dance ensembles as dean and chair, though not at the expense of other areas in the faculty or department of music. Programs with such deans and chairs tend to flourish even after tenures of their deanship or headship as the ensembles continue to thrive on the logistic and other foundations that the departmental heads ensured they benefited from. Further, because such administrators have established working relationships with other top university administrators, they tend to have stronger leverage when lobbying for support for their ensembles.

However, some administrators from the preceding category tend to arrange takeovers of the ensemble or instructions in drumming and dance by somebody else for two main reasons. First, administrative work may weigh too heavily on them, especially when combined with too many commitments. Such relief thus enables focus and attention for the demanding administrative role. Second, they invite experts, who can take the drumming and dance programs to another level, to take over. Classic examples are the great West African drumming and dance programs at the University of Toronto and York. In my interview with Russell Hartenberger, the (2010) dean of the music faculty at Toronto, he related that he was the one who introduced the teaching of West African drumming (without movement) at this university. Later, he invited one of his students who had visited Ghana, Cathy Armstrong, to study dance to add the teaching of the dance component. Before Kwasi Dunyo, the gifted instructor I met, took over and developed the program into a really enviable one, Joseph Ashong, another Ghanaian ensemble director, expanded the program (Interview, January 2010). Though not the chair of the music department, Robert Simms started the West African drumming program at York. After a few years he pushed for the hiring of experts in Ghanaian—Ewe, Akan, Dagbamba—and Mande drumming traditions in order to grow the program. He has since relinquished his position as the coordinator of West African drumming at York to Kwasi Dunyo, who works with Anna Melnikoff, Larry Graves, and Isaac Akrong who all provide vibrant instructions in drumming and dance.

A third category of administrators, where Olly Wilson belongs, is Africanist professors who are not directors of ensembles but whose research experiences in Africa—during which they experienced traditional drumming and dance within their original contexts—yielded friendships with talented master drummers who were subsequently helped to come to America to establish the African drumming program in their universities. Although not then the chair, Wilson was instrumental in bringing Christopher Ladzekpo to Berkeley and later, as chair, witnessed the fruits of the musical genre he assisted in planting. I have already mentioned how Mantle Hood's visit to Ghana concretized his friendship not only with Kwabena Nketia but also with the drum instructor he arranged to bring to UCLA about a decade prior to the Berkeley scenario.

When Africanists with vested interests in West African drumming and dance become chairs of music or ethnomusicology departments, they automatically become responsible for the perpetuation of world music ensembles that have already been established in their departments. For example, DjeDje, the chair of UCLA's department of ethnomusicology, was a member of Badu's UCLA ensemble as a student. An African American who conducted fieldwork in Ghana (albeit on fiddling), she has a strong love for West African drumming. As DjeDje asserts, "Whenever you think of African drumming as an African American, it is almost like, that's the soul, that's the heart, to the essence of being African" (Interview, July 2007). Eric Charry of Wesleyan is another Africanist who became a departmental chair for four years, even though courses in West African drumming were well established before he joined the music faculty. He briefly taught djembe drumming as a testimony of his passion for the Mande sub-region that he studies (Interview, December 2007). Charry shared other perspectives on the subject of study that I have drawn upon at various points of the discussion.

The majority of music faculty administrators are neither Africanists nor ethnomusicologists. While they are supposed to be fair to all areas within the department, there is a high probability of such administrators developing their own areas at the expense of others, including West African drumming and dance, which is obviously not one of the canons. Another phenomenon that C. K. Ladzekpo metaphorically describes as an ensemble becoming an "orphan" involves a situation in which a previous chair or dean who lent an ensemble his/her fullest possible support is replaced by another chair or dean who is not as supportive. Chairs who might not have developed a good sense of world-mindedness or overseers who are perpetuators of only the dominant culture are more likely to regard West African drumming and dance as not a priority. In schools located in regions that may not be very multicultural, the creation of multicultural awareness in my opinion must be a priority. And while some chairs could have capitalized on the presence of West African drumming in their schools by prioritizing support for it, they instead prefer to ensure that their programs rather resemble those offered in other major universities within the region. What they may not know is the extent to which those very universities are looking to each other to emulate the innovations they have put in place. Although some ensemble directors aim to lead the way in intensifying aspects of African studies in their universities, the economic meltdown has become a great excuse for some chairs to turn up the volume on their "not my priority" rhetorical song.

But who should decide the priority? Should not the priority represent the consensus voice of deans, chairs, faculty, students, and audiences of the

Figure 5.1 Charles Gates, chair, department of music, University of Mississippi.[Photo taken after interview by George Dor, October 2012]

ensembles, who in their patronizing numbers at various concerts are silently sending signals regarding sustained or shifting priorities? Perhaps, one needs to question what the determinants of priorities are. Are they activities that resonate with broader college values or with statewide needs? Schools have different traditions and demographic peculiarities, even though academic philosophies may be the same or similar. Should administrators simply work within the framework of such prevailing landscapes? Additionally, I think it may be rewarding for the university when administrators exercise their agency to include programs that reverberate world-consciousness, another pervasive global mentality of today. Nevertheless, there are exceptions to the preceding attitude and position and I must admit the dangers of total stereotyping in this case.

Given that the existence of a world music ensemble may constitute an important interdisciplinary salience for cognate disciplines within the same university, administrators of other departments normally support West African drum and dance ensembles in a number of ways. African studies, African American studies, international studies, and performing arts centers may co-sponsor programs by the ensemble. In universities with huge performing arts programs, the administrator may not be a music scholar or musician. However, it may not be surprising if an African drum and dance ensemble flourishes more under such leaders than under a conservative music faculty. Furthermore, one needs to recognize roles of college deans in the upkeep of West African drum and dance ensembles, because the employment of any drum and/or dance instructor partly depends on the approval of deans and other highly positioned administrators, who may at times depend on the advice not only of music chairs but also from appointed advisors on university multicultural affairs. The luckiest ensemble director is one who works under a college dean who is an ethnomusicologist, a musicologist, or a musician who has a passion and love for world music. Of course, several college deans who are not musicians can equally love music from other parts of the world. However, the most important consideration is for the dean to understand how an African ensemble fits within the operational philosophies of liberal arts colleges.

But to paraphrase Charles Gates, chair of the University of Mississippi music department, an individual administrator's personal interests should not override the institution's values, goals, and objectives they have been hired to uphold and pursue. When I opened my interview with him with the question, "To what extent do you think the African Drum and Dance Ensemble over here [at Ole Miss] resonates with the broader values, policies, and objectives of the College of Liberal Arts and then the Department of Music?" Gates responded thus:

> Actually, I will take it from the university level. University, liberal arts, and then the department. The University of Mississippi is committed to and very actively engages in access to cultural awareness, to stimulation of cultural engagement. Not just as an idea that students should read about the cultures. So from the top-down, university, college, and department, . . . we have been actively pursuing opportunities for students to actively engage in multiple cultures, not only as an academic activity, but also as a real-life experience. So the presence and activities of what was formed as the Ole Miss African Drum and Dance Ensemble, but now incorporated as an academic credit-earning course known as African Music Ensemble, is one of such possible expressions of African cultural participation. This is how I view it as a university ideal. (Interview, October 2012)

It may be observed that when administrators work with such informed and heightened awareness of university ideals, support for world music ensembles can be more consistently upheld, and not lacking because of a prevailing

Figure 5.2 Dean Glenn Hopkins, Dean, College of Liberal Arts, University of Mississippi. [Photo taken after interview by George Dor, October 2012]

economic landscape, but also because a new administrator wants to ensure visibility for his/her own projects at the expense of preexisting ones, even though world music ensembles' values might have been pragmatically proven. To borrow C. K. Ladzekpo's term, no African dance-drumming ensemble should become an "orphan" just because of a new administrator who is supposed to sustain the very university ideals discussed herein.

But before situating the ensemble within the ideals of liberal arts education, I asked Charles Gates, my chair, to share with me what he thinks liberal arts education is all about. He shared the following insights with me after strongly suggesting that I need to interview a dean of the College of Liberal Arts, a meeting he later arranged for me. Charles Gates thinks that

> The primary purpose of liberal arts education is not to train people professionally. Rather, it is intended to develop the whole person or citizen. Through different disciplines or various modes of thought, the student is helped to develop critical thinking, analytical skills, and both intellectual and ethical components of his/her life. Regardless of students' major area of concentration, exposure to various modes of enquiry characteristic of the sciences—natural and physical, humanities, literature and arts, and social sciences—is vital. For example, the way one explores the world through the sciences is going to be different

from doing so through the arts. Hence the liberal arts education requires students to take a variety of courses in all the areas of subject disciplines, but not necessarily expecting them to have comprehensive knowledge in all fields. Even when students are training in professional schools and aiming toward becoming an engineer, a teacher, a medical doctor, so that even in the liberal arts they are in fields that are more professionally oriented—chemistry, biology, and music education, for example—the undergraduate major, from a liberal arts point of view, is selecting a particular lens with which to engage the world. (Interview, October 2012)

When I interviewed Dean Glenn Hopkins, professor of mathematics and dean of the College of Liberal Arts at the University of Mississippi for the past fourteen years, his perspectives reinforced Gates's. In his response to my question, "Could you help me understand what liberal arts education is all about?" he opines as follows:

Although students must be informed about various components of liberal arts—physical and natural sciences, humanities, fine arts, and social sciences—study of liberal arts is far beyond that. It also involves learning to think across disciplines, interpret and use different ideas in places that may seem unusual. We will expect graduates of liberal arts to write clearly, take ideas and think critically, analyze and synthesize ideas, put them into perspectives and larger focus. Also, liberal arts graduates must be knowledgeable about the world, cultures, worldviews, and world challenges that prepare them ahead of probably visiting that country one day. Knowledge about different cultures is important, keeping in mind that different cultures have different guidelines, and although one cannot learn about all the cultures of the world, knowledge about different cultures provides broad thinking and thinkers. (Interview, October 2012)

In the light of the preceding ideals, Dean Hopkins is happy that the University of Mississippi has the African music ensemble that offers both students and faculty a way of understanding different African cultures. He notes: "it is a good thing that our students come from about sixty countries [in 2012], . . . and it is through endeavors such as this [the African drum and dance ensemble] that people come into contact with a particular culture." Hopkins thinks it is a great resonance with the ideals of liberal arts "to bring different cultures into a spotlight so that our students can be part of that and learn about the culture" (Interview, October 2012).

Since this world music ensemble belongs to the academy, I think it is important that all key players know how this caliber of administrators thinks about it. Also, I am positive that the viewpoints represented here apply to many universities and they will therefore serve as invaluable insights to readers. I consider it appropriate to close this segment with the passionate words of Dean Hopkins regarding the question of whether location or demographics affects a college or not. He uncompromisingly asserts:

> Freedom of inquiry, the idea of open and broad education, and thinking broadly is true in every college of liberal arts. The concept of liberal arts education is not a Mississippi idea, it is not a Southern concept, and it is not an American idea. It is all over the world. Liberal arts education that frees the mind is important. Certainly, where we are influenced are the resources, the amount of money we have. But, so far as what we stand for as a college, that does not depend on where we are. (Interview, October 2012)

While I have already touched on the importance of demographics to the patronage of student African drum and dance ensembles in North America, the above opinion rather encourages players in the sustenance of world music ensembles to boldly face challenges they may encounter irrespective of the locales of their universities. It is important to add that both Charles Gates and Glenn Hopkins have played major roles in the upkeep of my institution's African dance drumming ensemble.

AGENCY OF ENSEMBLE DIRECTORS

It will not be an overexaggeration to observe that the most important category of players in the presence of West African drumming and dance in the North American academy is ensemble directors. At times, their quintessential contributions are not fully appreciated and acknowledged. Yet, these directors or instructors have different cultural and academic backgrounds that reflexively inform their pedagogical philosophies and methods, a theme I discuss in chapter 3. Although I will revisit these differences, the central purpose here is to share aspects of directors' experiences on the job, touching on both strengths and areas in which they had to pursue personal development necessary to better discharge their duties.

The first consideration that qualifies these ensemble directors is their ability to demonstrate a substantial knowledge and competence in African dance drumming traditions. Naturally, some of the most skilled and accomplished drummers are those in African villages, whose gradual processes of enculturation often lead them into being custodians of specialized knowledge within their cultural communities. However, only drummers who have received formal Western education and speak the English language at a reasonably good level can instruct in the American academy. The command of the English language as a communicative tool is also a prerequisite for studying and performing in multi-ethnic dance troupes that are based in urban centers of Anglophone countries, just as French is required as an official language in some African countries. In my field conversations, one consultant recalled how in the early 1970s a talented African master drummer, though loved by the music faculty and students of an American university because of his genuine devotion to his art and his affable character, was relieved of his teaching job because of his inability to communicate his ideas to his students in English. This situation is not the same as the normal complaint that some lazy students give regarding the accents of their African teachers. Indeed, the preceding case was an isolated one. All the directors I have known personally, interviewed, or have spoken to about by their administrators and students have good command of language for instructing.

The first category of ensemble directors are great master drummers from Ghana, some of whom served as nationally acclaimed performers in the Ghana Dance Ensemble and other dance troupes before coming to North America. These are the classiest artists drawn from their ethnic regions and brought together to pursue a goal of national integration through the arts. These drummers and dancers not only performed their local dances but also taught each other to perform dances of other ethnic origins. Whereas this category of directors are virtuosi in their respective ethnic dance traditions, they have a rich knowledge in other Ghanaian dances. While all members of the Ghana Dance Ensemble had at least the equivalent of high school diploma, some members have higher diplomas before coming to North America. It must be emphasized that performance was their focus and not academic study of the performing arts. These directors, before coming to North America, had enviable performance careers at the forefront of national events and on numerous international performance tours especially to Europe, America, and other African countries. In spite of their stellar performance careers, they never relented in seeking personal development whenever necessary.

During my field conversations, one collaborator shared with me the developmental programs he had to pursue in order to be full-time faculty and to brighten his chances of tenure and promotion in the future. Coming to the United States with a bachelor's degree in music, this master drummer was encouraged and challenged to earn a masters degree in music from an American university. He was happy he did, and he reaped the dividends of these further academic courses in his career as an instructor in the university. Other directors in this category were happy that they became autodidacts or at times took informal lessons from friends aimed at a fuller understanding of notation of drum rhythms that they may draw upon as pedagogical tools whenever necessary. As they relate, the knowledge gained in these lessons was also translated into the writing of articles on the dance genres they teach, some of these posted on their personal websites. As I have shown in chapter 3, the use of notation is not a prerequisite for teaching West African drumming and dance for most instructors. However, it remains an asset for whoever masters it. While some have written and published articles on their art, others have collaborated with other Africanists in various written projects. But given the diversity and plurality of African ethnic cultures, directors of this category still need support from their administrators and art and cultural foundations should they express the desire to learn new dances from other ethnic groups within or outside their countries.

Some of my consultants from this category of instructors expressed concerns about the difficulty of fair placement with regard to rank, salary, tenure, and promotion. Given that the kind of cultural capital with which these guardians of traditional culture come to the American academy is different from those required of regular professors, the initial determination of rank for these African instructors poses challenges to administrators. Their tenure or promotion often requires different considerations, leaving some who have worked for several years at the rank of adjunct or assistant professor until their retirement. Only one or two of this category have been promoted to full professor. Of course, it can be argued that not even every university professor who holds a doctoral degree has been granted tenure and promotion. As such, nobody will be advocating a higher rank for all directors of this category of West African dance drumming teachers. However, it is important that administrators and faculty members value and reward the competence and productivity that these virtuosic musicians demonstrate in their respective spheres of traditional knowledge.

As I have mentioned elsewhere, a second category of ensemble directors is Africans who come to North America universities to pursue graduate programs in music. This category can be further subdivided, first into those who were very competent on the drums or knowledgeable in dance drumming traditions, performed in or with dance troupes, or taught drumming in Africa before coming to North America. The second subgroup comprises scholars, art music composers, and/or performers of Western instruments like the piano, brass, and/or strings who may not be well grounded in dance drumming as the preceding subcategory, simply because they had other focal areas while in Africa. However, they have sufficient knowledge in drumming and dance to start an ensemble in their new music departments in North America. Most directors of this group are normally teaching assistants or fellows, but some professors who may take on teaching African drumming as an added load may belong here. These directors are ready to relearn African dances more seriously and now as an added prioritized activity. As such, they either return to Africa during summer months for intensified drumming and dancing, or they seek help from competent African master drummers working in North America. Here, institutional support is crucial for the development of the instructor in this new engagement. Normally, directors of this category have good command of the English language and can therefore communicate their ideas clearly to their students. Also, although they may not be virtuosi on their drums, as in the previous category, they still are Africans. Accordingly, they operate with their general cultural consciousness as shaped by their ethnic and national heritages. Additionally, the bi-musical knowledge of these directors is more balanced, because they have acquired very high skills and knowledge in Western musical instruments, music history, theory, as well as African music components of their bachelors or masters degrees from African universities. All this habitus informs their instructional work in the American academy.

Yet, the lesson I have learned from my study is that it may be better for professors in this category to found and establish West African drumming and dance as a credit-earning activity, and then persuade their institutions to hire experts to take over from them. Certainly, such assistance will provide the former director more time to conduct scholarly research, develop and teach other ethnomusicology courses, thereby expanding the program. Admittedly, it may sound absurd suggesting hiring an additional instructor during these economically hard times. But then, suppressing lenses to certain cultural and intellectual engagements that have been tested as rewarding is a tough choice and call. Hopefully, the landscape will improve.

As I discovered in Toronto, complementary federal funding may facilitate the hiring of a new ensemble director. Also, grants could be written by a team of experts including institutional grant writers, ethnomusicologists, and multicultural officers in order to secure finances for the African drum and dance ensemble within a general world music promotional project. The University of Florida's African ensemble is a beneficiary of such huge grants. Other sources of support may include arts and fellowship foundations that can be explored for short-term projects and programs. In some universities, however, an incoming graduate student from Africa is purposely granted admission as a teaching assistant who is competent enough to direct the ensemble.

In spite of the preceding observations, categories, and suggestion, I want to assert that there are exceptions to the above descriptions. Some directors in the second category are very versatile and outstanding in dance drumming as well as their programs of study in North America. Similarly, I have known directors who have developed rapidly in their added role and may not need to relinquish their teaching of dance drumming if they and their institutions make that call. However, the hiring of a dance instructor in African dance will rather expand and strengthen the program in a significant way. The Wesleyan and Binghamton programs are classic cases of the preceding reinforcement.

The final category of directors is American Africanists, whether as researcher-performers or simply as performers. Two subcategories may be noted here too. The first comprises those American ethnomusicologists who spend substantial time, perhaps more than a year, studying a dance-drumming tradition in Africa. The second subcategory is former ensemble members and students of African dance-drumming directors at UCLA, Wesleyan, WVU, Toronto, or Pittsburgh later develop and become directors, a process I discussed in chapter 4. I have always been intrigued with the consciousness that directors of this category often express, be it in casual conversations, interviews, or implicitly in their scholarly writings. While I withhold names, most of them acknowledge the differences as well as similarities that exist between them and the first category of indigenous African master drummers and directors. Because culture can be learned, these American directors have acquired great levels of performance competence on their instruments and dances. However, nothing will erase the differences between an enculturated master drummer and an unenculturated lead drummer. This observation in no way demeans the outstanding efforts of American directors.

While such consciousness of these differences by American directors may be translated into positive energies, care must be taken not to overdo it, for it may have negative effects as well. I have admired the collaborations that some American directors of ensembles have initiated between themselves and their African teachers in joint projects including workshops and performances. On the other hand, the strong reflexive mindfulness on the part of the American director as performing the music of a different race, constantly asking questions on how others may perceive his or her devotion to the music of other people, especially when one situates the practice within the broader American history of racism, may be too burdensome on the overly cautious director. My fieldwork has revealed to me the extent to which some of these American directors respect the traditional knowledge and wisdom of the cultures they have specialized in, and they always celebrate their mentors in African music. At other times the self-probing may relate to the aesthetic nuances associated with West African drumming, and since these are also other domains of culture they can also be learned. Frequent returns to their field sites for further and followup research, collaborations with established African drummers and teachers, and invitations of their African teachers for workshops for short residencies have been rewarding to both teachers of this category and their students. Here, David Locke's model is exemplary. More recently, though, James Burns's program at Binghamton has benefited from his returns to Ghana, even when enabled by external grants.

It is encouraging and assuring to mention that the consensus from numerous audience responses, administrators' viewpoints, and returned student ensemble members' surveys indicate a high level of appreciation for the contributions from all the categories of directors I have discussed in the previous paragraphs. Yes, directors may have different backgrounds, but they are all contributing in diverse and significant ways to the global or multicultural landscapes of their respective North American institutions and their larger cultural communities. But given that the sky is the limit, ensemble directors need to develop in different spheres of the game, when consistent institutional support empowers them to do so. Self-introspection and pursuit of development are a necessary commonplace in all human endeavors. I am reminded of how some of our famous anthropologically trained ethnomusicologists had to intensify their musicological studies in order to become more grounded and rounded scholars and leaders of our field. Conversely, all ethnomusicologists know too well the required anthropology courses that were integral to our training. I find the personal narratives discussed here very inspiring, especially the relentless efforts that most ensemble directors make to take their works to higher levels of enterprise with the attendant self-gratifications.

FOUNDING, DIRECTING, SUPPORT/FUNDING

Founding

The stories of how West African drum and dance ensembles were founded in North American universities range from institutions with well-planned agendas for world music ensembles, initiatives of faculty researchers and performers who visited Africa, to innovation-driven actions taken by music faculty and teaching assistants and fellows. In some universities, the idea of founding a West African drum and dance ensemble is that of administrators. Taking UCLA for example, the account was part of a well-thought-out concept of having world music ensembles as part of the ethnomusicology program. Though a result of Mantle Hood's innovative drive and ingenuity, the entire faculty and college, I think, bought the idea. After ensuring that funds would be made available for the bi-musicality project, Hood consolidated his zeal and impetus for the project through his fieldwork experiences in Ghana in 1963. He had the opportunity to collaborate with Nketia, conduct research on drumming, and take drumming lessons himself. He not only witnessed the models already in place at the University of Ghana through the Ghana Dance Ensemble, but also made contacts with those who would become his future drum instructors at UCLA. According to Kobla Ladzekpo, Hood ordered the green-painted *Atsimewu*[1] in UCLA's Gamelan Room in 1963 through him toward the subsequent commencement of instructions in West African drumming. These steps seem to apply to the inception of instruction in West African drumming and dance in several other universities. They have broader world music programs, and although not as elaborate as Hood's bi-musical project, they may already have gamelan and other ensembles that make arguing for the addition of West African drum and dance ensemble easier. Berkeley, West Virginia, and Bowling Green American professors who went to Ghana, though with different agendas, all (1) experienced drumming within the original cultural contexts, (2) resolved to establish a program at their universities upon return home, (3) made initial contacts for the recruitment of founding ensemble directors, and (4) gathered background information regarding cost and the processes of acquiring and shipping the necessary instruments.

While Berkeley, like UCLA and Wesleyan, arranged for the employment of permanent ensemble instructors, most institutions rather depend on African graduate teaching assistants for the same job. For this reason, recruiters may go personally to Africa, normally Ghana, or work with a trusted ethnomusicologist or ensemble director in Ghana to do the recruiting of a suitable student for the drum and dance instructor position. Ghanaians who have already completed their African music diploma or B.Mus. and are good drummers and dancers often approach visiting American professors and make known their desires of studying in the United States or Canada. At the University of Pittsburgh, one of the African teaching fellows is normally responsible for the African ensemble until he or she completes the program. Yet, Pitt did not send anybody to Africa to recruit or base their admissions of African students solely on their ability to drum and dance. Rather Pitt admitted on merit and I remember years in which Akin Euba himself had to teach the course, and also when Pascal Younge traveled from Morgantown to teach in Pittsburgh on a part-time basis because the newly admitted African students were neither drummers nor dancers. Even William Anku, who founded the first African drum and dance ensemble at Pittsburgh, was not admitted as a drummer. It was his personal decision that led to the founding of that ensemble, though one would hope that Nketia, the Africanist then at Pitt, gave him his support. DjeDje informed me of how the expertise of particular African graduate students led to the introduction of drumming and other genres from other African ethnic groups. Thus James Makubuya gave instructions in ethnic cultures from Uganda, and Olatunjie Vidal taught *dundun* drumming from Yoruba.

Some professors who are percussionists and researchers of African drumming traditions founded their institution's ensembles. David Locke of Tufts is a classic example. After his fieldwork experiences and drumming lessons in Ewe and Dagbamba cultures, he founded and directed the African ensemble at Tufts for many years. Similarly, Russell Hartenberger introduced West African drumming to the University of Toronto. Though initially it was not a credit-earning activity, he taught interested colleague faculty and students drumming mostly during weekend rehearsals. He further recollects that their earliest performances were informal, at times during lunch breaks to entertain mainly music faculty and students (Interview, January 2010). It is revealing to learn about the humble beginnings that have led to the great West African drumming and dance program of University of Toronto today.

University of Colorado at Boulder represents another model in which the college of music was ready for an Africanist ethnomusicologist to be hired to teach relevant theoretical courses and found an African ensemble. In this scenario too, gamelan, taiko, and other world music ensembles were already part of the ethnomusicology program when the search for an Africanist was vigorously pursued. Kwasi Ampene's promise to found a West African highlife ensemble during his 2000 interview as a finalist was taken seriously before eventually offering him the job. When I visited Boulder in November 2009 to give a presentation on this book project and also have a conversation with Ampene regarding his ensemble, I was stunned by the degree to which he had changed the cultural landscape of his university and its region. In April 2010 his ensemble celebrated its tenth year of vibrant presence. The performance drew invited guests, as it normally does, and homecoming of former students. The ticket proceeds of this concert, as Ampene disclosed to me in October 2010, amounted to $20,000.

I include this ensemble in this discussion for the following reasons. First, though a popular music genre, it is from West Africa, with carefully selected repertoire from Nigeria, Congo, and Cameroon, though Ghanaian works predominate. Second, choreographed dancing complements the highlife pieces during performance, and Ampene had arranged for Ghanaian dance drumming instructors living in Denver to work with the students on movements, an integral component of the course. They include Agyei and Maputo. Third, the audiences, the majority being students, hardly sit in their seats. They dance their hearts out throughout the entire performance, some occupying the space between the stage and the seats of the auditorium, with almost everybody else standing and swaying or moving more gently but rhythmically to the beat.

Another admirable model and a success story is James Burns's agency as reflected in the West African drumming and dance at Binghamton University. In less than a decade the program has grown to four different courses (which I discuss in chapter 2) taught by two instructors, with a great image and visibility on campus and the university's surrounding cultural communities. Burns himself describes the enrollment for the courses as follows.

> For the class part of Nukporfe, they [students] have to pass an audition. Because all MUSP [music performance] courses like orchestra etc. are by audition only. This means they have taken one of the dance or drum courses or they have a background in the music. (We have many Ghanaian and Nigerian students.) In addition, we do allow alums and community members to sit in, and we do have about five or ten such people that come regularly. There are also many students who cannot overload with more credits, so they just come for the love of the music. Because our numbers are so high (forty dance students in each class, twenty to thirty drummers), we can let anyone sit in, (Interview, September 2012)

Although I will discuss the extent of support that Burns had received from the dean of his college, Burns deserves commendation for his zeal and dedication and sacrifice that have factored into the growth of this ensemble.

Capitalizing on opportunities such as being a sabbatical leave replacement, though brief, can lead to the path-finding agency translated into the introduction of West African drumming and dance into an institution. When Kofi Gbolonyo was appointed a visiting assistant professor at University of British Columbia, Vancouver, Canada, his term was to replace Michael Tenzer for a year, teach some ethnomusicology seminars in African music, and teach an African ensemble. Supported by the institution, he acquired drums from Ghana and taught a course in drumming and dance, drawing on his Pittsburgh experiences as a director. He impressed the university with the annual concert so much such that the college dean, chair, and music faculty arranged to extend his stay for another year. Whether or not 2013 or a later date will see the end of the West African drum and dance ensemble in that university, the memory of Gbolonyo's agency will linger in the collective minds of many in the university. The best-case scenario is the possibility of continuity in the West African drumming and dance ensemble that Gbolonyo founded.

As my last example of the narratives on founding of ensembles, I recall my own. Drumming was not part of my assigned load when I was hired to teach in the honors college and music department of the University of Mississippi. I was expected to teach area, theoretical, and topical courses in ethnomusicology and themed courses in the honors college. But as I came to Oxford and experienced the cultural landscape, and remembered the history of suppression of drumming during the period of slavery in the American South, I resolved that I would found a West African drum and dance ensemble for our own enjoyment and to send a signal to the world regarding historic cultural changes on campus. Though it took eight years (beginning in 2003) to become a credit-earning activity, one cannot deny the path-finding efforts of the Ole Miss African Drum and Dance Ensemble (OMADDE), which I discuss at different points in this book. Below, I would like to present two excerpts lifted from remarks by various university administrators during the ensemble's performance on March 6, 2007, commemorating Ghana50 in a concert at the Ford Center.

> There is an old Ghanaian proverb which states, do not follow the path. Go where there is no path to begin a trail. — Ghanaian proverb evoked

by Dr. Don Cole, Adviser to the Chancellor on Multicultural Affairs, University of Mississippi

... We live in an age when so much of our attention is focused on the things that divide us. Differences in race, age, gender, religion, political views, and there are so many issues that seem to separate us. So how special it is like tonight we can celebrate with the people on the other side of the planet our common national independence. Thanks to Professor George Dor, the distance between the nation of Ghana and the campus of the University of Mississippi has been bridged tonight. We can share in their joy of independence and their musical heritage. It is truly a small world after all. — Jeff Alford, Associate Vice-Chancellor for University Relations

The preceding assertions indicate the extent to which individuals construct their own readings into the innovation necessary for founding an ensemble on campus, the symbolism of collectively celebrating universal causes and virtues of liberation for humanity, irrespective of the place in the world, and the advantages of such promotions of international and multicultural relationships within a university community.

Directing

In this segment I discuss the agency of instructors of West African drum and dance ensembles aiming to explain the reasons for which they merit to be called directors. As the label suggests, a director is supposed to direct and lead his/her organization/group in their collective efforts at realizing their goals and objectives. Driven by the pursuit of maximum productivity and quest for perfectionism, the director must be anchored by ethically sound actions by which he/she plans, programs, and implements, ensuring the availability of tools and resources necessary for the accomplishment of goals, coordination of roles, sustenance of good working relations, atmosphere, and happiness, as well as the administration of rewards to deserving members in recognition of their outstanding work in the group. All ensemble directors will agree with me that what they do on a weekly basis entails the foregoing duties. And although the designation of director for somebody working within the ambit of the performing arts will obviously imply both administrative and artistic responsibilities, I choose to concentrate on the artistic.

But why should I even spend time unpacking "directing" as an aspect of these instructors' agency? Are they not simply like any other instructor in the music department? I argue that the designation is not at all superficial. It is earned through what they do. A further clarification of the differences in the nature of teaching West African drumming and dance in the North American academy will foster a deeper understanding of the subject at hand here. Four kinds of student participants in West African drumming and dance can be distinguished. First and the most common category is students who enroll for credits in drumming and dance classes, and at the end of the semester are required to participate in a concert that is factored into their grading requirements. In some schools, these students also form the African ensemble. Second, the best percussionists and dancers may be selected from among these students to join the university's African ensemble. At universities where African ensembles enjoy regional or national acclaim, this select group, resembling a quasi-professional team, normally performs off campus. Third, a separate group is organized as the university's African drum and dance ensemble to include students, alumni, faculty, and at times staff. Credit earning may not drive activities of such a category. Rather, members devote their time and participate as an extracurricular activity that enriches the cultural life of their schools and surrounding regions.

The fourth type is an independent ensemble formed by the director who teaches at a university as well. Such a group normally involves talented students, alumni, other drummers and dancers living at a driving distance from the rehearsal location. Such groups are organized more professionally and notable examples exist in Los Angeles, Medford/Boston, Berkeley/San Francisco, and Athens, Ohio. While some critique these independent ensembles as draining the university ensemble by feeding on it, others see such a development positively, as an opportunity for serious student percussionists and dancers to further develop and learn relevant professional skills to complement what they acquire at school. Given the demand for performances by African drum and dance ensembles in some urban settings, such affiliated groups honor invitations that could have taken too much of students' time. Also, these groups honor performance needs that may arise in the summer months when most students are away and the student ensemble is in recess. Some strengthen the student African drum and dance ensemble by contributing their expertise and resources when a particular music department has major celebratory events. In other contexts, they team up with student ensembles in fundraiser concerts for worthy causes or in festivals and other celebratory performances.

Directing an ensemble such as the West African drum and dance at a university entails a substantial amount of work, the nature of which is different from the theory classes that we teach. Given that performances culminate all drumming and dance classes, and that the organization of performance is crucial to the other categories I have distinguished above, then all the efforts that an ensemble teacher invests into having a good performance characterize his/her role as a director. I now subsume the directing roles under (a) classes and rehearsals, (b) programming, (c) performance space and other arrangements, (d) sponsorship and support, (e) publicity, and (f) documenting the event.

Classes and Rehearsals
Directors of African drum ensembles are teachers of their instrumental parts, dances, and songs. Hence, like many other world music ensemble directors, their work is more than rehearsing and executing the correct interpretation of notated music. Thus they combine the duties of a violin teacher and a symphonic conductor, or of a trumpeter and a jazz band director. The preceding observation is by no means intended to demean the challenging nature of directing other groups. Rather, I am alluding to the absence of written scores from which other ensembles rehearse. After selecting the repertoire for a semester, the director depends on his mastery of the oral tradition for his instructions. He may at times choreograph new dances, and may be responsible for recruiting some percussionists and dancers. I have discussed the qualities of a good director elsewhere and the process of translating artistic goals through deployment of appropriate techniques and setting of conducive relational tones.

Programming
The director plans and programs for the year, semester, or a specific performance. He/she will teach and rehearse items for a semester or for a particular concert, and arrange the participation of other key players including guest artists or even guest groups. Long-term programming must be distinguished from short-term programming. Short-term programming may involve the building of appropriate items for a particular program, the preparation, typing, and printing the program, as well as the program notes. All these various areas of directing are inextricably linked.

Performance Space and Other Arrangements
Whether by choice or limitation, some African ensembles routinely give all their semester ending concerts in the department's auditorium. Ensembles

Figure 5.3 Front page of the Ghana50 Concert program notes. [Program by George Dor, March 2007]

of other institutions change their performance spaces as necessitated by considerations such as timely reservation and availability of desired space for a specific performance. I have shown elsewhere in the discussion how a regular concert can be turned into a historic celebration that may have symbolism for the entire university, city, and region, or marking of a milestone in the ensemble's existence. Hence the size of the target audience is a determining factor in deciding and arranging for an accommodating space. Yet concern for better interaction between performers and audiences may prompt the director to match the physical nature of performance spaces with intended levels of interaction with the audience, leading to the choice of a band hall in which the physical barrier is nonexistent. Concerns for acoustical nuances of the various spaces, lighting and recording equipment, and technical staff, whether it is a ticketed or non-ticketed event, proximity of the space from the music department, and availability of changing rooms are among the other considerations. However, whereas the music department auditorium may not charge any fees for the use of its facilities, other performance spaces run by semi-autonomous or autonomous administrations may charge fees for the space, equipment, and technical team. These charges may not apply to events deemed university-wide celebrations, and some administrators may donate the space as their co-sponsorship so long as the space is available and the event is non-ticketed. When a performance involves ticketing, the ensemble director has an added assignment of working through his/her department chair to arrange the printing of tickets and providing information on the account into which money will be sent. Since some performance spaces may not have staff who sell tickets at the door, the director would have to make that arrangement and place trusted students at all the entrances. Such students must be trustworthy and must not be those who may let in all their friends without tickets. Figure 5.1 shows the front page of the program for the Ghana50 concert we organized at Oxford. As can be seen, we turned an ordinary concert into a historic celebration, and the number of cosponsors on the program can suggest the extent to which the entire university embraced the event. While some co-sponsors gave funds toward the event, others provided performance space and technical assistance in a program involving a high degree of collaboration (although I was still the originator and coordinator of the event).

Sponsorship and Support

Some regular semester-ending concerts may not need co-sponsorship. However, if grants have not been secured and money in the account of the ensemble is not enough, while the director wants to invite a guest artist who must be flown in, housed, fed, and given some honorarium, I think chairs may need to be flexible in allowing ensemble directors to look for co-sponsors in order to carry out programs effectively. Themes of some celebratory performances may resonate with the missions and responsibilities of specific university offices and cognate disciplines, who will be willing to contribute something toward concerts as cosponsors. West African drumming and dance have relevance for multiculturalism, international studies/programs, African studies, African diaspora studies, interracial relationships, promotion of diverse performing arts, and much more. What beats my imagination is for some chairs to be very possessive of a departmental ensemble even if university money can be meaningfully redirected toward a project that may provide interdisciplinary outcomes. The alumni association of my university and Walmart in Oxford have all supported my concerts in the past. I have already provided a list of such offices under my discussion of campus culture, and will provide more insights on sponsorship in the next few paragraphs. Here, I simply want to shed light on one of the responsibilities of the director.

Publicity

At the beginning of every academic year, secretaries of music departments provide information regarding dates of all performances, which are in turn coordinated with other campuswide cultural events into a university's cultural calendars. Information on events can be accessed on university websites, from box offices, and other sources. First, directors take advantage of the music department's website for announcing their ensembles' performances. Cross-listing of events with city calendars provides further publicity. Moreover, every American university has specific offices and assigned staff responsible for providing publicity of university programs, and I have mentioned such offices elsewhere in this discussion. Preparation of flyers, writing of stories by journalists after brief interviews, and publishing such stories with catchy action photos of the ensemble's previous performances in both campus and city newspapers are all rewarding in terms of reminding audiences of coming events. If funds exist, advertising too may be used and effective. Yet, the student ensemble members are normally helpful in disseminating news about programs by word of mouth or distribution of flyers. Written invitations or cards may be sent to top university administrators, mayors, and other dignitaries and cosponsors as a sign of respect and honor. However, the cheapest form of publicity, which demands no money from the ensembles resources, is for a campuswide e-mail to be sent to thousands of students, faculty, and staff of a university just a few days before the event. Using teachers of service courses, including music appreciation and world music, to spread information regarding concerts that they may attend and review as part of coursework has been helpful.

Documenting the Event

With the availability of funds, the arrangement for professional documentation of major concerts, including video and audio recording and photos, is a duty of the director. Personnel from various university offices normally do these at times with fees. Such recordings have led to the kinds of DVDs and/or CDs I spoke about previously. However, even without funding, amateur recordings can at least be used for teaching or for capturing the moment. Certain performances tend to end up better than expected. As such, directors will never regret making plans for the documentation of performances, which may have multiple uses in the future.

As can be seen from the preceding, the director's work is very demanding, although they do it with inner satisfaction and without complaining. But when one considers the holistic nature of African drumming and dance, it is easy to see how the instructor is compelled to combine the roles of a dancer and a drummer, especially when viewed within the prism of Western culture and epistemology, which are noted for their compartmentalization. Several directors go by the correct African aesthetic dictates of not separating this composite art into components. However, the teaching of West African dance drumming comes with the demands of the two integrated arts, which takes a longer period of time to teach and learn than drumming or movement alone. It is frankly overtaxing for a professor to direct an African drum ensemble in addition to his/her official teaching load. Although student members always lend their help to their directors or instructors, full-time faculty who are teaching other courses in addition to West African drumming may need the services of student assistants. All my consultants who know the amount of work involved in being a director of a West African drum and dance ensemble strongly recommend that it must be part of the director's official workload.

Support and Funding

The instructor's salary is a major consideration in establishing a West African drum-dance or any other world music ensemble as a course offering. Universities that create permanent positions first and foremost secure funding through a process that normally involves systemic decisions from top officials. Professor Emeritus Olly Wilson vividly recalled how he had to discuss with the dean the feasibility of bringing C. K. Ladzekpo to Berkeley, to explore the availability or garnering of funds for the director salary. Even though an instructor may be academically qualified or artistically competent, factors including the number of students that may be taking the course, and number of sections or different levels of the program that the instructor may be teaching, may partly determine whether the instructor is given full-time or adjunct faculty status. But as Eric Charry has observed, when the administration recognizes the importance of the African ensemble program, in terms of student enrollment with the attendant tuition fees it draws, or the contribution of the ensemble in attracting new students to the music program, it will continue to support the ensemble even in other situations, such as the financial implications of a regular instructor taking a sabbatical leave. But to ensure continuity in a vibrant program and to enable a diligent ensemble director take a well-deserved rest, Wesleyan, for example, granted Abraham Adzinya's sabbatical leave as Samuel Nyamuame temporarily replaced him (Interview, December 2007).

Figure 5.4 Ama Oforiwaa Aduonum, founder and director, African music and dance ensemble, North Illinois State University, Normal, IL. [Photo from Ama Oforiwaa Aduonum]

Figure 5.5 Kofi Gbolonyo, director, University of Pittsburgh (2006-2009), and University of British Columbia (2009-) African music and dance ensembles. [Photo from Kofi Gbolonyo]

Funding from the state and foundations established by alumni may provide supplementary money from which an instructor in the music department receives his or her salary. For student directors of ensembles, music departments tend to use tuition fellowships in which teaching is required from the awardee; at the University of Pittsburgh, the Andrew Mellon Tuition Fellowship supports graduate student instructors of the African ensemble.

At York, a university with a dynamic West African drumming and dance program—with no fewer than four instructors, some of whom teach two sections of the same level, while others teach three levels of the course—the upsurge in student enrollment for West African drumming and dance, thinks Robert Simms, serves as a complementary source of financial support for the program. Salaries of part-time instructors, acquisition and repair of musical instruments to meet the demands of the sizable number of student participants, and acquisition of costumes are all challenging to realize. But in addition to funds allocated to the music department, the Canadian cultural policy encourages federal financial support for universities in many cities with the aim of perpetuating the multiculturalism of cities such as Toronto through cultural programs (Interview, January 2010). Responding to my question regarding funding of the ensemble, Hartenberger revealed that the

Figure 5.6 Kwasi Ampene, founding director of University of Colorado's West African Highlife Ensemble (2000–2011), leading a performance. [Photo by Casey A. Cass/University of Colorado Photography]

University of Toronto receives funds from the Canadian government toward the implementation of those cultural policies. Also, Hartenberger shared how an Academic Initiatives Fund (AIF) award for which he applied helped the University of Toronto purchase new musical instruments and to meet other obligations.

Funds for the acquisition of instruments and costumes as well as logistic support for ensembles normally come from departmental or college funds, university-wide grants, external grants, proceeds from ticketed performances, and honoraria for participation in festivals and other off-campus events. In his answer to my question on how the West African drumming and dance ensemble is funded at Wesleyan, Charry explained: "There are two kinds of budget. Each ensemble has a budget. One is annual budget, part of which is used for bringing in visiting artists, costumes, and publicity. The second is capital equipment, for instruments." Wesleyan has quite a variety of ensembles and the allocation of funds to the respective ensembles are discussed and decided in a democratic process. Equitable distribution of resources seems to be the norm, and other administrators I interviewed told me that the same process applies in their respective institutions.

At Wesleyan, says Charry, "Ghanaian drumming and dance, symphony orchestra, gamelan, steel band, South Indiana ensemble are all on the same

Figure 5.7 Gideon Alorwoyie, Kobla Ladzekpo, and George Dor at SEM 2010 in Los Angeles. Photo taken a day after they and other Africanists remembered Willie Anku during a special and symbolic session. [Photo from George Dor, November 2010]

and equal footing." But how could the symphony orchestra, Ghanaian drumming and dance, and the gamelan be on the same budgetary footing? Yes, the symphony orchestra, Charry explains, needs to repair instruments, buy reeds, strings, and scores, among other financial needs. Similarly, the gamelan needs to be tuned every five years and experts have to be brought in to do this technical work. In the same vein Ghanaian drum heads and pegs need to be replaced, especially given the number of students that use the drums. Acquisition of new sets of drums may be necessitated by the instructor's decision to teach a new dance that may require a particular set of instruments.

Other expenses with the African dance ensemble involve costuming. Costumes need to be mended and new ones acquired, to meet the demands of about thirty to fifty dancers each semester. The fact that the program has existed for more than four decades may mean that the old costumes are torn and weak from overuse; and one set of costumes may not do for another dance, even when both dances are from the same ethnic group. Charry confirms, "I know Helen Mensah [the dance instructor] every semester had tough time getting the costumes for all the dancers." But luckily, "funding comes from the dance department too, and concert proceeds partly go into costumes." Cost sharing among departments can be relieving in terms of support. However, most African dance drumming ensembles are under

Figure 5.8 Alorwoyie and Isaac Akrong (extreme right), two ensemble directors, with African musicians and scholars (l to r) Chapman Nyaho, Kofi Agawu, Bode Omojola, and Agatha Ozah at SEM 2008, Wesleyan University, Middletown, CT. [Photo taken by George Dor, October 2008]

the ambit of music departments alone. University ensembles that have risen to pseudo-professional heights charge performance fees that go into the ensembles' accounts. Separate accounts are created for the ensemble and the funds it generates are not entered under broader departmental accounts. During major events organized by the ensemble on campus, some music department chairs even allow directors to look for co-sponsorship from other departments.

Binghamton University's West African dance drumming ensemble resembles Wesleyan's in a number of ways, but they markedly differ from one another in terms of funding. Like Wesleyan, BU has multiple levels of the course and also has a huge enrollment. The courses are cross-listed for music, dance, and African studies at BU. But while one would expect that cost sharing happens between these three departments in allocating funds for the repair of old instruments, and purchase of new instruments and costumes, that is not the case. All such support comes from the dean's office. Some of the departments may not have enough money, while the music department might have already allocated its funds among the major ensembles before the introduction of the African Performance Ensemble. In the long term, I think

Figure 5.9 Damascus Kafumbe and Frank Gunderson, directors of East African music and dance ensembles, Florida State University, at SEM Southeast/Caribbean Chapter Meeting, Tallahassee, FL. [Photo from George Dor, March 2009]

it will be very encouraging to the director if some form of financial support from the three departments goes to the African Music Ensemble too in the near future. But for now, any of the three departments can show that appreciation by assisting with program flyers, printing of programs, and other pre-concert advertisements that may not be very expensive.

Indeed, it is assuring that the dean's office continues to support BU's African dance drumming ensemble, and the director can only hope that some help can be forthcoming from other sources soon. However, the BU case presents another lesson of how diversely these ensembles are administered and that differences exist between the financial capabilities and endowments of similar departments at different universities. For example, University of Florida's African Studies Center partly supports the Agbedidie African Music and Dance Ensemble of that university. Such comparisons should not serve any basis of criticism, for the African Studies Center at Florida may be better positioned financially than the African Studies Institute at Binghamton.

186 PATH-FINDING AGENCY OF ADMINISTRATORS AND ENSEMBLE DIRECTORS

Figure 5.10 Regular percussionists of OMADDE (George Dor, David Carlisle, Ricky Burkhead, Shelter Dor, and Tim Burkhead) performing on the Ole Miss Grove Stage. [Photo by University of Mississippi Communications Photography, July 2008]

In some universities the distribution of departmental resources among a substantial number of world music ensembles may at times make support barely enough for operating the ensembles. Acquisition of new drums and costumes or the repair of instruments may become very difficult within the constraints of limited resources, which can be compounded by the current economic climate. Some directors of West African drum and dance ensembles have made fundraiser concerts, normally in the fall, a regular feature of their programs. Sowah Mensah, for example, shared with me the extent to which proceeds from fall concerts help him bring other drummers and dancers to the University of Minnesota to work with students, thereby enriching their perspectives as well as the programs for spring concerts.

I have already mentioned how huge grants support world music projects at the University of Florida.[2] This is an area many directors aim to explore. Art foundations and councils are also sources of funding for performing groups like world music ensembles. Directors may write grant proposals to these state or federal agencies to get support for their ensembles' activities. Furthermore, the production of CDs and DVDs of performances of ensembles may serve a dual role, marketing the university and providing support for the ensemble. Eric Charry, Pascal Younge, Kobla Ladzekpo, and Kwasi

Figure 5.11 Bagandan (Uganda) instruments at Florida State. Also, Ewe *atsimewu* in the corner, used by previous African music and dance ensemble directors Ama Aduonum and Frank Gunderson. [Photo by George Dor, March 2009]

Ampene have all given me professionally produced DVDs and VHS recordings of their respective ensemble's performances. I have given out free DVDs of OMADDE performances, produced by the University of Mississippi's media department, during my presentations at UCLA and Colorado. In the near future, however, OMADDE may have to sell such products; as the Ewe adage implies, we have to change our dance movements to match the changing rhythms and tunes of the economic landscape, speaking metaphorically.

In the previous few pages, I presented more photos of some of the ensemble directors I have discussed or alluded to at different stages of the book. While some were taken when I interviewed them, others capture moments during different conferences at which they were fraternizing or posed as African musicians or music scholars or simply Africanists. The final photo of this chapter provides evidence of my awareness of other African dance drumming traditions in the American academy.

6

A TRANSPLANTED MUSICAL PRACTICE FLOURISHING IN THE AFRICAN DIASPORA

In chapter 1 I provided a historical overview of the fate of West African drums and drumming traditions in the African diaspora, tracing the changes that marked its diachronic trajectory, and then contrasting the period of absence to that of presence. Chapter 6 focuses on the presence. It explores what I metaphorically call the "fertility of the new cultural soil," which resonates with the Ewe conception of establishing or founding a musical ensemble. Furthermore, West African dance drumming has developed into an important campus subculture of universities where it exists, along with other world music and canonic ensembles and bands. As such, this chapter will also situate the place of the genre within its immediate academic and cultural environment and life. Additionally, I examine audiences, post-colonial imprints, African American perspectives, and influence of regional demography to shed light on the manner in which these forces nurture the genre's growth. These themes complement human agency and other topics covered previously.

THE NEW AND FERTILE CULTURAL SOIL: RESONATING THE EWE CONCEPTION OF PLANTING A GENRE, *WUDODO*

I consider *wudodo*, the Ewe conception of planting a genre, an intriguing framework that can be used in explicating the suppression and the resurrection of traditional West African drumming and dance in the United States of America. *Wudodo* consists of two Ewe words. *Wu* refers to a musical genre that combines creative activities of drumming, singing, and dancing (Fiagbedzi 1977: 51–61; Dor 2000: 79, 2004: 27; Gbolonyo 2009: 136); *dodo* means the act and art of planting (Dor 2004: 45). This conceptual metaphor implicates commonalities between initiating, nurturing, and the growth of a musical genre or ensemble, on the one hand, and planting, nurturing, and the growth of a tree, on the other. Tree planting thus becomes the source domain of the conceptual metaphor that facilitates the visualization and cognition of the process of establishing a musical genre as the target domain. Apparently, the planting of a tree is contingent upon the availability of certain favorable conditions: (a) plant, (b) planter, (c) fertile and accessible land, (d) planting implements, (e) knowledgeable caretaker, and (f) climatic considerations including water and sunshine.

In the context of this discussion, dance drumming, the genre of my focus is the metaphoric plant, while diasporic Africans serve as our imaginary planters. Evidence presented by black Caribbean islanders and South Americans reveals that drummers, singers, and dancers, who represent the planters, were among the slaves taken from West and Central Africa. And these Africans, who uprooted their cultural plants of dance drumming and stored them in their collective memories, can be said to have found fertile lands in South America and the Caribbean where they planted and nurtured drumming traditions without much disruption. That was not the case in many parts of North America, although there were drummers and possible drum carvers among the African slaves who came to North America and who lived and worked in some regions abundant with trees that could have been used in making drums. Ownership or legitimate accessibility to land, then, becomes an implied question and problem here. For, like planting of a tree, if the land is unavailable, or if the owner of the land does not permit the planting of a different kind of tree on his/her land, the uprooted tree will simply die in the planter's hands (Dor 2006: 357–361).

In previous chapters I have elucidated the transitional forces and factors that ushered in the ascendancy of world-mindedness and world-consciousness that in turn motivated "new planters" of the genre in North America. Not only have I discussed the diverse groups of people who took advantage of the new and fertile cultural soil, but I also have illuminated ways in which the fruits of the genre have affected students, the focus of chapter 4. In the following paragraphs, I provide further examples of influences on and of the musical plant. For West African drumming and dance has produced experiences for diverse people who have constructed both their individual and shared meanings in multiple ways.

A UNIVERSITY CAMPUS MUSIC SUBCULTURE

Culture has been defined as the way of life of a people. It then follows that each university campus has an idiosyncratic way of life that partly consists of routine activities and the structures that support such behaviors. Although a campus culture comprises multiple domains, I will focus on music as a subculture. Colleges, faculties, schools, and departments of music are brewing spaces of universities' music cultures. Students, faculty, community ensembles, student- or university staff–run radio and television stations, and programs responsible for disseminating campus-related music and news are ubiquitous on American university campuses. In some cases, media services or departments facilitate the mass mediation of campus music. However, much of the music performed on campus is intended for the consumption of the performers and audiences in situ. Auditoria and other performance spaces are purposely built within or near music departments, schools, colleges, or faculties to serve the needs of both the department and the larger cultural community. Within every university's structure and system are a set of offices and university standing committees accountable for supporting and promoting campus music, and depending on the nature of specific performances, cognate academic disciplines may cosponsor specific campus music programs. With specific reference to West African drum and dance ensembles, offices charged with the promotion of multiculturalism, diversity, and internationalism are a regular source of complementary support. In addition to performances by campus ensembles and bands, university committees or individual faculty members arrange and coordinate the promotion of world-renowned groups and artists to campuses to enhance university cultural and academic life.

Performance contexts on campus include regular student and faculty concerts, ranging from mundane afternoon performances to semester-ending or annual concerts given by recognized university ensembles. Seasonal programs, including Black History Month, International Night, and Christmas, and special fundraisers to support university projects and programs are great sites for experiencing music on campus. Yet, other kinds of performances are organized on campus to identify and recognize musical talents or to encourage the development of musical skills among students of a particular region. These include summer instrumental and opera workshops and camps that may conclude with performances and concerto competitions organized at undergraduate and graduate levels. Other campus performances are intended to showcase what students, faculty, or ensembles have achieved in their various areas.

During national or international music conferences such as the annual conference of the Society for Ethnomusicology, it is a common practice for the host university to arrange performances by some of their finest student ensembles to entertain the visiting conference participants as well as to showcase aspects of their music programs. Also, composers on a specific campus premiere their works in concerts that may involve visiting instrumentalists. On the other hand, a well-established composer affiliated with a campus may organize regular concerts involving only his/her compositions; El-Dabh of Kent State University is a classic example. At times accomplished composers and/or performers who are alumni of specific universities are invited with pride to give homecoming concerts at their alma mater. For example, Nancy Van De Vate, a world-renowned composer and University of Mississippi alumna, was invited from Vienna back to Oxford in October 2005 to discuss her life and work as a result of a book that Laurdella Foulkes-Levy and Burt Levy wrote on her. A concert culminated the presentations and discussions.

Another category of campus performances belongs to symposia organized around specific musical genres or themes. Great examples include the Symposium on African Pianism that Akin Euba organized in 1999 at the University of Pittsburgh; the Living Blues Symposium organized annually at the University of Mississippi (the 2004 symposium ended in a historic concert by B. B. King); Africa Meets North America—A Dialogue in Music Project, held in 2009 at UCLA; and the Fourth Symposium on the Music of Africa, held in 2012 at Princeton and organized by Kofi Agawu. The programs of the preceding events partly comprised series of concerts in addition to scholarly paper presentations and workshops.

On a grander scale, the commissioning and celebration of a completed major performance space like the Gertrude Ford Center for the Performing Arts at the University of Mississippi campus is often heralded by historic performances that showcase some of the classiest groups on campus and alumni musicians who are national celebrities in a gala concert. On game days when members of the larger university community come to support their teams, marching bands become the most contextually important ensembles to spur on the athletes and then activate the patriotism of thousands of fans by playing specific college identity-related tunes and moving national songs, since campuses are sites for expressing and promoting national sensibilities and sentiments.

Music is always an integral part of other quintessential university events and ceremonies. During the rituals of universities' annual convocation and commencement, ceremonies may be deemed incomplete without the singing of the national and university anthems by the gathering, or the playing of marches or voluntaries, commonly Edward Elgar or from the Baroque period. A few universities have used their African drum and dance ensembles in graduation ceremonies to engage the attention of the arriving commencement audiences. Yet, a special occasion like the commissioning of a new chancellor or president attracts a high magnitude of celebratory splendor and sublime academic order. A university choir may be called upon to sing the national and college anthems as this pseudo-sacred ritual is performed with a strong sense of symbolism in which delegations from many universities as well as national and state politicians participate. A great example was the induction ceremony of Dr. Daniel Jones, the current chancellor of the University of Mississippi, which took place on April 9, 2010. Many North American universities have huge auditoria where these events may be held. However, universities' natural and beautiful groves allow for greater mass participation in events, some which may have a national magnitude. The performances on the Ole Miss Grove Stage by groups—student, regional and national professional groups—during the 2008 United States presidential debate represents another rare dimension of campus cultural life.

Returning to regular campus music subculture, one must mention performances by groups not formed under the umbrella of the music department. While some students form their own bands, campus associations including black student unions or sorority associations often form Greek and gospel groups, since only a few music departments house gospel choirs as one of their recognized ensembles. Generally, world music ensembles have become integral to many university campus subcultures, and the unique timbres of gamelan, steel band, taiko, and West African drum and dance ensembles add to the soundscapes of academic institutions that own these and other similar ensembles. But what differentiates one institution from the other are the number, type, and vibrancy of world music ensemble(s). While a visit to UCLA's Gamelan Room—named after Mantle Hood's first world music ensemble—provides empirical evidence of instruments for more than twelve music traditions from all over the globe, my visits to Wesleyan University at Middletown, York University in Toronto, and University of West Virginia in Morgantown provided evidence that each of these universities owns about ten world music ensembles. Although five is an average number of world music ensembles in most universities with great ethnomusicology programs, other institutions are very excited about the presence of a few or a lone world music ensemble, especially when their dynamism is far-reaching on campus-wide life. If I may not be viewed as an ethnomusicologist who is sacrificing his reflexivity, then I can observe that universities that do not have at least one world music ensemble may be missing something very special in this era of globalization. And this is by no means an act of romanticizing; to validate the preceding claim, and after recalling this broad landscape of partial musical activities on university campuses, I now redirect focus to the role of West African drumming and dance within this subculture.

It may not be an exaggeration to say that universities that do not yet have an African drum and dance ensemble may not understand the presence of this genre on campuses. Admittedly, audio-visual materials on these student ensembles can be accessed on television or as classroom teaching resources, and people who do not participate in these ensembles' activities could visualize the effect when West African drum and dance ensembles visit their campuses and give life-changing performances. Yet, the experience is never the same as the impacts discussed in chapter 4 and this chapter. I cannot imagine how different cultural life will be on some university campuses without the crowd-pulling and engaging West African drumming and dance ensemble performances that have become cultural emblems and norms.

In universities that offer West African drumming and dance as credit-earning courses, students are required to perform at the end of each semester as a partial fulfillment of their grades. Thus, fall and spring concerts are the most regular occasions for the performance of this genre. Furthermore, West African drum and dance ensembles actively perform as part of many university events, including Black History Month and African or International Night programs. To attract a more direct communal participation from the non-members of the ensemble but equally important campus audiences, Robert Simms and David Locke have discussed with me the deliberate strategy of ensemble directors who give some of their performances at open and natural spaces rather than in large auditoria. Ensemble members invite members of the audience to dance, and such participation captures the African village essence and spirit especially characteristic of the more inclusive social dances. Other regularly organized events where campus African drum and dance ensembles perform include festivals to encourage internationalism or multiculturalism; World Fest at Ole Miss and the African Festival at York University are classic examples. I still carry lingering memories of the performances of Pascal Younge's University of West Virginia's African Drumming and Dance Ensemble, especially during Black History Month in the late 1990s when I was a graduate student at the University of Pittsburgh.[1] Such enduring impressions informed my decision to garner support from the University of Mississippi, and we were able to bring the same ensemble to Ole Miss in November 2003 and they gave a compelling concert at the Ford

Center. Also, David Locke disclosed to me his initiatives regarding the intercollegiate festival of West African drumming and dance he organized a couple of times. He invited James Burns's Binghamton University African Music and Dance Ensemble, and Patricia Tang's MIT *Sabar* (Senegalese dance) group to join the African ensemble of Tufts in performances and workshops on West African dances.

Special events in which African drumming and dance feature prominently include marking of specific milestones in the lives of a department, ensemble director, or the ensemble itself. For example, while DjeDje recounts the celebration of the Year of African Music at UCLA in 1999–2000, students of Abraham Adzinya at Wesleyan organized a tribute concert in order to celebrate the dedicated work and service of their teacher at the same institution for more than forty years. Similarly, Kobla Ladzekpo's students at California School of Performing Arts organized a moving concert for him on his retirement in 2007, after teaching and performing at this institution as the director of the African ensemble for four decades. Similarly, Alfred Ladzekpo's students, friends, and aficionados celebrated him in a May 2011 concert for his dedicated service at the same institution for more that four decades. In April 2010 Kwasi Ampene and his West African Highlife Ensemble at the University of Colorado at Boulder celebrated their tenth anniversary of existence and powerful campus presence.

All these concerts brought accomplished guest artists to the various campuses to heighten the celebratory performances. Modesto Amegago recalls a vivid memory of his West African dance ensemble giving an outstanding performance during the commissioning of York University's Performing Arts Building. Currently, UCLA has organized a series of concerts aimed at raising funds to sponsor their ethnomusicology students to study abroad programs to empower them to participate in and experience world music cultures in their original contexts. Also, these concerts partly mark five decades of the ethnomusicology program at UCLA. The DVDs produced of these historic landmark performances provide the highest form of empirical evidence of the magnitude of the achievements of both the concerned directors and the programs of their respective institutions.

Later in this chapter I will discuss people's concerns about the predominance of Ghanaian dances in the North American academy. But for now, I share two situations in which knowledge of Ghanaian dances was put to extraordinary use to mark symbolic events. In 1999 Ghana's president, Jerry John Rawlings, visited the United States. After then President of the United States Bill Clinton honored him at the White House, President Rawlings visited Pittsburgh, where the Ghanaian community welcomed him prior to his other official business. Joseph Adjaye, a Ghanaian professor of history at the University of Pittsburgh, invited and arranged for the University of West Virginia's African Drumming and Dance Ensemble to perform music suitable for welcoming a Ghanaian head of state. Pascal Younge's ensemble lived up to everybody's expectations: they played courtly dances including *Fontomfrom* music, and Akan regal dance, often used in Ghana for kings and paramount chiefs as well as rulers of the modern nation-state. President Rawlings was stunned by the competence of this student ensemble, and he remarked that he felt as if he was at a state function in Ghana. Furthermore, I have already narrated how the Ole Miss African Drum and Dance Ensemble organized a commemorative concert to mark the fiftieth anniversary of Ghana's independence. The extent to which the university community joined the Africans in this celebration portrays how internationals are embraced and located in the campus culture.

AUDIENCES

Audiences are partly responsible for the growth in popularity of West African drumming and dance in the American academy. The aficionados of most student ensembles consist of students, family and friends of student performers, faculty and staff, alumni, and members of the immediate cultural community including a university town, or the county or sub-region where the university is located. Sampled diverse viewpoints from audience members as to why they frequently attend West African drumming and dance concerts can be subsumed under the following two major rubrics: 1) those who seek ephemeral pleasure, and 2) those expecting to understand cultural indexes or identity-based texts in this genre.

As the Ewe adage goes, *Detsivivi ye hea zikpui*—"It is the sumptuous soup that draws the stool." The Ewe believe the first taste of a delicious soup naturally compels the one eating the food to draw his or her stool closer to the table where the food has been laid. By implication, the effect of West African drumming and dance on audiences is metaphorically parallel to the taste of exquisite soup. Accordingly, I argue that it is the sweetness or pleasurable and consumable nature of West African drumming and dance that wins the affect of audiences. Pleasure is derived from all aspects of a performance, including the vibrancy and tightness of drumming, the virtuosic competence of the mother/master or lead drummer, the gratification that people who have "the love for gazing" or "scopophilia," in Laura Mulvey's terms (1975), from the beauty of the costumes, the beautified performers' bodies, catchy dance movements, and uniformity in the execution of the choreography while at the same time enabling the individuality of the dancers to show.

More telling is the pleasure the audience members experience when drawn into the performance as active participants. Although my world music students' reviews of West African drumming and dance reveal their initial reluctance to attend such concerts as course requirements, they often end up expressing their gratitude for being asked to attend, and they later become those who encourage their friends to attend concerts. Contrarily, some are enthusiastically driven by the zeal and desire to learn something about another culture as part of international or multicultural education. Writing on "Consumption, Duration, and History," Arjun Appadurai describes this new aesthetic regime as "ephemerality," a short-lived pleasure that satisfies the nostalgia of most trans-cultural communities (1996: 82–84). While Africans may attend such concerts as a way of quenching their nostalgic thirst for music from their continent, parents and friends of ensembles members participate to support their respective dependents or colleagues for their creative abilities at a foreign musical genre, often perceived as a novelty.

Ensemble directors' awareness of and sensitivity to what their performances can offer their various audiences facilitate the selection and deployment of appropriate aesthetic tones for their concerts and other contexts that may be aimed at deliberate goals and meanings. Like the function of the mass media, West African drumming and dance performances entertain, educate, and inform. Additionally however, performances are supposed to be inspirational, therapeutic, and motivational for individuals or a larger cultural community that may be undergoing some hardships in life. Hence, directors' knowledge about the general social landscape of a particular audience may be helpful in determining how he or she navigates the performance space with an informed, responsive, and ingenious stage behavior.

However, one important consideration regarding the choice of aesthetics for a West African drumming and dance performance in the American academy is whether an ensemble prefers African- and African American–oriented aesthetics over more Western-oriented norms. A director may contemplate whether to model his concerts along the lines of idiosyncratic symphonic, jazz, or popular music performer-audience behavioral codes. It may sound obvious that an African genre should first and foremost employ African modes of performance practices. Nevertheless, such concerts are often situated within acceptable behavioral codes often associated with other music department ensembles that tend to uphold strict formality and protocol. On the other hand, African and African American aesthetics favor showmanship, individuality of performers, interactive engagement during performance—first among the dancers, drummers, and singers and then between performers and audiences. Scenes from popular music concerts with huge crowds seem to corroborate this highly interactive nature of performance in which pop stars engage their audiences in a manner that is markedly different from established Western classical concert behavioral norms.

Nketia noted "musical performance as play" as another underlying aesthetic practice and concept pertaining to African musical practices (Nketia 1991). Both the Akan and Ewe of Ghana provide aesthetic appraisal of specific performances through sayings including "Agro ye de" (Akan) or "Fefea vivi" (Ewe), literally meaning "the play was sweet," thus conceiving inclusive musical performances as play. This play mentality pervades a typical recreational musical performance in which young and old, rich and poor, can all come together to express their communal ethos and indeed experience their shared cultural life. However, serious dances (Agawu 1995: 92–99) including war and religious dances are not performed with the same "play" mentality, because they serve other purposes than entertainment. The preceding aesthetic considerations and choices inform the decisions of ensemble directors when setting the aesthetic tones for their performances.

Peculiarities of the demographics of regions or cities where these ensembles are located also inform the aesthetics and expectations that audiences bring to a particular performance space. While a majority of the audience for a specific performance may be returning fans who were impressed and encouraged by previous performances, a substantial composition of the audience may be first-timers. As such, they come to a West African drum and dance concert with mixed expectations, not knowing exactly how to behave aesthetically. This is a common feeling that my world music students express in their written reviews on my ensemble's concerts. It is for such a partial reason that an ensemble director's setting of the aesthetic tone of every performance is crucial.

Greetings or opening remarks for a performance can help the audience have a fair idea of what to expect artistically, a sense of what they will be learning, how their presence is appreciated and important, and how their attendance will not be a waste of time but rather a meaningful experience. Introductory remarks can be done in a variety of ways, depending on the nature of the performance in question. It could be at a regular annual concert or a commemorative concert like Black History Month, a showcasing of newly acquired musical instruments or costumes, a celebratory performance marking a milestone in the life of the ensemble, music department, or school, or freedom-related historic anniversaries of nations to which any aspect of the ensemble may be linked. On special events that broadly implicate the music department or the entire university, I have asked chairs to do the greetings. For example, Professor Steve Brown, a previous Ole Miss music department chair, greeted the audience when we "outdoored" our first set of costumes in 2005 at the Meek Hall before an enthusiastic audience who were receptive and happy about the cultural innovations the ensemble's presence had signaled at the University of Mississippi. Similarly, Professor Charles Gates, the chair of the music department (2005–06 and 2012–13), welcomed the audience to the Ghana50 commemorative concert at the Ford Center on March 6, 2007. Such introductory comments from relevant administrators suggest to the audiences the extent to which the African drum and dance performances fall within the broader values of music education and university objectives regarding diversity, multiculturalism, globalization, and internationalization. For, although the perpetuation of genres indigenous to universities' situated regions will always remain a priority, most people are excited whenever sharing rich and cultural experiences of humankind. Likewise, Professor Jacqueline DjeDje, the chair of the department of ethnomusicology, introduced the 2010 spring concert of UCLA's African music ensemble, since it partly marked the fiftieth anniversary of ethnomusicology at UCLA. Kobla Ladzekpo, the director of the ensemble, sent me a DVD of the performance.

My recollections from several West African drumming and dance concerts I attended in North America reveal that ensemble directors often use the services of narrators so they can concentrate on their artistic roles offstage as they prepare for smooth progression from one item to the other. In such a context, detailed program notes are written out by the ensemble director to be read aloud by the narrator. Prior to performance, the narrator has to spend some time with the director to work on the appropriate pronunciation of foreign terms relating to concert repertoire, instruments, genres, and other words. This option has advantages as well as disadvantages. While the ensemble director under such an arrangement will have more time to focus on the performance of the pieces, it constrains the opportunity of interaction he/she could have with the audience who often look toward the director as the most informed person regarding the details of performances. I now discuss the dialogue that the director can engender in the absence of a narrator, specifically drawing on cases from my own ensemble's performances.

Figure 6.1 Explaining aspects of the construction of Ewe drums. I lifted the Anlo *kidi* to show how its bottom is sealed with wood that affects its sonority. [Photo from George Dor, 2007]

I have never ritualized the way in which I greet my audiences for our performances. But I always welcome them in the name of the music department, co-sponsors of a particular concert, and the ensemble itself. I will think of something to say to make audiences know their participation is appreciated, at times using typical Ghanaian or American phrases or catchwords. For example, rather than say, "Hey, how is everybody doing?" or "Ladies and gentlemen, lend me your ears," or "May I have your attention," I sometimes use "Agoo" as a call-phrase, and teach the audience to respond with "Amee," or a variant phrase, "agoo ee" with "amee ye" as the corresponding phrase. I will normally do this call-and-response phrase, which is a typical Ghanaian way of inviting and engaging the attention of an audience prior to addressing it, at least three times, requesting the audience to emulate the intensity at which I say the "agoo." As simple as this interaction may seem, it has proved very effective. First, the audience learns something new about another culture; second, the director initiates a dialogue between him and his audience; third, the repeated phase done in an increased intensity synergizes the audience as well as promising an expected positive interactive participation during the performance.

Before formally welcoming the audience, I normally step forward on the stage, gazing with a smiling face or nodding my head as I stare without verbal utterances at the entire audience. These nonverbal gestures suggest my satisfaction with something and prepare the expectations of audience members in

Figure 6.2 In contrast to the *kidi*, I once again lifted the Ewedome *wuga*, the second master drum in *Borborbor*, to show the hollowed trunk is left open while the playing end has a membrane. [Photo from George Dor, 2007]

anticipation of good things. The moment I make statements including "Look at these wonderful people," "What a great gathering," "Special people," or "All I can see are kings and queens," I normally see many contemplative faces change into smiling and joyous ones. On a number of occasions I have told audiences I imagine them representing the chiefs, queens, and other elders in attendance at a typical indigenous African performance setting. Communicating respect for the audience is an important way of acknowledging the presence of professors, deans, top university administrators, and other staff. Yet, students and other audience members from the city or county also need to hear something positive. To some, such opening comments may promise them an inspirational encounter, a partial reason why they may be attending.

To throw more light on praising the audience as kings and queens, I now provide four different contexts. In April 2008 I was invited by second grade teachers of Lafayette Lower Elementary School, Oxford, Mississippi, to bring my African drums and talk about them as a way of introducing the students to Africa. Coincidentally, Yawa, my daughter who dances in my African ensemble, was one of the students. In my introductory remarks I addressed these young girls and boys as kings and queens, and immediately I saw glimmering faces of elated students. I had a wonderful time interacting with them, each having his or her turn on a drum and some tried some simple but beautiful creative dance movements. It was not until these second graders wrote their individual thank you letters to me when I realized the impact of my interaction with them, especially regarding my calling them kings and queens. One of them wrote, "Thank you for calling me a king, my parents never called me a king."

Teachers, motivational speakers, preachers, politicians, and other public communicators all understand the importance of conditioning the minds of addressees, creating the right atmosphere, and stimulating the interest of a target audience before introducing the main message. Most directors of African dance drumming are not excluded from this preparatory exercise, which has psychological effects on the audience. Another context where I used the "queen and kings" reference for my target audience was the workshop OMADDE gave on the Grove Stage at the University of Mississippi in July 2008, and which I discussed in chapter 4. To encourage students of around ages eight to twelve, who were visiting from summer camps in Oxford for the Yocona Children's Festival, I translated their curiosity and interests into a celebratory and participatory mood after I welcomed them with a high level of energy in which I designated them not only as "kings and queens," but also as "great future American leaders." As can be seen from figure 2.29, one can imagine the enthusiasm and joy with which these students actively engaged in learning to perform basic movements from two of our dances we taught them during the workshop.

The two other contexts in which I invoked the "king and queen" reference involved African Americans. One was at Clarksdale during the workshop OMADDE organized for high school students who were predominantly black. Capitalizing on my knowledge of the demography of Clarksdale as a great home of the blues, but economically underdeveloped by American standards, I decided to use the workshop to challenge and advise these black students to study harder. After introducing them to a brief cultural background of Ghana, which included my discussion of the symbolism of the *kente* cloth as bodywear of kings, chiefs, and queens in Ghana, I placed a female kente cloth (which belongs to my wife) on a few of the female students as I reiterated the "You are queens" assertion. It proved very effective as a way of winning the attention of these students prior to my discussion of what it takes to become a chief or queen in a contemporary Ghanaian city or village. Of course, to become a ruler or leader in any part of the world, one needs to be educated, have great morals, and develop exemplary leadership skills. I challenged the students to aspire to these virtues and to believe that they could become outstanding personalities through diligent perseverance. We followed this introductory talk with two dances by OMADDE, after which I invited the students to join in the drumming of the Kpatsa dance.

Figure 6.3 The workshop audience, mainly students with a few teachers and staff. [Photo from George Dor, July 2008]

During Black History Month concerts at the University of Mississippi, I do not limit the recognition of African Americans to key players in the performing arts domain. Rather, I choose to celebrate all African Americans because I believe in the power of communities as well as the agency of unsung heroes who must be equally valorized. Hence, by greeting everybody as queens and kings, I am invoking that communality before the performance. Also, it is important for me as an African director to show how I love and respect everybody, and those familiar with the history of African Americans can imagine that some of their ancestors were from royal families in Africa. And I think using any activity to aggrandize the image of people who have been marginalized in the New World is consistent with the rationale behind the celebrations during Black History Month. In any case, I am careful not to make statements that allude only to African Americans. The same assertion designating audiences as being important personalities can receive other multiple constructed meanings. While anybody will be happy for being called a king or queen, the same designation of informed African Americans engenders symbolic significations that seek to redeem their distant past in present and renewed consciousness. By extension, a concert audience may include people from lower classes or internationals from so-called underdeveloped countries. As such, these categories of people will not be constructing their meanings along ethnic lines.

A higher level of interaction with the audience involves inviting them to the stage to participate in a dance. The Gahu dance seems to be a favorite for mass participation. At Ole Miss, I invite volunteers to do the dance, which I lead as the ensemble members are changing their costumes for the next item on the program. However, I have observed the same dance used at Wesleyan and during Alfred Ladzekpo's farewell concert as the final dance of the concert that draws massive participation from previous students and even first-timers.

Further, inviting the audience to sing catchy, brief, and repetitive call-and-response phrases as part of a song during performance, or inducing the audience to clap simple recurring rhythms as the ensemble is playing, invigorates the performance. A couple of such moments remain indelible on my mind. Once when my ensemble was performing the Kpanlogo dance at the Ford Center, I invited the audience to join us by clapping the fourth and first of every four regular quarter notes and to rest on the second and third beats. Thus on beats 1-2-3-4-|1-2-3-4-|, they must clap-rest-rest-clap-|clap-rest-rest-clap-|. Those familiar with the Kpanlogo rhythm will know that the clappers have to throw their left and right hands sideways with palms open and alternately on the resting beats—clap-throw-throw-clap-|clap-throw-throw-clap|. To my pleasant surprise, this special audience clapped throughout the entire piece, almost ten minutes. This activity added another dynamic to the communal involvement of the audience, invoking a typical African aesthetics that there was no psychological barrier between the performers and the audience.

At other times, ensemble directors may have to delegate the act of inviting the audience to participate in an activity to a dancer or dancers because the director is busy drumming or the dancers are doing solo dancing. A classic example was during our 2009 annual concert at the Nutt Auditorium. Samuel Nyamuame, our guest artist, taught the group to perform the *Bambaya* dance of the Dagbamba of northern Ghana. During the performance, group dancing gave way to three intermittent solo dances. But to invigorate dancing and to take the performance to a level of heightened groove, each dancer invited the audience to clap a simple repetitive rhythmic motive. Interestingly, each dancer displayed their individuality and never repeated the other in the rhythmic motives they introduced and requested the audience to clap. While dancer 1 preferred claps on off beat quarter notes with intervening quarter-note rests [rest-clap-rest-clap-], dancer 2 changed the motive to rests on the first two quarter-notes followed by claps on two eighth notes [third beat] and the fourth quarter note. So, 1-2-3-and-4-| was played as:

rest-rest-clap-clap-clap-|. Finally, dancer 3 changed the clapping to the easiest motive, which is, all the four quarter notes, adding a driving momentum to the rhythm for dancing. The three solo dancers, I-nassah Crokett, Emanuel Johnson, and Elikem Nyamuame, were motivated by the participatory atmosphere we created during the earlier stages of the concert to intensify even more this important spirit of communal creativity.

During other performances, the audiences will voluntarily explode with their own initiated clapping of the steady beat in sync with the drum music if they feel the groove of the performance emotionally. The performance of OMADDE at the commissioning of the Powerhouse, a performance space at Oxford, climaxed in clapping from the audience amidst vibrant drumming from the men and eye-catching dancing from the female dancers of the Kpatsa dance. Thus audiences use such opportunities to register their satisfaction with the performance even before the final long applause or standing ovation.

POST-COLONIAL IMPRINTS

The progressives who often advocate revolutionary breakaways from rigid colonial hegemonic legacies and their imprints will be the first to acknowledge the extent to which West African drumming and dance and other world music ensembles fulfills such ambitions for change in the academy. Given that the music curricula of North American (like African) universities were for several centuries purely Western (Campbell 2006: 228) before the advent of ethnomusicology and world music, the presence of West African drumming and dance in American universities brings and intensifies diversity and multiculturalism in academic programs. I have earlier in this book pointed out how Wilson, DjeDje, Hartenberger, Locke, Simms, Charry, and other American musicians and scholars decided to study African music and apparently go to Africa because of the feeling of insufficiency of the solely Western-oriented education they received. In this respect, it is fulfilling to see the spread of West African drumming and dance in many North American universities in which the foundations for further artistic and professional pursuits are laid, even though a good number of universities are yet to embrace or promote this direction.

Indeed, Robert Simms considers the presence of West African drumming and dance as a powerful statement on North American universities' initial efforts at affirming and embracing other forms of the world's rich knowledge the academy is willing to explore. Resonating with perspectives from Solis (2004), Simms draws on his own experiences and conviction as he asserts:

> A fundamental thing in North America is the need to decolonize education for all public schools and at different levels. I think there is a revolution going on, but we still have a long way to go. We need to have the same kind of respect, same kind of resources toward non-Western music. We are still suffering from tokenism, mentality of exoticism, still a colonial mentality that hinders us from reaping the full benefits of richness of other knowledge systems. (Interview, January 2010)

He further observes that the imprints of colonialism still exist in subtle ways in independent North American universities, and he is hopeful that a day will soon come when all youth will be given the kind of education that helps them open their eyes and minds to different ways of thinking and respect for other cultures. He is specifically excited about the West African drumming program at York as it serves as a site for "cultivating a positive energy for people to interact in." Simms is not surprised that Toronto is playing a leading role in this regard given its makeup as a "highly multicultural city" and reiterates that "Toronto is United Nations," a rhetoric I have heard from other informants when alluding to this city's diversity.

Responding to my question of what he would like me to emphasize in this book, which I asked all major consultants of this project, Simms thinks readers may be interested in my political analysis of the post-colonial legacy as it pertains to music education and affects West African drumming and dance in the academy. Wilson, Hartenberger, Locke, DjeDje, Charry, and Charles Gates, my department chair, all anxiously anticipate reading how my Ghanaian cultural background informs this book project. In the same vein several Ghanaian ensemble directors and ethnomusicologists expect me to provide a fair Ghanaian perspective, but also as an ethnomusicologist who is required to engage in balanced reflexivity. Specifically on the theme of post-colonialism, Simms points out what my Ghanaian perspective can bring to the debate.

As a Ghanaian, I am well informed about the advocacy of decolonizing African cultures and its germane thought processes, and it is interesting to know that Americans are equally concerned with the effects of such mental enslavement, though from a different trajectory. At times, it is simply a problem with the manner in which people rigidly adhere to predominant hegemonic traditions and their slowness to embrace change. I am impressed when non-African ethnomusicologists, like Simms, out of honesty say things one would more likely hear from indigenous African (Akin Euba, Meki Nzewi, and Kofi Agawu) and African American (Olly Wilson and Jacqueline DjeDje] scholars. But one of the colonial canons in the North American academy and elsewhere that Simms mentions is the seemingly strong preference of academic qualifications over artistic expertise when hiring directors of West African drumming and dance.

Not all types of cultural capital are recognized through certificates. Unfortunately, this colonial dogmatism in the academy affects even ways in which administrators have to grapple with the initial ranks, salaries, processes of promotion, and recognition of competent indigenous African musicians hired as ensemble directors. Admittedly, equating two different systems can always be challenging, if not also problematic. However, since I have already discussed this issue earlier in chapter 3, I now focus on another side of the post-colonial vestiges that have transcontinental implications within the framework of West African drumming in the academy.

A close reading of the dances predominantly taught in the North American academy will reveal an importation of the colonial legacy from Africa into the North American academy. Moreover, the fact that West African colonial territories (and later the independent modern nation-states) can be classified as Francophone and Anglophone is both an advantage and disadvantage. For, the introduction of the English language as the official language in Ghana, Nigeria, and Gambia by the British, and the American presence in Liberia and Sierra Leone in the nineteenth and twentieth centuries have given some native West African teachers of drumming and dance as well as some native African music scholars a common language with which they can communicate with the Canadian[2] and U.S. academic community. Here, the same colonial legacy of the English language makes it possible for North American music scholars and musicians to go to any of these Anglophone West African countries to conduct field research, perform, or simply visit, if permitted by other factors to do so. Not only have I been compelled by language constraints to leave out Mexico, which is part of the regional scope promised in my title, but language has also constrained the teaching by Anglophone African drumming and dance instructors in a Spanish-speaking country.

Dances and teachers from the Francophone countries of Africa are not well represented in the North American academy. I have already discussed Anna Melnikoff of York, and would like to add MIT, where Patricia Tang directs a *Sabar* dance ensemble originally from Senegal. Also, the University of Florida performs dances from Mali taught by Mohammed DaCosta, although Samuel Nyamuame has resurrected the Ewe dances the late Godwin Agbeli, the founding director, used to teach. Eric Charry informed me of a strong dance program at Brown University in which Mande dances are offered in classes without drumming. The drummers come from the cities when invited to accompany the dancers.

Dances and performers from Francophone Africa abound within communities of sizable population of immigrants from Senegal, Mali, Guinea, Cote d'Ivoire, and Togo living in major North American cities. Further, Melnikoff hints that France and other European countries are home to many outstanding drummers and dancers from Francophone Africa. Obviously, the enabling power of language as a necessary tool for instruction is again evident here. I will later under "Models from Africa" discuss the role of African national dance ensembles. But suffice it for now to mention that although great drummers and dancers could have emerged from the Guinea Ballet Nationale as teachers in the American academy, the language constraint made it impossible. In comparison, I will soon discuss the impact of the Ghana National Dance Ensemble on the American academy in terms of directors and other considerations.

Given the preceding discussion, then, it may look as though I was homogenizing the dance drumming cultures of West Africa in my title. However, that is not the case. I have included insights from Mande and Wolof drumming, and further will discuss at length the reasons for the predominance of Ghanaian dances, offering suggestions of what to do and hope for the future with the belief that the situation will change one day. Here are a few descriptive labels for some of the ensembles I have discussed or mentioned previously. I also provide my thoughts about each name.

African Music Ensemble

Those familiar with the challenge of designing a new course will agree that it is a stringent process, receiving the scrutiny of the departmental curriculum committee and later that of the faculty before it is subjected to the rigors of the college and undergraduate committees. This process safeguards the course's alignment with broader departmental and college learning objectives, and ensures its reinforcement of other courses within a program and avoiding recycling or duplication. Awareness of this somewhat cumbersome nature of designing a new course has led some directors to settle for the broader designation of "African," leaving it open to the director to decide what to teach. This label gives room for the inclusion of chordophones like the *kora*, tuned idiophones including the *mbira*, *balo*, *gyile*, or *akadinda*, beyond drumming. Admittedly, the expression suggests an overgeneralization on what Agawu (2003: 60–61) calls the "unanimist" approach to African music. However, it accommodates the need of who is around as the director. Classic examples from the histories of ensembles at Pittsburgh, Florida, and Florida State prove how helpful this general term has been. Among the teaching fellows who have directed the African ensemble at the University of Pittsburgh, Anku founded the ensemble by teaching Ghanaian dances, Mundundu went Congolese, Nannyonga-Tamusuza made it Ugandan, and Kofi Gbolonyo reverted it to Ghanaian dances. At Florida, Godwin Agbeli founded the Agbedidi ensemble with Ghanaian dances, and after his death Mohammed DaCosta introduced dances from Mali and Guinea, and currently Samuel Nyamuame has resurrected the Ghanaian dances as he co-directs the African music ensemble with Mohammed, thus enlarging the repertoire. Florida State has moved from Ethiopian, to Ghanaian, and then later from Tanzanian to Ugandan dances as the directorship changed hands from A. Kebede (Ethiopian) to Ama Oforiwaa Aduonum (Ghanaian/American), Frank Gunderson (who studied the music of Tanzania), and Damascus Kafumbe (Ugandan). Traditionally, all directors from eastern and southern African countries introduce chordophones and tuned idiophones into their ensembles, thus justifying the advantage of leaving the broader label for flexibility and more possibilities.

African Drum and Dance Ensemble

This label is slightly specific in terms of the kind of ensemble, that is, dance drumming. However, it promises to be overly ambitious, given the enormous spectrum of African dance drumming traditions. This name also allows some room for future changes of focus in case of a substitute director. I use this designation for my university ensemble, hoping that I could teach a few dances or a visiting artist could be invited to teach a dance from a different region of the continent besides West Africa.

African Drumming and Dance Ensemble

This designation is pretty similar to the previous, except that the act and art of drumming is emphasized rather than the instruments of the ensemble. Here the technique of different types of drumming are ostensibly distinguished—African drumming from Indian tabla or Japanese Taiko. Yet there are different drumming techniques used by various African ethnic groups and even for different dances, notwithstanding the overarching structural organizational similarities of sub-Saharan dances.

The Music and Dance of West Africa

University of California at Los Angeles has the most specific name in terms of the origins of the dances that Kobla Ladzekpo teaches as well as the equal importance he places on dance (movement), drumming, and singing. As I have noted under my discussion of pedagogical approaches, Kobla Ladzekpo strictly adheres to this symbiotic nature of music and dance to reflect traditional African aesthetics and practice. Seasoned Anlo Ewe master drummers who are directors tend to teach some of the older Ewe dances that belong to the coastal Ewe of the sub-region that inhabit Anglophone Ghana, but also Francophone Togo and Benin.

AFRICAN AMERICAN PERSPECTIVES

I explored the suppressed state of African drumming during the period of slavery in chapter 1, and in subsequent chapters illuminated how the presence of West African drumming in the American academy is a resurrection and a novelty for many aficionados of this genre. African Americans who treasure their ancestral African heritage often express their shared identity through participation, passion, support, and acknowledgment. At the end of a presentation I gave on this research project at the University of Colorado's college of music in November 2009, I decided to play an excerpt from "Sounds of Blackness," drawing on the sentence, "We are the drums, Africa to America, We are the drums," to prove a point that even today, the nostalgia about African drums and drumming in the consciousness of some informed African Americans is real. Accordingly, some see the performance of African drums in the United States within any context as a demystification of a suppression that lingered in their collective memory for centuries and generations. Though wishful thinking, some would have expected that African Americans resurrected West African drumming after slavery as a reinvented tradition with ancestral connection. That could not happen, for they have given the world other rich music traditions that they continue to perpetuate. Rather, they have found alternative outlets for their rhythmic sensibilities including step dancing and African influenced modes of playing Euro-American drums, a preoccupation that seems to affect the level of interest and participation of African American male students in West African drumming at the university (Dor 2006: 356–366). While I plan to return to this claim later, I now share a number of experiences that affirm African Americans' love and respect for West African drums, drumming, and dance, even when they express this in subtle ways.

I had an African American friend named Major Albert Mason when I was in Pittsburgh from 1996 to 2001. In 2000, he visited Ghana and brought back some drums and other souvenirs from his ancestral homeland. Although to a Ghanaian these drums may be regarded as not one of the consecrated serious drums associated with royal courts, religious and warrior groups, Major constructed an elevated meaning of these drums, raising their symbolism to him to near sacred. Here, my friend Major has allowed his historical consciousness as an African American to inform his admiration for these drums, celebrating his acquisition of drums that could have been confiscated during the time of slavery. He invited me to his home to see the well-crafted carved drums and I played a few rhythmic motives on one of them after fine-tuning it. Major, who had a profound passion for African Americans, organized events in which he ensured West African drumming featured prominently. He never finished sharing his positive impressions about African culture with me before I left Pittsburgh for Oxford.

Writing under the Ole Miss Africa Drum and Dance Ensemble (OMADDE) in chapter 2, I mentioned our percussionists' August 20, 2005, participation in a tent meeting involving two thousand Episcopalians led by Bishop Gray at the Gray Center, near Jackson. What I now want to add is Rev. Ollie Rencher's role and what led to our ensemble's invitation. Rev. Rencher, an African American, had attended performances of my African drum and dance ensemble prior to his ordination. For his ordination, he requested the percussionists (without dancers) come to grace the solemn occasion by drumming as guests were arriving for the ordination service. According to him, he heard such drumming when he visited Kenya and intended to re-create it during his ordination. But most importantly, he wanted something symbolic from his ancestral home during this milestone and consecratory event. It was this performance that impressed Bishop Gray, who officiated the ordination, so much such that he asked Rev. Rencher to arrange our participation during the August camp meeting. Yet, I have other stories to share in order to validate my claim that many African Americans honor the symbolism of African drums and drumming.

Some audience members view identity as the quintessential consideration that draws them to West African drumming and dance performances. For example, I know an African American family in Oxford who has never missed a single performance of my ensemble on campus. They are not simply driven by the traditional pan-African identity as their quest to satisfy rather a sustained nostalgia for a heritage that their immediate ancestors were denied. In another development, I vividly recollect a scenario in Oxford after our ensemble had performed at the Powerhouse as part of the Yocona 2008 International Festival of Folk Music. An African American man approached me with excitement about our drumming and dancing, and with great curiosity about the drums as he asked me whether they were authentic and from Africa. I answered in the affirmative, and as he was about to further express his experiences of the evening, his waiting wife discouraged him from doing so and rather convinced him to walk away from me. My readings into this scenario were that of mixed feelings, especially when I remember what I read regarding the love that most African American have for Africans, whereas a few other people of African descent have a bitter resentment against Africans for taking part in the slave trade, though they did not initiate it. Did the husband represent the love and the wife the resentment? In his famous video *Wonders of the African World*, Harvard professor Henry Louis Gates Jr. asked questions related to this resentment upon his visit to Ghana before later wrapping himself in kente cloth with pride, thus conveying the mixed feelings similar to those this couple inspired after our performance. In any case, my reading into this scenario may be right or wrong.

In 1997 I participated in a symposium on African music and dance organized by the University of Michigan's International Center for African Music and Dance (ICAMD). As part of the meeting Pascal Younge's African Drumming and Dance Ensemble was invited to perform along with a number of local Ann Arbor groups. Coincidentally, the auditorium for the concert was located near a black neighborhood; many African Americans who heard about the event came with very high expectations, particularly of the West Virginia group. But as the group was getting ready to perform, a cross-section of the predominantly black audience wanted to boycott their performance, contesting that with the exception of Younge all the other drummers were white students, whereas most of the female dancers were African Americans. Luckily however, the organizers of the symposium had to intervene in order to soften the anger of the concerned audience before the ensemble could perform. Happily, this incident did not affect the countenance of the performers, who gave a spectacular show. Also, it was helpful that several people did not know of these backstage developments, and I would not have known if my friend Pascal had not told me. But why did this Ann Arbor scenario occur?

It seems to me that African Americans who were nostalgic of the drums, drumming, and dance traditions of their ancestors came to the concert looking for such a desire to be met. While the name of the group may be misleading to those who do not know such university ensembles are available to all students, irrespective of their ethnic and racial backgrounds, the complaining audience members might not have immediately put into perspective the differences between the demography of Morgantown on the one hand, and that of Ann Arbor on the other. The black population in Michigan is proportionally larger than that in West Virginia. Admittedly, such issues may not matter to African Americans who were conversant with the history of the suppression of African drums and drumming, and contrary to their expectations to view and experience black drummers, they were going to be disappointed. As Younge further revealed, the protesting audience members viewed predominantly white drummers as a kind of performed hegemony in which black female dancers were commanded by white drummers performing on the blacks' ancestral instruments. But as a matter of fact, the only one "commanding" the dancers to change their movements or motives was the master drummer Younge who was and is a black African, the teacher and director of the group, and thus the fear of authenticity and hegemony does not seem to come into play here.

The student ensemble members do not think along such lines, and even if they did initially as they joined the ensemble, their symbolic interactions, discussed in chapter 4, might have mediated such differences. While some may describe this scenario as an extreme racial reaction in the late 1990s, Monson (2008) has stressed the importance of understanding the interplay between musical practice, social structure, and forms of discourse coexisting in a given time and space. Here, the social spaces of Morgantown and Ann Arbor, university campus and black neighborhood are all implicated, suggesting a context of converged physical, mental, and experienced social spaces that initially conflicted but were later negotiated in order for the performance to go on. Also, it is abundantly clear that the African Americans involved in the aforementioned scenario were not operating with a typical university campus sub-cultural mentality because that is not their spatial domain. Further, the next chapter discusses the kind of world-mindedness, trans-cultural, and transnational conception of recontextualized performances within the framework of modernity and globalization with which other audience members of the Ann Arbor concert received the performances.

In resonance with my point that African Americans attach special symbolism to African drums and drumming, the Ann Arbor incident again reminds us of hermeneutical constructs relating to drums as instruments of power, whether used as tools for articulating power or as emblems of authority. Notwithstanding the legitimacy or otherwise of the concern raised by the black audience, and taking cognizance of the demographic landscape, one other observation that could be made is the need to interrogate the reasons for which most African American male students do not want to take West African drumming and dance as a course in some universities. Younge used what he had, and he would have used black drummers if they had enrolled for the course. But later in 2003 when Younge's student ensemble came to the University of Mississippi to perform, I remember that his immediate assistant lead drummer was an African American.

Luckily, I do not have this problem in my ensemble because Ricky Burkhead, the main professor of percussion at the University of Mississippi, is a pioneering member of our ensemble and remains a regular member of our ensemble, always using his influence to educate several of his students (both black and white) to join the African drum and dance ensemble in order to add that experience to their career development processes. However, at other universities including Pittsburgh, African American male students tend to be satisfied only with membership in jazz and gospel ensembles. Understandably, these are African American music genres that they need to perpetuate, and as such, my concern may simply stem from an unfounded wishful thinking. It was indeed legitimizing to learn that other people have been asking similar questions about the lack of interest on the part of students from certain identifiable groups in other world music ensembles like Taiko or gamelan.

When one compares the strong identity-based nostalgia that the immediate generation of African Americans, especially during the Pan-Africanism era, express in relation to the lack of interest shown by younger black male students in West African drumming and dance, I am inclined to accept an explanation that an African American professor gave me. A generational gap is at play. Most of these students were born in the 1970s, 1980s, and 1990s, after the civil rights era; some have been consumed by global and urban popular culture and lifestyles dictated by large cities in which they were born—New York, Houston, Chicago, Washington, and Los Angeles. Therefore, to maintain the identity and love for African heritage, the professor of African American studies suggested that parents have a duty to constantly educate their kids about their ancestral history and genealogy. Professors can also advise students on courses to take leading to deeper understanding of the realities of their world beyond hip-hop life and youth culture. Taking courses that privilege perspectives of W. E. B. Du Bois, Melville Hertskovits, Marcus Garvey, and Kwame Nkrumah, for example, may generate some degree of interest in "Pan-Africanism." Furthermore, assisting black students to understand concepts like "Negritude," "Pan-Africanism, or "Ethiopianism" may restore some consciousness of African linkages and apparent interest in African culture.

Two narratives will further illuminate the importance of consciousness on the part of an African American of the connections between his/her cultural heritage and African culture. After I raised the issue of why African American youth have not been patronizing West African dance drumming in the academy to a degree that an informed Africanist would expect, an African American ethnomusicologist approached me to express his regrets that he did not take advantage of the West African drumming offered when he was a student at his university. Now that he teaches courses on the music of the African diaspora and Africa as a professor, he realized what he had missed. Had somebody given him the needed consciousness, not a superficial awareness, of the identity-related relevance of African drumming to his own heritage, I believe he would have considered taking the dance drumming class (Personal Correspondence, October 2009). Here, a cultural gap is also at play. The tastes and priorities of youthful African American students are diverse, and they could change when they grow older and gain a deeper understanding of African cultural, historical, and biological links.

James McLeod, a graduate student at my department who has joined the Ole Miss African Drum and Dance Ensemble, emphasizes the cultural gap as the major reason, explaining that the lifestyles of several African American youth are different from those of his generation. Yet he admits that most students are concerned with the completion of their programs at the earliest possible time. Accordingly, they will concentrate more on taking courses that are required than on electives. As such, those universities that have ethnomusicology programs and require students' participation in at least two world music ensembles, or institutions in which taking an African music and dance course for two semesters fulfills a liberal arts elective requirement for undergraduates, have a higher probability of students of all racial backgrounds participating in this genre. Further, course scheduling can make participation incompatible for interested students, and these are understandable reasons.

I mentioned earlier that Ricky Burkhead is an African American percussionist. And although he started his enculturation as a drummer at an early age of eight, had his first drum set from his mother at twelve, and grew into a musician that is attracted to all types of drums and drumming traditions from the world, his subconscious awareness of having an African ancestry shapes his reception of African drumming in a special way. He reminisces the memory of the induction of Babatunde Olatunji in the Percussion Hall of Fame after he gave a talk with musical examples on his life and legacy of

African drumming and dance in the United States of America. According to Burkhead, this touching event was during one of the Percussion Arts Society conferences he attended a few years before Olatunji passed. That moment deepened Burkhead's feelings about his connectedness to his distant African linkages and a factor that intensified his love for West African drumming beyond the intrinsic aesthetic gratification it offers him. And yet, since I came to Ole Miss and continued to explain the connections to him, he observes, a stronger consciousness now informs his interpretation of West African dance drumming. Burkhead remarks, "In my spirit there is drumming, and it seems I have connection with the African ancestors" (Interview, July 2011).

There are certainly other African Americans who reason along similar lines as Ricky Burkhead, and one such staunch proponent of African dance drumming is John Price of Los Angeles. I have discovered him to be one of the most passionate former students of Kobla Ladzekpo, who after completing his program at UCLA is now a member of his teacher's professional group ZADONU. At SEM 2010 he performed in the group, and supports his teacher with his technical knowledge of recording and production of professional videos. He plans to produce a video recording on the life and work of Kobla Ladzekpo; such a project speaks volumes about the other category of African American participation is a musical genre of their distant ancestral homeland.

Realizing that a stark difference exists between John Price's unflinching commitment to West African dance drumming and the lack of interest from other African Americans in the genre, I asked his opinion on this attitude. My request for his views: "It has been observed that many African Americans fail to take advantage of the West African dance and drum ensembles in their respective schools. Please give two factors that you attribute to lack of patronage by several other African Americans in what may be described as a genre from their distant ancestral land." His response:

> One factor that contributes to lack of patronage in African music and ensembles by my brothers and sisters is simply shame. Another factor is ignorance. Unfortunately sometimes shame and ignorance work together against an African American trying to embrace his or her ancestral culture.
>
> People have to first understand that it is OK to be black. It's OK to be African. It's OK to not be black or African as well. It doesn't matter the class or geography of the person, you always run into a divide between African Americans and Africans that is usually imposed by the

party that perceives or desires benefit from the division. If you begin to go to the trendy popular clubs or eat at the best places no one will question your taste or choice. If anything you will be rewarded or at least acknowledged as a person with high culture. People will want to be around you and you feel good because people want to be around you.

Once you begin to act on your interest in Africa (that is if you're not some rich celeb adopting a baby or a cause) you have to express it by participating more in things that are African such as activities, discussions, classes, dress, food, people, music, etc. These things aren't trendy or popular and you won't find a lot of friends that will envy you. Most will try to shame you or question your motives or tell you that you're not African and you're wasting your time trying to get involved with African stuff or people. They will usually keep to the more trendy and acceptable places and activities and tend to ignore you more.

Involving oneself in things African and things black must be expressed internally and externally and many are truly afraid to admit their love for Africa for fear of being found out. As my mother would say "That would be too much like right." (Personal Correspondence, December 2012)

I now return to other younger African Americans whose attitude toward African dance drumming is nothing near that of Burkhead or Price.

Encouraging the youth to view videos featuring (1) master drummers Babatunde Olatunji and Kofi Ghanaba performing with key African American jazz musicians, (2) collaborative performances by Louis Armstrong's band and Philip Gbeho's dance ensemble in which Kobla Ladzekpo danced in 1956, or (3) images of Maya Angelou performing at the 1994 PANAFEST in Ghana in which she dressed in the queenly kente cloth, reciting her poem on Africa immediately after a performance by the Ghana National Dance Ensemble can make positive impact on younger African Americans toward African culture in general and West African drumming and dance in particular. All these artists witnessed the 1950s and 1960s, a time when there was an increased awareness about Pan-Africanism. Yet their children and grandchildren belong to a different generation, hence the need for education. It may be helpful if the younger generation of black jazz musicians and classical music composers could be guided to know the different degrees to which their forbears engaged with West African drumming or drum rhythms.

Luckily, Robert Simms of York has noted that not only are West African drumming and dance classes exciting, challenging, and stimulating artistically and academically, but they also provide "different kinds of energies with which students are familiar." By implication, it should be easy for African American male students to be guided to transfer the kind of passion they have for contemporary American popular music to West African drumming and dance, because the energies of both genres should be affective to the youth in a like manner.

More importantly, programs that engage students at an earlier age before entering university will foster a sustained interest in West African drumming and dance. During my fieldwork travels in the summer of 2007, I became aware of youth music projects and programs. One of them is housed in Berkeley's department of music. It comprises talented youth between age ten and sixteen, both black and white kids, who have been identified in the Berkeley, Oakland, and San Francisco sub-region, and through the support of an art foundation, the young students receive instructions in jazz and West African drumming. They are being gradually transformed into future outstanding performers because recordings of their concerts and studio-produced CDs are nothing less than phenomenal. When such youth enter universities that have West African drumming and dance programs, it is highly probable they will continue to intensify what they have already studied. Similarly, DjeDje informed me of summer world music programs she led at UCLA to put in place for youth from the region. Although the 2007 camp did not include West African drumming because the director traveled that summer, giving the students the opportunity to learn to play in a world music ensemble engages their interests in both the genres they have performed and UCLA, a possible school to consider for their university education.

West African drum and dance instructors in universities also have done outreach to middle schools of their communities. Sowah Mensah has, for example, conducted workshops concurrently in large auditoria for hundreds of middle school students in Minnesota. Similarly, Pascal Younge has on a number of occasions worked with particular middle schools when he was at Morgantown, and I have witnessed some of his concerts in which about five different middle schools performed a Ghanaian dance each before intermission, and then the university ensemble took over during the second half of the concert. Kofi Gbolonyo, who was the University of Pittsburgh's African Music Ensemble director from 2004–2009, is also noted for his visits to numerous middle schools in and outside Pittsburgh. Normally, these directors visit middle schools because they have been invited, or they have initiated and expressed their desire to extend their art to the youth. I know certain school districts in Texas and elsewhere have West African drumming programs for their middle schools, especially djembe drumming. I have personally visited Bramlett Elementary School, Lafayette Lower Elementary School, and Oxford Middle School in Mississippi with my drums and engaged them in drumming and dance, and given them information about Ghana in particular or African culture in general.

My conversation with Kwasi Dunyo when I visited Toronto reveals that beyond his work at York University and University of Toronto, the Canadian government has contracted him to teach West African drumming and dance to students at selected pre-university schools in Toronto. This project, which is supported by a federal grant, is predicated upon the Canadian cultural policy on diversity and the government's commitment to extending the spirit of the multicultural composition of Toronto to the schools as well. While I will be exploring this program further under the next section, I cite it here to strengthen the importance of early exposure and participation in West African drumming and dance before students enter universities in creating the possibility of continuity and development in the same art and its attendant impact.

INFLUENCE OF CITY/REGIONAL DEMOGRAPHY ON WEST AFRICAN DANCE DRUMMING

Each North American university that has a West African dance-drumming ensemble is located at a particular city or region with a unique demographic identity or aura. Such an idiosyncrasy would not be limited to the size, density, distribution, birth and death rates, growth or decline in that habitat's population, but will also include ethnic, national, and racial composition and degree of interaction among inhabitants of a city or people of a particular region. Multiculturalism and international fervor of dwellers of New York, Los Angeles, Pittsburgh, and Toronto for example, are conspicuously noticeable in a body of respects. Honestly, multiculturalism is not only a conceptualized awareness among people of multiple cultures coexisting in the same city. The second level of multiculturalism is consciousness of the extent to which multiple cultures of a city can provide better states of living when people take advantage of such diverse cultural forms. The third level of multiculturalism is experiential, a state in which people live the positive ideational views they hold about people from different cultures of the world. Put differently, the behaviors of inhabitants of highly multicultural cities also partly reflect the demographic traits of such cities in cultural terms.

Cities and their universities reciprocally reinforce the cultural lives of each other. While centers of performing arts and other auditoria are available to students for accessing music from different places of the world, students in different contexts can experience performances staged by resident groups of a particular city. These include nightclubs, concerts, international festivals, carnivals, fairs, contests, and parties. Visiting different sites of worship can offer the curious multicultural listener the opportunity to experience music originally from Asia, Africa, Oceania, or Europe in a North American city. Student performing groups also participate in off-campus activities that may capture the cultural landscape of a particular city. Cities or regions where universities are located serve as sites and social spaces from which majority of students are recruited. Accordingly, students in an internationalized city bring lifestyles that exemplify heightened multiculturalism to campus. Furthermore, inhabitants of multicultural cities form a good percentage of the audiences for world music ensembles including West African drumming and dance. Cities not only serve as fertile grounds for the flourishing of world music ensembles and classes, but they also support specific world music ensembles beyond receptivity to performances.

Reciprocally, campus ensembles perform during events organized by groups that culturally identify with specific ensembles. While DjeDje has discussed the impact of the large Asian population in Los Angeles on UCLA's world music ensembles from Asia, Kobla Ladzekpo similarly mentions how the African community in the same city patronizes both his student and professional ensembles. David Locke and Patricia Tang have also discussed the same interplay between city and university as it applies to Boston. Similarly, Christopher Ladzekpo vividly shared his experiences of the extent to which the city lives of San Francisco, Berkeley, and Oakland are central to his work as a Ghanaian master drummer and promoter of the performing arts. Using Pittsburgh as an example, I can still remember how the university and Indian associations living in Pittsburgh jointly sponsored some of the Indian Hindustani (North Indian) classical music concerts I attended at the University of Pittsburgh in the late 90s. In the same vein, West African drumming and dance concerts were well patronized by the large number of Africans and African Americans who live in this city. Yet, as a result of the migration of the Balkans of southeastern Europe to Pittsburgh because of its flourishing steel industry of the early twentieth century, Duquesne University houses the popular Tambouritza Orchestra since the early 1990s as a group whose membership and performances mediate and perpetuate their regional identities. I still carry the enduring picture of the international rooms at the Cathedral of Learning, University of Pittsburgh, where various nations or regions of the world have been given spaces to decorate with iconic symbols. Indeed, multiculturalism is a lifestyle in many cities.

In addition to my previous discussion of the multiculturalism of Toronto at different sections of this book, I now share how Russell Hartenberger recalled a graduate student's decision to visit different neighborhoods of the city to listen to diverse musical types from different parts of the world. The student based his selected sites on his knowledge of the concentration of nationalities at spaces that included their expressive art forms. The outcome of the project revealed that people from almost everywhere in the world live visibly through various forms of cultural behavior. The multiculturalism of Toronto was evident in the behaviors of the students I saw in all the classes I observed at York and the University of Toronto. I have elsewhere in this book discussed how the Canadian federal government supports the multiculturalism of Toronto through specific grants for the promotion of the diverse arts, and the work that Kwasi Dunyo does in Toronto schools teaching students African dance and drumming. The racial and national composition of the students I met during the classes I observed at York and the University of Toronto were very diverse.

Although I could not visit New York as part of my ethnographic research on which this book is based, I cannot resist making an observation, especially when discussing multiculturalism; for it is well known that New York is one of the most internationalized cities in the world. While nightclub music abounds in its multifarious manifestations, hundreds of cultural festivals, world-class international dance troupes' tours make New York a favorite destination. But specifically in connection with West African dance drumming, the performances of West African migrant communities in New York are noteworthy. Djembe drumming can be accessed from dance troupes and Mande popular music bands that combine guitars and trap set with *kora*, *balo*, and other instruments of the sub-region in music that is stylistically distinctive. As mentioned in chapter 2, West African dance drumming was introduced into Columbia University in 1964, the same year as at UCLA. Both Kobla Ladzekpo and David Locke have mentioned their participation in this early ensemble, with Ladzekpo as an instructor and Locke taking classes from Alfred Ladzekpo, Kobla's brother. At SEM 2006 and 2010, I met Philip Yopovsky who had taken West African drumming under Kobla Ladzekpo, and the degree to which Phillip and Kobla have sustained the teacher-student bond for almost five decades was very revealing to me. Although I could not discuss Columbia's early ensemble in detail in chapter 2,

Figure 6.4 Philip Yopovsky and Kobla Ladzekpo at SEM 2012 in Los Angeles. [Photo by John Price, SEM 2010]

the photo of Philip Yopovsky and Kobla Ladzekpo in Figure 6.4 visually recalls a lasting friendship that started in 1964 at Columbia, and in 2010 when this photo was taken, the bond was still very strong. Furthermore, Kobla Ladzekpo and Gideon Alorwoyie have mentioned that they once instructed at Brockport State College in New York. Yet while Kwabena Nketia's name is associated with UCLA, Professor Opoku, the other pathfinder of the Ghana National Dance Ensemble and a leading authority in African dance scholarship, worked at Brockport State College for several years in the 1970s and 1980s before returning to Ghana. I suggest that the multicultural landscape of New York contributed to interest in the study, learning, and reception of West African dance drumming. Multiculturalism of a city informs students' interest in taking culturally diverse classes, and serves as a repository of cultural experiences that electrifies patronizing audiences whenever activated. It is no coincidence that Nukporfe, Binghamton University's African performance ensemble, continues to benefit from the multiculturalism of New York, as discussed in chapter 2.

Reciprocally, West African dance drumming is a transformational tool that is and can be used in creating, intensifying, or affirming multiculturalism on university campuses and in its immediate cultural environment. As such, in demographical zones of smaller college towns that may not be as readily multicultural as large city-based universities, the ensemble can be used to construct that cultural landscape and soundscape on campuses. Internationalization and multiculturalism is a major role of the West African dance-drumming ensemble.

It may be helpful to use my own ensemble to buttress this argument. The Ole Miss African Music and Dance Ensemble is the first and only African dance drumming ensemble in a university in the state of Mississippi. While some have behaved toward this ensemble as though they were continuing the disruption and suppression of African drumming in the American South, as I discuss in chapter 1, others have captured the symbolism of this ensemble, a theme I mention in chapter 2. Given the history of the University of Mississippi in the 1960s, and the degree of change that has taken place in terms of diversity and inclusiveness, multiculturalism and internationalization has since then remained one of the university's objectives. Some administrators have captured the transformational value of the African dance-drumming ensemble beyond changing the cultural landscape on campus to partial empirical signs of change. I have discussed the dynamics of the ensemble fostering interracial and ethnic and national interactions. To the outside world, a DVD of the African ensemble will send signals to the world about the changes that are taking place culturally, academically, and socially in our demographic region. Hopefully, all administrators, students, alumni, politicians, and even grant foundations can catch this proven transformational capacity of a university ensemble constructing the needed multiculturalism. I conclude this section with an excerpt from a remark of my university's administrator about how he considers the use of our African drums and the dance-drumming ensemble a transformational tool in our institution.

> I think back to fifty years from this age on this very site, and what a beautiful thing it is that we are celebrating the diversity of our cultures on this campus.... As we look back fifty years, the people at that time will look in awe at us.... So truly, the holiest place on earth is where ancient hatred has turned into present love. So, we thank you all for bringing that to our campus. That is a celebration of hope. (Michael Johanssen, Director of International Programs, University of Mississippi, during Ghana50 Concert at Ole Miss, March 6, 2007)

These two documents (see Figs. 6.5 and 6.6) suggest the articulation of communality during the celebration of the historic Ghana50 concert. Figure 6.5 is a copy of the proclamation that the city of Oxford presented to me and other Ghanaians as an expression of solidarity from its citizens to

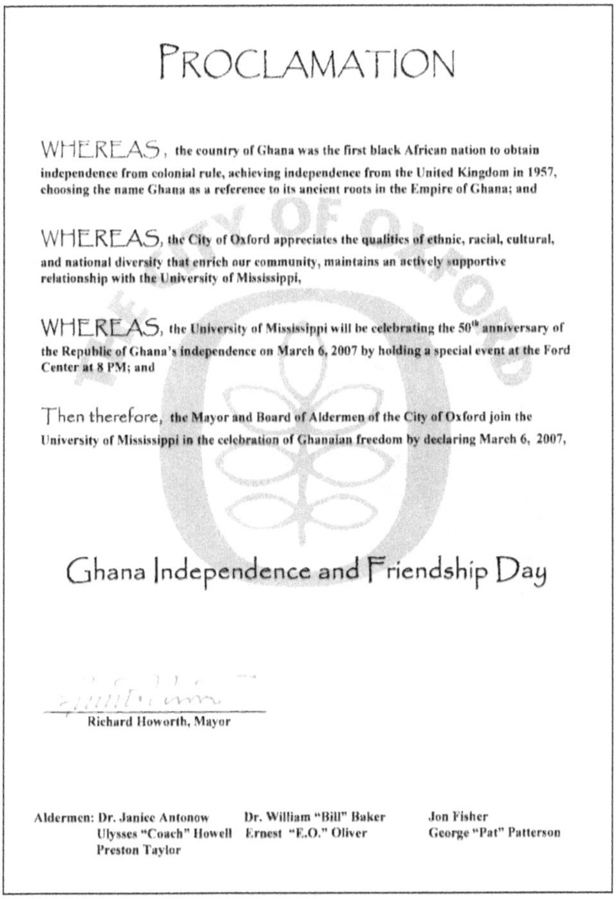

PROCLAMATION

WHEREAS, the country of Ghana was the first black African nation to obtain independence from colonial rule, achieving independence from the United Kingdom in 1957, choosing the name Ghana as a reference to its ancient roots in the Empire of Ghana; and

WHEREAS, the City of Oxford appreciates the qualities of ethnic, racial, cultural, and national diversity that enrich our community, maintains an actively supportive relationship with the University of Mississippi,

WHEREAS, the University of Mississippi will be celebrating the 50th anniversary of the Republic of Ghana's independence on March 6, 2007 by holding a special event at the Ford Center at 8 PM; and

Then therefore, the Mayor and Board of Aldermen of the City of Oxford join the University of Mississippi in the celebration of Ghanaian freedom by declaring March 6, 2007,

Ghana Independence and Friendship Day

Richard Howorth, Mayor

Aldermen: Dr. Janice Antonow Dr. William "Bill" Baker Jon Fisher
Ulysses "Coach" Howell Ernest "E.O." Oliver George "Pat" Patterson
Preston Taylor

Figure 6.5 Proclamation from the mayor and alderman of Oxford on the celebration of Ghana50 (1957-2007) by the University of Mississippi and the city of Oxford. [Presented to George Dor on March 6, 2007]

internationals living in the city and studying and/or working at the university. Figure 6.6 is a flyer we used to advertise the program. Further, the office of the vice chancellor for university relations paid for advertisements of the program published in the Oxford *Eagle*, and that concert remains my highest point of experienced love from the entire university. On the other hand, this and other performances promote collectivism, multiculturalism, and common virtues of humanity including love and liberation. The Ghana 50th Independence Anniversary Secretariat now holds a DVD, program notes, and related items I sent at its archives in Accra.

Our awareness of the reciprocity between a particular demography and an ensemble shaping each other should inform our strategies and challenges as ensemble directors and administrators as we continue to seek growth in our respective West African dance-drumming programs. As Dean Glenn

224 A TRANSPLANTED MUSICAL PRACTICE FLOURISHING IN THE AFRICAN DIASPORA

Figure 6.6 Flyer for Ghana50 contains images of OMADDE in performance, political and cultural symbols from Ghana, and other details. [From George Dor, March 2007]

Hopkins has uncompromisingly asserted in chapter 5, the broader ideals of liberal arts education are the same everywhere and they must be pursued with utmost dedication and ingenuity that may include how we handle our challenges and take advantage of available resources.

7

WORLD MUSIC AND GLOBALIZATION

West African Drum-Dance Ensembles

Economic and political ideology stubbornly assume center-stage thematic positions in discourse on globalization. Accordingly, it is not surprising when a student who walks into my world music class after leaving a class discussion on the global economy at an International Studies Institute, for example, challenges his world music teacher (myself) for "falsely claiming" globalization for the domain of music cultures. Certainly, such may not be the reaction of students from cultural studies, diaspora studies, ethnomusicology, anthropology, and other culture-related cognate disciplines. Yet, the lesson I learned from this classroom scenario is not to take the understanding of popularly used concepts for granted and not to presume all my students have a working understanding of the scope of globalization. Luckily, I was able to convince my curious student and the whole class by providing preparatory insights after citing the five "-scapes": (a) "ethnoscapes," (b) "mediascapes," (c) "technoscapes," (d) "financescapes," and (e) "ideoscapes" that Arjun Appadurai (1996: 33) proposes as a rubric for discussing facets of globalization. Given the interdisciplinary nature of ethnomusicology, all the five "scapes" intersect with various aspects and themes of our field, although ethnoscapes is the main rubric. However, beyond citing an authority to intuitively legitimize claims regarding the scope of globalization, a general definition of the concept itself is central to the understanding of globalization's wider applicability. It was exactly my effort at that task that became most compelling for my students.

Globalization involves worldwide processes and conditions in which human beings have become more transnationally connected in various departments of life. This large-scale interaction among people of the globe has been characterized by an increased circulation of goods and ideas, resulting from swifter communication through advanced technological means, mass migration, and operating with increased world-mindedness and interdependence. More importantly, people everywhere in the world are embracing, appropriating, and domesticating these global phenomena, which they use along with local ones. The practice of West African dance drumming outside Africa captures our global imagination and validates this worldwide trend, trajectory, and landscape.

Writing on the new aesthetic paradigm during the era of globalization, Appadurai has observed that pleasure is a more important motivating factor than leisure in the context of consumption of different kinds of products—goods, media, and metaphorically, art forms (1996: 83–85). These days, people relate to the music of cultures other than their own for reasons beyond identity-related ones to other constructed meanings. The following excerpt is from remarks made by Charles Gates, chair of the Ole Miss music department, regarding his experience of the performances of the Ole Miss African Drum and Dance Ensemble (during Ghana50 Concert on March 6, 2007).

> ... This music and dance is expressive of and truly rooted in a particular culture. Yet, like all great arts, it transcends mere cultural boundaries. What it communicates is undeniable. You find it virtually impossible to listen and watch passively. I feel I become part of the performance in an organic sense. It draws me in. We have a real experience of the communities whose stories are told, and that is the point of the performance.

In the next paragraphs, I will point out different ways in which people from different parts of the globe engage in West African dance drumming.

WEST AFRICAN DRUMMING AS A GLOBAL SOUNDSCAPE

While this study has focused on the North American academy, it must be added that some degree of West African dance drumming is practiced in a few universities or colleges in France, Britain, Germany, Australia, China, Japan, and Hong Kong, to mention a few. For example, Anna Melnikoff confirmed during our conversation that Famoudou Konate, her djembe teacher, spent several years in Paris teaching drumming to people of all walks of life, including students. Friedberg (2001) provides a summative profile of Konate that includes the phenomenal 2000 workshop he conducted at the University of Chicago, in which he "came with 30 plus drums" and taught and performed Mande music. More importantly, Friedberg reports that Konate was awarded an honorary professorship in 1996 at the Academy of Arts in Berlin, and suggests the substantial impact Konate must have made on his students in Berlin: "In the first few years, Konate has offered several drum workshops here in Berlin, and it was the students who participated in them who said, 'We want him as a professor,' and it worked."

Academic conferences are sites for workshops and performances of West African dance-drumming genres in parts of the world beyond North America. An excellent example was Africa Meets Asia, which Akin Euba initiated and coordinated in 2007 under the collaborative auspices of the Center for Intercultural Musicology, Cambridge, U.K., the University of Pittsburgh, and Beijing Central Conservatory of Music. Both Pascal Younge and Kwasi Ampene gave presentations on aspects of West African dance drumming. Normally, a festival component of the event is reserved for the performance of different kinds of music.

The genre has become a favorite research theme for music education students in Australia for exploring cross-cultural pedagogic models. Admittedly, some have studied the practice of West African drumming in Australian communities outside the campus; Corney (2007) and Joseph (2005) are classic examples. Today, music education has become an area in which the use of African drums and drumming as pedagogical tools is increasingly reaching global appeal. I have previously discussed this theme and Kofi Gbolonyo's advocacy in this interdisciplinary enterprise.

Outside the academy, international cultural festivals of global magnitude in which African dance-drumming groups participate abound in the world. Opening ceremonies of international sports contests may involve African dance drumming. While one would consider it normal for an African drum and dance ensemble to perform during such a global game in Africa, such as during FIFA 2010 in South Africa, it takes great accomplishment and popularity for an African dance-drumming ensemble to be invited from the United States to perform at a global game held in Asia. Pascal Younge reports, "The group [Azaguno] also represented the U.S. at the FIFA World Cup opening ceremony and games in Seoul, Korea in 2002.¹" Younge founded Azaguno when he was teaching at West Virginia, and the team of expert percussionists and dancers was comprised of Ghanaians—Younge's past students—as well as a selected few from the student ensemble to form a formidable group. Interestingly, Africans and Americans constituted an African dance-drumming ensemble based in a U.S. university that represented the United States in Korea. What a global matrix!

In chapter 1 I mentioned how Babatunde Olatunji performed during the 1946 New York World's Fair. Similarly, a number of African countries participated in the 2010 Shanghai World's Fair showcasing their national dances and other expressive cultures.

International performance tours by African national dance troupes are avenues for sharing rich dance-drumming traditions globally. Famoudou Konate, in an interview in Friedberg (2001), relates his numerous international performances with Les Ballets Africains (Guinea National Ballet) as master drummer. This group, which was founded by order of Sekou Toure in 1958, toured both North America and many European countries. Similarly, I have mentioned the role of the Ghana National Dance Ensemble in this discussion and will shed further light on this ensemble's international tours later in this chapter.

Three articles written on Mande djembe dance drumming, Charry (1996: 66–72; 2000: 1–8), Polak (2000: 7–46), and Hill (2011: 4–10), are relevant here for a better cross-ethnic cultural understanding of this sub-theme. I choose to subsume these texts under "global dimensions," although they all pass for research, and Hill's is particularly germane to pedagogy. Raimer Polak's article, "A Musical Instrument Travels Around the World: Djembe Playing in Bomako, West Africa, and Beyond," provides a comprehensive discussion of the geo-cultural source, the processes that have made the djembe the second most widely played (after conga) African or African-derived drum. In addition to Polak's being the lead article in Volume 42(3) of *The World of Music*, the editors put an action photo of Jali Madi Kuyate playing the djembe on the cover. Kuyate was a master drummer of Ballet National du Mali from 1966.

In his "The Dancing Djembe: Resources for Exploring Guinean Drum and Dance Connections," Matthew Edward Hill succinctly advocates a holistic approach to teaching the genre. An added value of this article is the list and discussion of excellent videos produced on djembe drumming and dancing by virtuosic musicians. The target beneficiaries of these instructional resources are Americans, Europeans, and beyond, and as Hill rightly emphasizes the importance of vision and imitation in learning West African dance, learners around the globe will find these videos very useful and accessible.

Though brief, Eric Charry's article is insightful, covering a range of themes pertinent to the djembe drum. These include the agency of individuals and groups who popularized the instrument, the ethnic origins of the drum, explanation of its delayed international impact, especially in the academy, as well as reasons for the varied spellings of the instrument. Furthermore,

Charry touches on West African methods of teaching the djembe and the challenges djembe teachers face that may necessitate modification of teaching approaches. After discussing the instruments of the ensemble, Charry illuminates the djembe repertoire, drawing a distinction between styles played in the villages, modernized ballet choreographies that draw on ethnic dances into a suite, and pieces that simply use motives from any ethnic dance to create a totally contemporary piece. Charry notes that national djembe drumming styles are a post-colonial legacy. He also provides some bibliography and discography that can offer accessible information on this globally ubiquitous drum and its related genres.

Other means through which West African dance drumming has become a global soundscape include the United Nations' efforts to preserve intangible forms of knowledge through exhibitions such as the March 2009 event held in New York on African drums. I have already discussed changing demographics of cities where West African migrants now perform their social dances on foreign lands. Mass mediation of West African dance drumming is ubiquitous, be it through radio, television, or film. While the recording industry has produced CDs, VHS, and DVDs, iPods have become a portable, global tool for accessing different forms of music. Further, a myriad of recordings of West African dance drumming exist on YouTube, including some by the ensembles discussed. Additionally, media components of world music textbooks include coverage of representative West African dance-drumming genres. One should not forget the impact of world music courses that help students listen to the genre wherever they may be in the world. Finally, the international or global composition of students in North American universities facilitates such students' participation in the genre.

Drawing on the case evidence of Olly Wilson and Russell Hartenberger in chapter 4, I have discussed the importance of practical hands-on knowledge of West African dance drumming to art music composers in their exploration of new compositional resources. Also, I have mentioned how Steve Reich's study tour to Ghana, where he studied drumming with Gideon Alorwoyie, equipped him with partial creative resources derived from Ghanaian dance drumming. Similarly, Gyorgy Ligeti's minimalist compositions have their partial ontology from the dance-drumming music genres he studied in Ivory Coast. But while world-renowned composers had to go to Africa to acquire knowledge of these idioms, African-born composers of art music, especially composers of piano and/or symphonic music, have extensively drawn on the idiosyncratic features of dance-drumming genres—both drum rhythms and song forms—from their ethnic, national, and/or sub-continental cultures. In addition to local cultural knowledge of some of these dances, most of these composers have to critically study the structures of these dance genres in order to gain deeper understanding of their features prior to applying them in their intercultural music pieces. Classic examples include Joshua Uzoigwe, Kwabena Nketia, Akin Euba, Fela Sowande, Nicholas Nayo, and Gyima Labi, who have written works that are now performed in different parts of the world (Nyaho 2009; Dor 1992; Omojola 2009). These African art pieces are a symbiosis of African and Western music, or African and Asian, or the three.

RESEARCH AND WEST AFRICAN DANCE DRUMMING

Research and West African dance drumming in North American universities have dialectically influenced each other. While it is known that the most researched theme in African music scholarship is rhythm, studies conducted on drum ensembles of the Guinea Coast have remained a major focal point of interest and attention (Ekwueme 1975/76: 28). But with the advent of world music ensembles in American universities, mature ethnomusicology students have the option of studying aspects of their student ensembles or traveling to West Africa to conduct field research on dance-drumming practices. I point out in chapter 4 how American students who actively participate in ensemble drumming end up researching West African dance drumming. Evidently, some of the well-known names in African rhythm research began as drummers in African ensembles of UCLA, Wesleyan, or the University of Pittsburgh, among others; James Koetting and Philip Harding of UCLA, Hewitt Pantaleoni, David Locke, and John Chernoff[2] of Wesleyan, and Willie Anku of Pitt[3] are classic examples.

Research from within the academy without embarking on a field trip has been one of the outcomes of Mantle Hood's bi-musicality-oriented programs. Such studies tend to focus on analysis of rhythm based on music performed by campus ensembles or on complementary use of recorded music held at institutional archives—methodological issues including transcription and notation—though university campus cultures at times may inspire themes for critical investigation. Subject themes include recontextualization in genres and cultural practices (Mundundu 2005), African pedagogical approaches to teaching drumming and dance, and ensembles' roles in the construction of new cultural communities. Conducting research in a backyard environment comes with its advantages as well as disadvantages for the aspiring ethnomusicologist. The advantages include cost-effectiveness, since fellowships or grants for field work in Africa may not be available.

While North American universities have served as the field sites for some studies on African dance drumming or rhythm, ethnographic research in Africa is inevitable for certain kinds of study and degrees. In addition to ways in which research themes may dictate the need to travel to Africa, having specific consultants in Africa gives credibility to researchers' findings; performance or social contexts the researcher may observe, and the experiences the ethnographer partially draws on in reaching his/her conclusions, are in Africa. An American ethnomusicologist who wants to understand the processes involved in making Akan or Ewe drums does not have the option of researching from his university campus. Hood (1964) studied drum making among the Akan, while Galeoto (1985) studied "Drum-Making among the Southern Ewe People of Ghana and Togo" for his master's thesis. It is fair to observe that it was Galeoto's participation in Ghanaian drumming at Wesleyan that inspired his interest in the subject.

Throughout this study I have discussed or mentioned the relevance of the Ghana Dance Ensemble to the subject of this book. It is gratifying to know this ensemble has received a body of critical studies, of which Hirt-Manheimer (2004) and Schauert (2011) are great examples. The methodology of Hirt-Manheimer's pursuit of "Understanding 'Fast Agbekor': A History of Ghana's National Dance Company and an Analysis of Its Repertory" did not involve travel to Ghana, but depended on the knowledge of his drumming and dance instructors at Wesleyan, Abraham Adzinya and Helen Mensah. Understandably, Hirt-Manheimer's study was a master's thesis, and as such he chose to depend on the expertise and memories of his teachers who were former members of the national dance ensemble. It is important to note that he decided to use "... National Dance Company," the troupe's original name, to suggest an emphasis on the formative stages of the ensemble, as well as a perceived authenticity associated with performances of the pioneering members. Furthermore, it was the conviction of some of those original members of the national dance company, when working in the American academy, to represent repositories of the original dances their group used to perform in Ghana, but also as part of the repertoire they impart to American students.

Conversely, a doctoral dissertation demanded that Paul Schauert travel to Ghana and conduct a thorough ethnographic research in which he interviewed many informants and observed rehearsals and performances as he sought a contextual understanding of the Ghana Dance Ensemble.

The Dagbe Cultural Institute and Arts Centre, which Godwin Agbeli founded in 1982 at Kopeyia in the Volta region of Ghana, has become a popular research focus that has yielded articles and even a master's thesis (McCall 2010). This center, which continues to offer practical instructions in dance drumming, provides researchers the opportunity to intimately experience Anlo Ewe culture. While it draws tourists from different parts of the globe, a reflection on the number of nations and universities in which the center's founder has taught or given workshops on Ghanaian dance drumming provides another window into the global dynamics of the genre. These institutions include New York University, Tufts University, Boston University, Brooklyn College of Music, Berklee College of Music, Harvard University, University of Toronto—all colleges in North America—as well as at Auckland University and Victoria University, both in New Zealand.[4] The preceding discussion is central to the focus of this book elucidating the presence of the genre in foreign universities.

Hopefully, future researchers will consider exploring other similar cultural centers established by individual Africans to facilitate the perpetuation of West African drumming and dance to global patrons. Other researchers may consider working on detailed biographical works of these quintessential virtuosic gatekeepers into traditional African music traditions. On a broader scale, I think the time is ripe for writing on the contributions of distinguished musical families including the Ladzekpos of Anyako and Agbelis of Kopeyia. Such studies that focus on West African virtuosic musicians will be consistent with the ascendancy in the ethnomusicology of the individual which may take the form of a biography, whereby individual's agency and subjective culture can be situated within his/her objective culture that recognizes personhood within values of communality.

STUDY ABROAD AND WEST AFRICAN DANCE DRUMMING

The interplay between West African dance-drumming programs and study-abroad programs can be discussed on three levels: (1) short-term programs in which drumming and dance are part of the course activities, (2) short-term programs that make drumming and dance their focal point, and (3) long-term programs that prioritize West African drumming and dance over other course activities. In the first category, students from American universities travel to Ghana, Senegal, Mali, Guinea, or other West African countries and pursue short-term study-abroad programs in the summer, lasting from two to five weeks; drumming and dancing are partial course activities along with other, equally important components of culture- or history-related themes. Here, performance is not the primary focus of the course, and drumming and dance reinforce the understanding of the broader themes of the courses

Figure 7.1 Drumming and dance class for my 2006 study-abroad students at SYTO (Student Youth Travels Organization) Headquarters in Accra. [Photo from Annette Holloway, May 2006]

as well as consolidate any previous participation in West African drumming and dance by students on campus. In other cases, study-abroad visits to West Africa have been aimed at helping the American student experience the cultural roots or sources of the music of the African diaspora. My study-abroad programs (and, I think, those of Daniel Avorgbedor and Kwesi Amepene) mostly fall under this class.

In the second category, the focus of the course for exploring an African country's culture(s) is dance and drumming, African rhythm, or the performing arts. Hence such courses are designed for students to perform different dances of a particular ethnic group or region. For most of their stay, students remain in a particular ethnic region where they can experience the broader holistic culture, differentiate village life from urban lifestyles, and experience the communal ethos of African social and cultural life by interacting with Africans during and outside performance contexts. Arrangements are made by course planners to ensure these students also travel around the country to help them understand the cultural diversity of an African nation through experiential performance, observation, and other forms of active participation in dances. Workshops and performances by the Ghana National Dance Ensemble, for example, are arranged and organized for students to experience

Figure 7.2 An Ole Miss student dances to music played by Dagbon musicians in Tamale, northern Ghana. Susan Swindall was a member of the student ensemble before the study-abroad trip. [Photo from Annette Holloway, May 2006]

the dynamics of Ghanaian indigenous dances repackaged for urban and international or contemporary performing contexts and their attendant determinants. For some students, the opportunity will provide insight regarding how some ensemble directors were trained prior to being hired by American universities. Pascal Younge's study-abroad programs, from West Virginia University and now Ohio University, epitomize this category. Akosua Addo's study-abroad program is similar in a number of ways, in that she focuses on dances of the Akan people while the students primarily stay in the central region. However, her focus is on pedagogical approaches indigenous African musicians and dancers use in teaching their arts and gaining insights from narratives of these cultural custodians as they relate to their processes of enculturation—all concerns of music education, Addo's area of specialization.

The third level is a long-term program that may last a semester, term, or year. Through exchange programs or federal financial-support programs, arrangements are made for an American student to be affiliated with an accredited African university as well as a knowledgeable master drummer and/or great dancer whom the student will understudy during the duration of his/

Figure 7.3 George Dor doing the same dance as his students in Tamale. [Photo by Annette Holloway, May 2006]

her study abroad. David Locke has mentioned to me that Tufts has put such a long-term study-abroad project in place that enables students to spend a semester in Ghana.

West African drum and dance ensembles on North American campuses are sources of inspiration that create intensified awareness of African cultures among students, frequently engendering pursuit of study abroad. Such student members of their institution's ensembles long to experience the dance-drumming tradition in its original context. Other students might have taken theoretical courses in world music or African music that spark interests leading to study-abroad programs in Africa. Some might not have been in the African drum and dance ensemble prior to their visit to West Africa; however, it is usual for such study-abroad students to join their institution's drum-dance ensemble following their return. Here, it is the zeal of such students to continue an engaging aspect of the life-changing cultural experiences they encountered in Africa. For other students, habitual attendance of West African drumming and dance concerts is sufficient to generate interest that culminates into a study-abroad program. Naturally, there may be other students

Figure 7.4 Annette Holloway dancing in the OMADDE, which she joined after returning from her study-abroad trip to Ghana and tasting dancing there. Drummers: George Dor (L) and Ricky Burkhead (R). [Photo by University of Mississippi Communications Photography, March 2007]

who may join a study-abroad class to Africa through other windows, including cognate African studies courses in literature or history.

To realize the minimum number of enrollments required by many universities for a study-abroad program to pass as cost-effective, teachers may recruit from neighboring state or regional campuses that enable students to earn transfer credits. Some of these students may not have participated in African drum and dance ensembles because they may be nonexistent on their campuses.

UCLA, a source of inspiration for the development and spread of world music ensembles in the American academy, sees the wisdom in empowering their students to study abroad to Africa. Accordingly, the African music ensemble has been part of an advocacy project that seeks to raise funds for students to benefit from programs similar to those in other schools. As Eric Charry has rightly observed, visiting Africa should be the goal of students for whom African music may promise to become a defining component of their future professional enterprises.

Another ongoing summer activity, which often takes place off campus but locally, is summer workshops. While some universities' study-abroad offices may coordinate such programs, other organizers plan these workshops outside the auspices of the study-abroad offices. But to facilitate the transfer of credits for participating students, it is imperative that a university office is involved in the enrollment process, thus explaining the inevitability of the study-abroad office's or music department's role. Summer workshops involving world music ensembles are organized in various ways; the most common ones may include a variety of ensembles such as Indonesian gamelan, Japanese taiko, Hindustani classical music with tabla and sitar, or West African dance drumming, offering students the opportunity to learn to perform in two ensembles of his or her choice. These workshops may feature up to four different West African drumming traditions, with invited instructors responsible for each dance genre. Thus students find themselves studying under different accomplished African master drummers and dance directors. Normally, these workshops are a week of intensive drumming and dancing. An advantage of such a workshop is for a student member of a West African drum and dance ensemble to learn new dances not available on their campuses. Also, students from universities without West African drum and dance ensembles seize the opportunity to participate in an engaging experience.

David Locke has in the past brought together three or four student ensembles in the Boston area to Tufts to participate in an intercollegiate African music festival. Each director gives a workshop on a dance, and the ensembles perform toward the end of a three- to four-day collaborative meeting. The regularly featured ensembles include Binghamton, directed by James Burns, performing mostly Ewe and other Ghanaian dances; MIT's *Sabar* ensemble, directed by Patricia Tang; Berklee College Ensemble, led by Joe Galeoto; and Tufts, directed by Locke, specializing in Ewe and Dagbamba dances. For universities that may not have West African ensembles and their instructors, summer is a great time to enlist the services of a visiting expert from another school to broaden the horizons of their students.

Some American students go to African countries not to study abroad, but for other projects including those inspired by volunteer causes. The spirit of offering assistance to one's community through service, David Locke observes, has become a very strong American virtue. By extension, some students who plan to extend their community services to people living in countries beyond the USA often select African countries they consider as being in need of their assistance with specific projects. Accordingly, some students take Africa-related courses, including dance drumming, as a means of gaining preparatory knowledge of the countries they may be visiting in the near future. When these students go to Africa either through federal agencies or as members of churches, dance drumming is again one of the activities their love most.

MODELS FROM AFRICA

In chapter 6 I metaphorically compare West African drumming and dance to a plant that continues to spread globally and is consumed culturally by many. It may be appropriate to look at the source of the seeds of this musical fruit. Still speaking figuratively, when people talk about mighty rivers and their phenomenal importance to lives of humans downstream, they normally tend to forget the sources of such rivers, which are small but beautiful streams. By implication and extension, talking about the global dynamics of West African drumming, especially within the past four decades, may require retrospective acknowledgment of the foundational factors and processes that have contributed to this global or transnational phenomenon. Having shared perspectives of ensemble directors—including their countries of origin and enculturation, where some administrators pursued further studies in African music and received inspiration for founding of their institution's ensemble, and how ethnomusicologists researched into West African dance drumming traditions and understudied their consultants as performers who are now teaching the genre—I now reflect on a few models from Africa that shaped the presence of this genre in the North American academy. My areas of focus are (1) path-finding personalities, (2) state cultural and academic institutions, (3) national dance ensemble models, and (4) indigenous institutions and musical practices.

Philip Gbeho and the Promotion of Dance at the National Level

Philip Gbeho is a household name in Ghana as the official composer[5] of Ghana's national anthem "God Bless Our Homeland Ghana." And because I became a cellist, composer, and briefly a resident conductor of the Ghana National Symphony Orchestra for which Gbeho was the founding director, I am well informed about his other contributions to the Ghanaian musical landscape. For example, the symphony orchestra often played his arrangements of Anlo Ewe pentatonic melodies with typical Ewe drum-rhythmic accompaniment. Yet my interviews with Kobla Ladzekpo, Christopher Ladzekpo, and Gideon Alorwoyie revealed another important legacy Gbeho had left: the promotion of Anlo Ewe drumming and dance under the auspices of the Arts Council. In the next few paragraphs, I use Alorwoyie's narratives to explain the Gbeho legacy, aiming to argue that the partial ontology of the strong presence of Ewe dances and ensemble directors in the North American academy may be viewed as an enduring result of Gbeho's legacy stemming from the research group he supervised and his recruitment of traditional musicians.

In an interview I had with Gideon Foli Alorwoyie, he vividly recalled his childhood musical enculturation. Because of the signs of tremendous musical talent Alorwoyie showed at a very early age, his parents arranged a divination ceremony to be performed for him in order to ascertain paths of his destiny. This traditional Ewe practice revealed that he had two gifts, composing and drumming. He was deemed to be a reincarnation of Nuxo, a maternal relative who was a phenomenal composer. For drumming, Alorwoyie had inherited that from his paternal parents from Anlo Afiadenyigba, but also with partial ancestry from Anexọ in Togo. But because he was staying with the dad in Afiadenyigba, his paternal uncle ensured a consistent nurturing of Alorwoyie's drumming gifts at the expense of composing. Yet, the spirit of song was within him, and as he further related, he was really tormented by the spirits of song and drumming. At a time, he remembers, he was singing and fume was coming out from his mouth, and when his mother felt pity on him, she arranged and sought the assistance of a traditional priest, who concluded that it was difficult to receive both spirits of song and drumming together. "So, a ritual ceremony was performed for me in order to shut the door on composing so that I could focus on drumming" (Interview, November 2007).

Alorwoyie's *Tọde* (junior paternal uncle) took up the responsibility of training him into a great master drummer; immediately it became clear through divine intervention that drumming and not song has been privileged. He started to play lead drummer roles at both home and school when he was in middle school. His recognition as a promising master drummer came in 1961 during the Hogbetsotso Festival that commemorates the migration history of the Anlo Ewe. Customarily, all Anlo towns and villages attend this festival held at Anloga, the capital of the Anlo, with their representative performing groups, and the Afiadenyigba group prepared ahead of these festivities. Alorwoyie further narrates that on their trip to the festival site by road, specifically from Keta to Anloga, his uncle gave him the drumming sticks so Alorwoyie could take over the lead drummer role from him. The young Foli yielded to his uncle's insistence and drummed until the group reached their destination. His uncle had other surprises for him, and it would later become evident that his uncle had decided Alorwoyie should lead the drumming even during the morning's activities.

Such festivals, among other things, are sites for the display of creative talent, and Alorwoyie's uncle was not simply challenging the young drummer to aspire higher. He also was showcasing the youngster to the entire Anlo nation of an up-and-coming virtuoso drummer in the making. It therefore was not surprising that his performance caught Husunu Adonu[6] Ladzekpo's attention. As Alorwoyie vividly recalled, "That was the first time I would see Husunu Adonu of Anyako, the first master drummer of the Ghana National Dance Ensemble.[7] They were playing *Atsiagbekor*. But when he saw me he noticed my talent although I was still a boy. He placed money on my forehead to register his appreciation[8] and admiration for me" (Interview, November 2007). This scenario was indeed an affirmation of the divine prediction and a recognition that had a compelling effect on both Alorwoyie and his uncle.

When the celebrations resumed in the afternoon, his uncle, contrary to Alorwoyie's expectations, asked him to continue his role. Amidst concurrent drumming and dancing from several performing groups emerged Philip Gbeho, who came to where Alorwoyie was lead drumming. He was so impressed that he came and told Alorwoyie's dad that his son should come to the Arts Centre in Accra immediately after he completed middle school. So in 1964 after Alorwoyie finished his middle school education, he left for Accra and started working the next day as an assistant drummer/coach to the master drummer Robert Anani Ayitei,[9] from Adafienu in the Volta region. Alorwoyie's duties included assisting his immediate boss in supervising the performing groups that registered and rehearsed at the Arts Centre, including those formed by schoolchildren.

Like Alorwoyie, both Christopher Ladzekpo and Kobla Ladzekpo have, in my separate interviews with them, recalled Gbeho's leadership role in the performance of indigenous dances during national events, especially around the time that Ghana gained its political independence. Christopher remembers how he was at the Arts Council of Ghana, where there used to be a very dynamic set of activities involving drumming and dancing. These included

> all kinds of groups, and they used to call them amateur groups. One group in particular, Gbeho Research Group, was named after him, the composer of the Ghana national anthem, and the head of the Arts Council. That group performed basically Anlo Ewe dances, reflecting Gbeho's ethnicity, and one would find that group in a lot of very prestigious activities. Even during the independence celebrations in 1957, Gbeho Research Group was one of the groups in the forefront of the celebration. (Interview, July 2007)

I have mentioned elsewhere in this book how Kobla Ladzekpo recalled a performance of the Research Group to welcome Louis Armstrong when the

African American jazz icon visited Ghana. The then youthful Kobla Ladzekpo was dancing.

The Arts Council of Ghana

The discussion in the previous paragraphs has hopefully suggested the role of the Arts Council of Ghana in the promotion of dance drumming as a state cultural institution. In addition to the Gbeho Research Group, C. K. Ladzekpo further recalls the activities of other groups under the auspices of the Arts Centre, as well as the enabling cultural landscape:

> At the Arts Centre, we come to know other groups doing dances from all parts of Ghana. The whole political climate then was an encouragement for us to go back to our indigenous traditions. "Sankofa" [Go back and retrieve it]. It was a very dynamic and a very encouraging time period for us young people. So we picked up the challenge and learned as much as you can from our other neighbors, tribes, [ethnic groups]. Now we had formed all kinds of groups at the Arts Council. One of them that I really liked was the Asiedu Ketete Cultural Troupe. (Interview, July 2007)

Responding to my curiosity to know more about the membership and dances that this group performed, C. K. explained that it was a group of talented musicians from different ethnic groups. Among them was the master drummer Mustafa Dataade, whom C. K. really admires, and although Mustafa is a Ga, "he is not only a Ga. He is a Ghanaian because he knows all the dances." Mustapha was then a true embodiment of a national artist who became versatile by learning to play numerous dances. He is noted to have choreographed stylized dances I observed being taught both at Colorado and University of Toronto during my field research trips.

Christopher Ladzekpo pointed out that it is incredibly revealing to recall the degree of converged skillful artists that formed the Asiedu Keteke Cultural Troupe. They included George Konu, who was the director of the Adzido Pan-African Dance Ensemble based in the U.K. for several years. Although Konu is now retired and in Ghana, he reportedly is still functioning. The late Godwin Agbeli was another key member of the group. Thus, the Arts Centre as a cultural site partly provided the continuity in the foundations on which Agbeli would be drawing later for his work in American colleges, including the University of Florida, Gainesville, as the founding director of the Agbedidi. The list of Asiedu Keteke Cultural Troupe members continues with Gideon Foli Alorwoyie [now Togbe, or a chief]; Emmanuel Tagoe, the famous Ghanaian drummer in the U.K.; Yakobo Addy, who now leads Odada, a group in the New York area; and a lot of other young and energetic people, most of whom are scattered around the world now. It was highly memorable that all these talented artists were in the same group at one time (Interview, July 2007). Also, the Art Centre was a venue that attracted foreign researchers and learners of Ghanaian drumming and dance. In both the notes to his 2005 essay and his 2007 interview with me, David Locke confirms that he took drumming lessons from Godwin Agbeli at the Arts Centre in Accra.

Albert Mawere Opoku and the Ghana National Dance Ensemble

Professor Mawere Opoku is world renowned as an authority in scholarship and performance of African dance. More related to the subject under discussion here, however, is his meritorious contribution as the founding director of the Ghana National Dance Ensemble, which was called the Ghana Dance Company. Founded in 1962 at the order of Dr. Kwame Nkrumah, Ghana's first prime minister and later president, the Ghana Dance Ensemble was established as the performance wing of the Institute of African Studies at the University of Ghana, Legon. Kawbena Nketia, who was also involved in the founding of the Dance Company, co-directed the group with Opoku, but with other defined roles. While Opoku was the artistic director, Nketia was responsible for the administrative needs of the group when he was appointed the director of the Institute of African Studies in 1965.[10] But Nketia's collaboration with Opoku included brainstorming of cultural and creative ideas, resulting in a team effort that phenomenally contributed to the realization of the aspirations, goals, and challenges set before them by Nkrumah. To illustrate the degree of collaboration with which the two friends worked, Foli Alorwoyie informed me that both Opoku and Nketia interviewed him before he became a member of the Ghana Dance Ensemble (Interview, November 2008). But beyond the strength that resides in harnessing the expertise of two great personalities, Opoku and Nketia used their ideological awareness of the inextricably integrated nature of African dance and music as an underpinning impetus for concretizing their collaboration. It is not surprising therefore that Professor Emeritus Kwabena Nketia writes in his *African Art Music*, "This book is dedicated to Professor Albert Mawere Opoku for his distinguished contribution to the performing arts of Ghana."[11]

Opoku's duties as director of the dance ensemble included recruitment of the best drummers and dancers from the various regions of the country.

Traveling to festival sites was a normal occurrence for the identification of prospective members of the group. For example, Beatrice Ladzekpo, Kobla's wife, told me that Opoku spotted her as a talented dancer during a festival, leading to Beatrice later becoming a member of the dance ensemble (Interview, October 2009). Also, Olly Wilson recalled how he enjoyed traveling with the dance ensemble to festivals and other performances when he spent his fellowship at the University of Ghana in the early 1970s (Interview, July 2007). Another task assigned to Opoku was to ensure that the recruited artists shared their ethnic dances with each other with the intent of the construction of the nation through the arts. Here, the authentic cultural custodians were the teachers of the dances to their colleagues in an environment of sharing and exchange of traditional knowledge. The desired ethnic integration resulted in the creative activities and life of the group.[12]

During a panel session on modern African state dance ensembles at SEM 2010 held in Los Angeles, an Africanist wanted to know the source of Nkrumah's inspiration that led to the idea and ultimate formation of the Ghana National Dance Ensemble, one of the ensembles discussed in the session. Geo-culturally, some argued that Nkrumah was influenced by the Soviet Union's Folkloric Dance Company's project, especially given the objectives of (1) uniting various regions of a nation through the performing arts, (2) preserving the rich cultural forms of a nation, (3) showcasing these sublime artistic genres to the whole world through international performance tours, and (4) providing an outlet ostensibly for articulation of subtle political agenda. Furthermore, Eastern European countries were noted for expressing their nationalism through cultural performances during and after the nineteenth century. This ontology is quite convincing, considering that Nkrumah was a founding leader of the Non-Aligned Movement who could have used ideas from both the so-called East and West. Nevertheless, Nkrumah is a well-informed Africanist, and as such, the preceding Soviet Union case evidence, I think, could only serve as a partial model.

A more convincing ontology for the formation of a national dance ensemble resides in the model from the court music traditions of the pre-colonial African ethnic state. This may be called the original, local, national, political, or revitalized model of forming a group that may be compared to the court music practices of the Ashanti or the Dagbon. Thus, the Ghana National Dance Ensemble could perform the Akan *Fontomfrom* court music or a Dagbon *Salima* (praise name dance for the head of state), for example, as a recontextualized or reinvented tradition. But with a shift of focus from the ensemble's local functions to that of increased international, modernizing choreography aimed at contemporary staged performances, and meeting global tastes rather than remaining true to concerns of traditionalism, the previous model may become more convincing. But how did Opoku set the aesthetic tone of the original ensemble?

One of Opoku's duties was to choreograph dances for performance in diverse contexts. Almost all my informants who worked under Opoku describe him as a traditionalist. These consultants maintained that Opoku remained as close as possible to traditional village renditions of Ghanaian dances even as he choreographed them for stage performances. This advocacy for authenticity in African dance as an embodiment of the lives of those who perform them is a hallmark of his scholarship. I have earlier in this book mentioned how he was respected as a leading authority and custodian of his ethnic dances to the extent that he was chosen to train and educate a prospective Asantehene[13] in relevant Akan courtly dance-related culture prior to his enstoolment.[14] For traditionalists and preservationists, Opoku's philosophy of perpetuating indigenous dances with less foreign elements idealizes the true meaning of a national dance ensemble. Accordingly, some do not fully support the contemporary choreographies by Nii Yartey, Opoku's successor, who draws on Western creative ideas in his choreography. Certainly, Nii Yartey appeals to the many so-called progressives and advocates of modernity. For the purpose of this book, however, one may realize that this debate, which I discuss in chapter 3, is actually a ubiquitous conundrum.

Alorwoyie shared an anecdote regarding his experiences working with Opoku about the aftermath of an impressive state performance by the Ghana National Dance Ensemble for General Acheampong, the head of state at the time. Impressed with how well drummers and dancers could perform music from different parts of the country with such a high level of competence and versatility, Acheampong wanted to show his appreciation by granting any feasible request from the ensemble. Alorwoyie remembers that he and his colleagues requested a bus, and when the head of state granted it, Opoku invited Alorwoyie to accompany him as they went to a factory to select a Neoplan bus for the group.

Another defining period in Opoku's career was his move to the United States to be a dance professor at Brockport State University. And although he left the Ghana Dance Ensemble behind, Kwasi Amevuvor (an Ewe drummer and a former member of the Ghana Dance Ensemble) accompanied Opoku to Brockport as the resident teacher of African drumming. Opoku became a facilitator for visits by key artists from his home ensemble, including Nii Yartey, Edna Mensah, and Gideon Alorwoyie. He not only attracted younger Ghanaian artists to North America but also ensured a strong presence of

Ghanaian dance at his university and in the New York area. Further, he was a consultant to administrators of American universities who wanted to introduce African dance into their programs.

I vividly recall Mawere Opoku's return to Ghana in the mid-1980s when I was a student at the University of Legon. He was highly venerated by his former colleagues, dance ensemble members, and students who knew him very well. He remained a consultant to many groups and individuals regarding African dance, and as the saying goes, he never allowed age to be a barrier for him whenever he was inspired by a good performance to dance. In the *JVC & Smithsonian Video Anthology of Music and Dance*, Vol. 2, number 17, one can see Opoku dancing *adowa*, an Akan funeral dance. In the same video, members of the then Ghana Dance Ensemble perform *Fontomfrom* as part of a program that partly valorized Opoku and Ephraim Amu, the father of Ghanaian art music, for their invaluable contributions to the performing arts of Ghana.

Kwabena Nketia and the University of Ghana

Kwabena Nketia, the most eminent African ethnomusicologist in the world, turned 90 in 2011, a milestone that the University of Ghana, the government of Ghana, and many Africanists around the globe marked through a symposium held at the Institute of African Studies, University of Ghana, and a Festschrift based on papers presented at this celebratory event. But while participants from different parts of the world continue to reflect on different aspects of his titanic legacy, I think it is fair in the interest of this book to examine his contribution to the presence of West African drumming in North American universities—whether he acted directly or as a facilitator. I have already discussed Nketia's collaborations with (1) Opoku with regard to the Ghana Dance Ensemble, and (2) Mantle Hood with respect to the inception of West African drumming and dance at UCLA. However, a true appreciation of the influence that the University of Ghana had on the future of West African dance drumming in the American academy is located in the phenomenal foundational work that Nketia did as director of the Institute of African Studies, and of the School of Music, Dance, and Drama, which later became the School of Performing Arts. In actualizing Nkrumah's idea of the need to revitalize the deconstructed African culture in the academy, a reason for which the Institute of African Studies was created, Nketia promoted the scholarly study of the performing arts as an integrated expressive form as idiosyncratic of traditional African practices. While I do not attribute all innovative curricular contents in the performing arts to Nketia, I think it fair to argue that he partly laid the foundations, especially in the domain of the holistic African music.

Also, Nketia advocated a balance between theory and practice, or the scholarly and practical study of the performing arts. In addition to rehearsals and performances of the Ghana Dance Ensemble at the university, different caliber of students took/take drumming and dance courses as program requirements at the University of Ghana. These students may include those pursuing diplomas, masters, or doctorates in African studies—studying in the institute with a concentration in music, or students majoring in music, dance, or drama, who may be working on their diploma, bachelor of arts, bachelor of music, masters, or master of philosophy. Further, students across the board, but excluding students of the School of Performing Arts, may take either African dance or drumming as African studies electives, popularly called "AfroStuds," a requirement necessary to receive a diploma from the University of Ghana. Both Ghanaians and visitors alike can readily notice these visually and sonically conspicuous student activities of dance drumming at the university. These dance and drumming courses to some extent compare with liberal arts electives in the United States, though the constructed underpinning meanings of these course offerings differ.

Since the mid-1960s, past students of the School of Performing Arts or the Institute of African Studies have come to North America with the models from which they have accessed dance drumming at home. William Amoako, Kwasi Aduonum, William Anku, Pascal Younge, Modesto Amegago, Stephen Gbolonyo, Samuel Nyamuame, and others who had taken and/or taught dance drumming in the North American academy have partly drawn on their Legon experiences. The preceding constitutes a wave of exchange in which Africans share their knowledge of dance drumming with American students as they gain new insights from North America. A second process takes place as visiting North American researchers, administrators, or professors interested in West African dance drumming are influenced by or participate in the models available on the Legon campus, and which they may take back after their stay. But what is Nketia's role in this process?

I have in previous chapters discussed the importance of American Africanists—ethnomusicologists, administrators, percussionists, and composers—in the lives of their respective university African dance-drumming ensembles. Most of the preceding Americans came to Ghana, and Kwabena Nketia, in his capacity as the director of the School of Music, Dance, and Drama, and of the Institute of African Studies (1965–79) was a personality

Figure 7.5 Professor Emeritus Albert Maware Opoku, founding artistic director, Ghana Dance Ensemble, University of Ghana. [Photo from Dance Department, School of Performing Arts, University of Ghana]

who drew several prominent Africanists to the University of Ghana. Nketia's international travels as a student, teacher, and leading African scholar provided additional impetus for such dialogues and exchanges. Some visitors spent their fellowships as affiliates to either the school or institute; others whom he taught in the United States came to Ghana to further their studies in African music or to conduct their dissertation fieldwork; and still other notables came to Ghana as visiting professors. While I have already discussed the impact that visits to Ghana by Hood, Wilson, Locke, Hartenberger, and DjeDje made on their careers as ethnomusicologists, Akrofi (2002: 39–41) draws on DjeDje and Carter (1989: 10–13) to give a more comprehensive list of distinguished academics who visited Ghana and were associated with the university and Nketia. These include Maya Angelou (poet), Eileen Southern (musicologist), William Carter (musicologist), and Klaus Wachsmann (ethnomusicologist). Undoubtedly, the founding of African drum and dance ensemble was one of the ideas that some of them took home.

But thanks go to Nkrumah, who encouraged Nketia to promote such visits in order to foster cross-fertilization of ideas among these renowned astute thinkers. Here too, the immanent political landscapes of the 1960s,

Figure 7.6 Emeritus Professor Kwabena Nketia greets the Ghana Dance Ensemble drummers who play *fontomfrom* as he arrives at the Institute of African Studies, University of Ghana, for the conference honoring his legacy. [Photo by George Dor, September 2011]

which favored exchanges between Africans and Americans as well as the atmosphere of African renaissance in Ghana, must be acknowledged. In chapter 1 I suggest the extent to which the Pan-Africanism movement and its attendant heightened identity-related consciousness led to a better reception of African dance among African Americans. Similarly, the civil rights movement of the 1960s coincided with a period of political independence in Africa. These new landscapes provided the impetus for the reconstruction of the African personality, image, and dignity that included the resurrection of indigenous African culture as a field worthy of academic study. And as all these transformations were concurrently taking place with an increased world-mindedness, they led to the inception of world music ensembles in the American academy.

Writing on "Diaspora Studies and Pan-Africanism," St. Clair Drake explicitly provides the inextricable symbiosis between political agency of Pan-Africanists and fortifying of their advocacy in academic and scholarly discourse (Drake 1982: 341–402). Kwame Nkrumah's contributions to discourse on changing the political, economic, and cultural lives of all peoples of African bloodline are well known. Even before becoming Ghana's first prime minister and president, he forcefully advocated for the redemption of the African image from the shackles of colonialism, and for liberating Africans' minds from the vestiges of colonialism after political independence. The reconstruction of African culture was one of his pivotal concerns. In addition to his leadership in pan-African agency through conferences, Nkrumah, as part of this African renaissance agenda, authored and wrote on a set of relevant theories and concepts, of which "African Personality" was key. The tenets of this concept included the need to make Africans aware of the urgency of recognizing and celebrating their worth, capabilities in all fields of life, and the richness of their cultures. One of the nurturing sources of the African Personality concept is African communality, as opposed to Western individualism with its attendant economic and cultural implications. To Nkrumah, the consciousness must be created with a revolutionized synergy that favors heightened awareness. It is then not surprising that state cultural ideology and institutions spearheaded the momentum that the African Personality concept needed. But more relevant to this book is the study of Africa and Africans in the academy, specifically the establishment of the Institute of African Studies at the University of Ghana in 1962. Today, the institute has been named after Kwame Nkrumah to immortalize his legacy, and a Kwame Nkrumah Chair for Pan-Africanism has been established to be filled by world-renowned scholars from across the globe. Yet, Kwabena Nketia's role as the first African director of the institute has also been acknowledged in a variety of ways including the Kwabena Nketia Lecture Hall in the IAS, Legon.

INDIGENOUS INSTITUTIONS, MUSICAL PRACTICES, AND CUSTODIANS OF MUSICAL KNOWLEDGE

My conscience tells me not to limit the discussion of models from Africa/Ghana to cultural and academic institutions of the modern nation-state and selected contemporary Ghanaian intellectuals and/or art administrators, even though their scholarly and artistic enterprises may epitomize reflexive modernity that draws on African traditional cultures. Rather, the true ontology of models relating to West African dance drumming should be inherent in the indigenous social, cultural, and political institutions that support the practices of these very genres. While I mention these institutions briefly in chapter 1, and choose not to discuss them here, I strategically acknowledge the importance of the ingenuous indigenous African musicians who ontologically are responsible for the dance traditions that I have discussed throughout this book. It does not matter whether they are described as "villagers," "locals," or "oral traditionalists." Cosmopolitan African scholars who have not yet had the revelation about the richness of their indigenous knowledge, because these intellectuals have not yet liberated themselves from the shackles of colonial mentality, may out of ignorance even downplay the creative worth of these indigenous artists. To me, they are heroes in terms of the profound musicality they demonstrate and have institutionalized. In this book I praise the virtuosic capabilities of some of the master, mother, and lead drummers who are university ensemble directors. Furthermore, I note in chapter 2 how Christopher Ladzekpo honestly reminded me to thank his ancestors who had established the tradition they taught him. Consistent with this spirit, I celebrate the creativity and the quintessential roles of these simple but creative musicians. They not only trained most of the ensemble directors, but also gave them the knowledge and ability to share with American students. Indeed, they deserve our gratitude.

Yet, a bewildering novelty that frequently torments my imagination and comprehension, though on a good note, is the sublime creativity, inventiveness, innovation, and artistry with which these musicians have originated the intricate design that characterizes the polyrhythmic structure of West African dance drumming. Whenever I listen to good West African dance drumming, of *Atsiagbekor*, *Fontomfrom*, or *Bambaya*, *Bawa*, *Djembe*, for example, I am always reminded to laud the local knowledge of these custodians. Some may consider my preceding valorization as a mere romanticizing or essentializing of my culture after being overwhelmed by patriotic bias. But those familiar with the scholarly works of Jones, Nketia, Nwezi, Euba, Anku, Locke, Koetting, Agawu, and Chernoff on West African dance drumming will view my position as a reaffirmation. Accordingly, those who have been deceived into thinking that the classroom traditions of Western formal education are the only sites for accessing the highest forms of knowledge are being unrealistic. Acknowledging the indigenous knowledge that their custodians disseminate is equally important. It is not tangential to observe that when an informed listener attends a good symphonic concert, he or she may first commend the orchestra and its conductor, but the greatness of Haydn, Mozart, Beethoven, Brahms, Mahler, and Tchaikovsky as composers of the pieces cannot be overlooked.

Unfortunately, the originators of some of the very old West African dance drumming genres are unknown because of the oral tradition within which they operated. Yet, a younger generation of the guardians of West African dance drumming cultures that serve as perpetuating bridges between the originators discussed above and the teachers discussed in the book include Madi Kuyate and Fomoudou Konate (Mande). Further, each time the students of Kobla Ladzekpo and Alfred Ladzekpo give a great performance, they need to remember Kofi Zate Ladzekpo and other master/mother drummers who passed on the art to Kobla and Alfred. Similarly, I know that David Locke, and for that matter the Tufts Kiniwe Group are, though indirectly, grateful to Godwin Agbeli and Gideon Alorwoyie for Anlo Ewe genres, and to Abubakari Lunna for Dagbon dances that they play. And every time the Ole Miss African Drum and Dance Ensemble performs the *borborbor* dance, I should not forget Kodzo Nuatro of Kpandu, who initiated this dance genre.

That said, I once again recall my favorite Ewe metaphor *Detsivivi yehia zikpui* (It is the sumptuous soup that draws the stool). The aesthetic appeal of the musical plants (genres) that local African artists nurtured and planted have now spread globally, bearing aesthetic fruit that people of diverse racial backgrounds now enjoy. Traditional composer-poets and indigenous choreographers also deserve our gratitude, because West African dance drumming is an integrated art that comprises components of singing and dancing in addition to drumming.

I have predicated the entirety of this chapter on the conviction that a continuous interaction is at play between Africans and Americans, specifically in the histories and lives of the various West African dance-drumming ensembles in North American universities. Further, these flows, sharing, and embrace of cultural ideas have intensified within the framework of globalization. Through these trans-cultural and cross-continental interactions, the reinforcement, re-rationalization, and re-validation of the efforts of forebears in the 1960s and 1970s, with respect to West African dance drumming, occur. Thus this book exemplifies connectivity of phenomena that transcend times, spaces, histories, and people—partial defining properties of humanity.

WEST AFRICAN DRUMMING AND DANCE AND ETHNOMUSICOLOGY TODAY

To dilate the extent to which the privileged genre and the subject matter of this book intersect with a body of themes and other interests in ethnomusicology today, one simply has to recall a constellation of themes I have discussed throughout the study. Yet, a legitimate related question is, what are the current themes in our discipline, and through what means does one know them? Naturally, while scanning through the topics in ethnomusicology journals may provide partial clues, a retrospective cataloguing of the themes of the past five annual conferences of the Society for Ethnomusicology (SEM) can also hint at what may be important for ethnomusicologists today. Current seminal publications or specific articles that review our discipline may be helpful in this regard. West African dance drumming belongs to both world music and African music, an area or regional focus of ethnomusicology, though with its global dimensions. Given that "Sound Ecologies" was a theme for SEM 2010 at Los Angeles, this discussion has demonstrated the extent to which West African dance drumming has become a global phenomenon. The relationship between music and dance was the main theme for SEM 2011 at Philadelphia, and the resonance of this book's theme is conspicuous.

The 2011 International Council of Traditional Music (ICTM) held in St John's, Newfoundland, drew participants from more than fifty countries of the world. Participants came from diverse interdisciplinary backgrounds—musicians, dancers, choreographers, choreologists, and ethnomusicologists. My presentation on the teaching of West African dance drumming at York University, Toronto, and the University of Toronto received very positive responses, along with challenging calls from participants to me to consider looking critically at the same presence of the same genre in Australia and Asian countries. Further, the sub-themes for the next ICTM to be held at Shanghai Conservatory of Music in 2013 include research methodologies in choreology and ethnomusicology—thereby consistently accommodating aspects of music and dance.

Since 1966, when Wachsmann[14] coined the term "African musicology," the academic community's attention continues to be drawn to the peculiarities in the challenges of studying African music and the interplay between African music research and that continent's cultural and artistic aspirations and goals. This advocacy is copiously expressed in Wachsmann (1966; 1967; 1969; 1970), Nketia (1970; 1998), Nketia and DjeDje (1984), DjeDje (1992; 2005), DjeDje and Cater (1989), and Euba (2001), among others. As such, locating West African music in ethnomusicology today requires this genre's specific significance to directions in world music and African musicology. I have in this chapter shown the seemingly inextricable connection between scholarship and performance on the African continent, on the one hand, and the same activities as they relate to West African dance drumming in the diaspora, on the other hand. An added dynamic resides in the fact that the

African diaspora is the geo-cultural region and a partial hermeneutic site of this study. As can be seen, this book has covered the absence of the genre during the period of slavery in North America, the presence of West African dance drumming in the academy as a new form of African music in the diaspora, while anticipating a comprehensive research on the ways in which new West African immigrant communities in North African cities are using dance drumming to mediate their diasporic identities.[16] Furthermore, representation of African music (whether pedagogically or intellectually), the construction of meanings into this genre by different groups of people, and several other themes intersect with directions in ethnomusicology today. Certainly, this study has provided insights on under-researched subject matters that are worth exploring in depth in the near future.

POSTSCRIPT

This book reverberates a body of phenomenological truths about traditional African music, and these include West African dance drumming (1) is one of Africa's most compelling expressive art forms, (2) is the most researched subject matter (specifically, its rhythmic structure), (3) was a suppressed genre during the period of slavery in parts of the African diaspora, and (4) is a resurrected genre in the North American academy under the auspices of ethnomusicology and world music. And although the fourth point is the central focus of this book, my awareness and/or partial discussion of the other preceding truths have helped me in shedding light on the main subject matter. Further, the trajectories through which African dance drumming genres have reached other continents of the world are diverse, and this book is a classic evidence of trajectory of ethnomusicology and world music. But what were some of the specifics about this book?

Given that analysis and description of the West African dances that American students learn to perform abound in other literature, this discussion focused on other perspectives—issues, themes, challenges, debates, agency, and directions as they relate to the strong presence and practice of this genre. Conclusions reached in this research stem from the examination of multiple voices that matter in the lives of West African dance drumming in the American academy. Indeed, this genre thrives not only on the agency of ethnomusicologists. As such, the book's methodology paid equal attention to the voices of other instructors (who may not be trained ethnomusicologists), administrators, student participants, and audiences, all of whom provided rich insights that I have shared. Sources of data from which I inductively reached these conclusions include interviews, surveys, participation and observation of concerts and workshops, and visits to selected classes. The preceding is reinforced by my long-term interest and engagement with drumming and dance in the academy, whether as a student, founder and director of an ensemble, or organizer of events concerning the genre. Admittedly, my cultural and historical consciousness as a Ghanaian ethnomusicologist—a teacher of world music and topical courses on the music of Africa and its diaspora in an American university—have reflexively shaped my decision to begin the discussion of the genre from its "absence" during the period of slavery.

Dislocation of African musical practices from their homeland's social and cultural structures and systems, the role of Christianity—the religion of many American Southern slaves—in discontinuing African drumming in the New World, and the slaveholders' prohibition of drums and drumming are engaging illuminations that strategically prepared the reader for the novelty that the current presence of the genre at certain universities provide. Beyond situating the study historically and thus exploring immanent landscapes both linearly and vertically, other dialectical interplays that this discussion has explored include the richness of drawing on multiple and both Western and African interpretive frameworks as deemed appropriate throughout the discussion. Another dialogism involves the continued interactions between Americans/America and Africans/Africa with regard to the perpetuation of the genre.

With reference to instructors and their pedagogical approaches, the study examined and recommends a selective usage of the labels of "master drummer," "mother drummer," and "lead drummer." These designations have semantic nuances that are dictated by the cultural background and enculturation of a particular teacher/director, his/her level of competence, and artistic role during performance.

Whenever possible, the ideal approach to teaching the genre is for an instructor to teach all the three related aspects of the dance drumming—drumming, dancing, and singing, as reflective of its African conception. Every class participant must be led to learn all the three components of the art, and no room should be given to early or premature specialization, assignment, or choice of roles. The mentality that certain students cannot drum, sing, or dance must be discouraged, as student participants are happier when they are all taken through the three aspects of the art. It is understandable if roles are assigned a few weeks before a major performance in order to ensure a good performance in which assigned roles may change from item to item, depending on the capabilities of the students or on how much time has been invested in empowering students to ably execute any of the related roles. Developing oral, aural, and visual approaches to learning West African dance in an experiential atmosphere is desirable.

Related to the subject of performance roles is the ensemble teacher's selection of repertoire that may include roles that are culturally constructed and prescribed as gendered. Some of the African dances taught to students in the American academy are all-female, all-male, or genres in which one gender plays dominant musical roles while the other plays subordinate ones. Certainly, there must be exceptions to the suggestion that students must be taught all aspects of the art; it may sound strange teaching boys to do female puberty dances, especially if the objective of the course is to use dance to teach about an African culture. As such, it may be advisable to ask the boys to do the drumming and leave the dancing to the girls, who are singing and dancing about womanhood and socially constructed femininity. Another dance genre exclusively for men can be learned for the sake of balance, if the ensemble practices multiple genres within a semester. The conflict is compounded in a case whereby an ethnomusicologist studies a female genre and gives instructions, first paying attention to gendered roles, but later relaxing the restrictions. In a co-educational institution, should male students be encouraged to take part in this all-female African ensemble, including dancing? If yes, representation has been compromised; if no, male students are denied the opportunity to participate in what they desire to learn. Teachers should use their discretion and sound judgment in dealing with such conflicts, but compromising some defining aspects of a genre for the sake of re-contextualization and seeking exoneration in theoretical frameworks such as reinvention of tradition will inevitably attract and yield complex hermeneutic conundrums.

Another important consideration regarding directors' selection of genres is their inclination to exclude religious dances from their repertoire. It is important to ensure that one does not violate the separation of religion from the American classroom or academic activities and/or events. Student ensemble participants, and in some cases their parents, would not encourage the faiths of American students being threatened by newer religions. It may be argued that such performances are simply a secularization of religious practices and only the artistic aspects of the music are privileged during performance, and no rituals are performed on stage. However, it is widely believed that African and African-derived religious dances can induce possession to which directors who are not practitioners may have no antidote. And yet, some directors choreograph beautiful dance motives from sacred dances and perform them outside of their original contexts. Furthermore, since the age of the students is normally a determinant in the selection of dances, some directors prefer dances that are athletic in nature. They have been found to be very appealing to both participants and audiences.

In addition to ensuring that all student participants are given the opportunity to learn the three components of the genre, the experienced consultants of this study recommend that instructors must observe reciprocity between drumming and dance in their pedagogical approaches. Students must be guided to understand how specific drum motives instruct the dancer to execute corresponding movements and gestures, and must learn which drum motive or language they must play for a particular dance movement. This is an advantage of teaching the students all three aspects of the art. For, when they are drumming, they know what is required of the dancer or visa versa. This interplay is critical to laying the foundations for students who may eventually become future ensemble directors.

Another theme within the authenticity, representation, and traditionalism/modernity debate involves the question of whether or not African practices of teaching and learning are rigorously retained in the North American academy. There is wisdom in holding on to African approaches of teaching by both African and North American ensemble directors. However, flexibility should allow for the use of some degree of new or Western pedagogical procedures or behaviors that may be deemed central to achieving specific course objectives. Yet, utmost rejection of African traditional models of teaching is untenable. Responses from student surveys do not report African approaches of teaching to be ineffective. I have observed classes in which African teachers' use of their indigenous teaching approaches, with some amount of modification, earned my admiration. Accordingly, when North American Africanists place a premium on Western modes of teaching West African dance drumming, that must be viewed as an alternative pedagogical choice, not necessarily because it is better.

A number of consensus opinions of directors include the following positions. First, practitioners acknowledge the existence of what some have called "the right thing," or "the real thing," relating to authenticity. But while consultants advocate the perpetuation of the "right thing" in the American classroom, they admit that there is no single "right thing," given that stylistic variants of the same dance-drumming genre occur at sub-regional or even town-to-town levels in Africa. Notwithstanding, these stylistic nuances should never validate an anything-goes mentality, because serious teachers expect that what they have imparted to their students will be affirmed by reputable practitioners of the genres in Africa, as well as the students when they have the opportunity to visit Africa. Second, a difference exists between the "village style" and the urbanized, modernized, and contemporary choreographed dances that are meant for other contexts. Although performing West African dance drumming in North America already implies re-contextualization, directors must indicate in their programming whether they are presenting the dances in the traditional "village style" or in re-choreographed renditions. Generally, the study reveals the need for teachers to be flexible in response to the dictates of the contexts within which they work. However, it would be hoped that their choices are informed by their consciousness of the preceding debate.

The option of teaching multiple or limited dances within each semester comes with advantages and disadvantages. Considerations comparably at play include individual teachers' philosophies, knowledge of dances, capabilities, course goals, and the general nature and outcome of survey or in-depth themed courses. In any case, each type of course undergoes a process of stringent scrutiny before an academic institution approves it. Certainly, a great deal of constructed meanings or values must be articulated in the designed course, which in turn is considered a reinforcement of general college goals prior to that course's approval. As such, students and audiences will gain substantial, though most probably different, insights from either a comprehensive study of a single dance or the study of multiple dances in a semester.

Considering that a host of factors informs the varied pedagogical approaches that individual instructors employ in teaching both drumming and dance, conclusions based on overgeneralizations that lump teachers into cultural or academic groups are likely to be inaccurate. Accordingly, the practice of passing general value judgments that celebrate the pedagogical approaches of trained ethnomusicologists over and above those of enculturated African ensemble instructors, for example, is untenable. Evidence from this study has encouraged me to suggest that accounts of world music ensembles published in journals and books must reflect the realities of the competence of other caliber of music teachers in the classrooms and on stage. Undeniably, academic disciplinary training equips cosmopolitan ethnomusicologists with some strengths and classroom tools that other caliber of ensemble directors may not have. On the other hand, enculturated master drummers come into the academic profession with equally unique strengths that they have imbibed from their various cultures.

Conversely, it is unfair to generally underestimate the teaching and performance capabilities of American Africanists who have spent years in Africa and understudied reputable master drummers. Although they may not possess some aspects of African ethnic cultural knowledge that most African dance-drumming teachers do, many have produced students who are also good dance-drumming instructors. In the same way, I contest the prejudices often held by some ethnomusicologists as evidenced in their simplistic binary outsider/insider opposition as a woefully inadequate framework for interpreting today's world music ensembles. Conclusions reached through such frameworks may be logical but not truthful, especially when applied for discourse on themes of representation and authenticity. Multi-layered or multi-dimensional paradigms are more appropriate for such problems, combining considerations of transmission, re-contextualization, appropriation, and/or representation.

This book has explained the nature of processes implicated in the interactions among people at intra-continental, international, and trans-cultural levels that informed the agency associated with the founding and sustenance of the dance-drumming ensembles in North America, noting the prevailing landscapes that favored dialogues, collaborations, study, and practice of the genre. Further, discussion of models from Africa has provided underlying factors that explain the predominance of Ghanaian dances as the repertoire of dance-drumming courses taught in most American universities. Juxtaposing the practices of indigenous Ghanaian dance drumming in North American universities on the one hand, to the same course at the University of Ghana, on the other, one better comprehends the similarities as well as differences in the constructed meanings of the same academic activity.

Impacts of bi-musicality, use of the course as a means of understanding structural elements of African music or theory of music, acquiring pre-compositional resources, deeper understanding of elements of today's percussionists' standard repertoire, developing both individual and team performance skills, or building a future professional career, whether as a teacher, scholar, art administrator, or artist—all are commonalities obtainable in Canada, USA, Ghana, or Mali. Pedagogical approaches and perceptual norms accessible to course participants, as well as aesthetic gratification that both participating students and audiences derive from good performances, are other common and general meanings constructed on West African dance drumming in both North American and African universities.

However, depending on the participant's historical and cultural background and consciousness, the place of practice, and the philosophical underpinnings of dance-drumming courses within a program, individuals may have their personal readings into taking West African dance drumming as a course at the university. Those who participate in the course for the sake of identity-related motivations may include African Americans, with heightened consciousness about their ancestral roots, which may view drums and other African instruments, music, and dance as symbolic or iconic homologies of their distant bloodline. Further, African students studying in the United States or Canada, whether visiting, migrants, or North Americans by birth, may take West African drumming with a sense of ethnic, national, or continental identity, often accentuated by nostalgia. And yet when African students are encouraged to take dance-drumming courses at one of their home universities like the University of Ghana, reasons that support their identity-related motivation may differ from those that inspire their fellow citizens studying abroad. Admittedly, the invocation of ethnic or national identity may be at play here as well. However, ethnic integration, revitalization of African music culture that was deconstructed and suppressed during the period of colonialism and missionary activities, preservation of indigenous practices through performance and collective memories, repackaging of indigenous knowledge forms for the needs of contemporary African communities, and showcasing and marketing African performing arts at the global terrain are convincing factors that inform such a course in Ghana, for example.

On the other hand, American and international students who have no ancestral connections with Africa may participate in the course primarily because of its affective appeal, students' general embrace of multiculturalism, or a desire to satisfy one's creative edge by performing in a variety of world music ensembles within the spirit of world-mindedness, or driven by the worldview that the arts belong to humanity and citizens of the globe. Certainly, advocacy for American students' participation in such a world music ensemble is not intended to diminish the study of local American genres; there is virtue in being patriotic about one's own culture. On the other hand, patriotism that myopically promotes the study of local culture but neglects or rejects courses of global dimension is not a virtue. Luckily, using the ensemble as a site for understanding other domains of African culture is a common motivation to all my student informants. This is a move in the right direction, because most of today's students do not want to live in provincial rigidity. It is then important that this book offers a deeper understanding and appreciation of the importance of multiculturalism, cultural diversity, and world music on our campuses.

We are all products of historical landscapes of our times. Today, West African dance drumming is available as a class and/or ensemble to students studying in North American universities with strong ethnomusicology, world music, and performance studies programs—thanks to the path-finding agency of the key players I have discussed. I have explicitly explored the phenomenal impact that participation in this world music genre can have on students' future individual careers. And yet, it is important that students of these privileged universities take advantage of these opportunities, for the choices students make in terms of courses they take shape their life experiences in significant ways.

My intent in this discussion is not to romanticize instruction in West African dance drumming over other world music ensembles, canonic music courses, or other strengths of universities that may not yet have an African ensemble. As a research consultant for this book has observed, every institution—college, school, or department of music—has its focus, and as such, a particular program may not necessitate the founding of an African drum and dance ensemble. With the kind of awareness that this book provides, students studying in universities without African ensembles can access this experience through multiple ways, including study abroad programs if deemed necessary in realizing their career dreams. In any case, this discussion offers an explanation of the multiple and far-reaching areas with which West African dance drumming can intersect in providing and contributing to an enriched synthesis, cumulative and well-rounded musical training, education, musicianship, and experience.

Admittedly, the predominance of Ghanaian dances and ensemble directors is not happenstance. While Locke has attributed this concentration to the fact that Ghana uses the English language, other factors must explain the absence of dances from other Anglophone West African countries. In retrospect, the foundational efforts of Mantle Hood, Kwabena Nketia, Robert Anani Ayitei, and Robert Bonsu at UCLA, which privileged Ewe and Akan dances, are central to this continuum. Similarly, at Columbia University, Willard Rhodes and Nicholas England, together with Kobla and Alfred Ladzekpo, also focused on Ewe dances. Writing on the "Structural Levels of Rhythm and Form in African Music," Laz Ekwueme, a Nigerian music scholar, notes, "the music of the West Coast does tend to show a more sophisticated structure in rhythm and formal organization . . . in particular Ewe dance rhythms, than the rhythm of probably all other areas of Africa combined" (1975/76: 28). Perhaps this sophistication is a factor that attracted A. M. Jones in the late 1950s, and attracted several other researchers of the dance rhythms of Ghanaian ethnic groups. I have discussed the important roles played by Philip Gbeho, Mawere Opoku, and Kwabena Nketia, who served under the auspices of Ghanaian cultural and academic institutions including the Arts Council, Institute of African Studies, School of Music, Dance, and Drama (now School of Performing Arts), at the University of Ghana. Furthermore, the Ghana Dance Ensemble provided models and prepared some of the future teachers of the genre in the American academy. Also, the academic and cultural environment at the University of Ghana prepared Ghanaians who would later pursue ethnomusicology degrees in American universities while at the same time teaching Ghanaian traditional drumming to American students.

The continuity and rate at which American ethnomusicologists—researchers, composers, and percussionists—have visited Ghana for the conduct of their various dance drumming–related projects is another important factor. Certainly, the stability of Ghana's political climate with its emergent peace necessary for the pursuit of the preceding projects, coupled with the hospitality that my non-Ghanaian informants often acknowledge, cannot be taken for granted. Ghana continues to attract exchange and study-abroad programs, most of which are led by Ghanaian native directors or ethnomusicologists during summer months. In addition, Ghana is one of the countries selected by American federal grant-awarding agencies for short-term international studies, and some recipients do drumming and dance while there. On a different note, a Nigerian ethnomusicologist thought that the number of instruments involved in typical Ewe, Akan, and Ga dance drumming ensembles encourages teamwork. Accordingly, it is aesthetically satisfying for five to seven students to each play a distinct part as they collectively contribute to a polyrhythmic sonic nexus. There are not that many parts in some ethnic dances of the sub-region.

Whether or not one calls it serendipity, I believe this book provides readers with revealing insights that may help them understand Ghana's leadership role in the presence in the North American academy of dance drumming in particular or African music study in general. Additionally, Kwame Nkrumah's leadership role in Pan-Africanism, in both political and cultural spheres, is well known. In this book I have discussed his support for Babatunde Olatunji, the famous Nigerian drummer who became the "cultural ambassador" of Africa in the United States in the 1960s. This book has also acknowledged Nkrumah's African revivalist philosophy and vision that underpinned the establishment of the Institute of African Studies at the University of Ghana, Legon.

A related theme concerns nomenclature of the ensembles in the American academy. Why should they bear the name "African" when they may be learning or performing dances from only a country at a time? The rationale for maintaining this broader geo-cultural name is not to suggest any monolithic African culture. I am convinced that those who named the courses did not intend to engage in unanimism (Agawu 2003: 60) by characterizing African dance-drumming traditions as though they exist without diversity. Rather, course designers are prospectively aware that directors may change hands, and different genres from other countries may be introduced or emphasized by new directors, or the same director may later learn to teach a dance or two from a different African country, while a visit by a director from a sister school to teach dances from another sub-region of the continent may validate the foresight behind this broader name of the ensemble. I have discussed classic examples of the preceding possibilities, as well as two directors collaborating at the same university, each from a different cultural background contributing ethnic dances from Anglophone and Francophone countries.

Hopefully, university administrators will understand the degree of diversity in African music cultures, and the Herculean challenges that confront any ensemble director who may seek to master the numerous dances of even a single modern nation-state. Accordingly, expecting an ensemble director to teach or perform any African dance without him or her spending time and resources prior to adding that dance to the repertoire is a wishful consideration. Although this study has provided a number of cases in terms of the countries of origin of the dances that constitute regular class repertoire, dances from a single country seems to be more common. Other avenues through which a student may participate in dances beyond those offered at their schools include study-abroad programs to other African countries. Dance drumming under such programs can be undertaken under state academic or cultural institutions, or students may be affiliated with national or private cultural centers. Traveling around a country to participate in diverse ethnic dance-drumming activities is very rewarding for the visiting student. Also, summer intercollegiate cultural festivals in America, such as the one Locke organizes that brings together four student ensembles to participate in workshops and performances, are noteworthy and recommended. Yet, for the sake of learning about the culture of other ethnic cultures, students may consider taking other courses in African music available to them.

African American perspectives discussed in the book include divided positions on the suppression of dance drumming during the period of slavery. Although African dance-drumming traditions could not be reinvented for almost a century after Emancipation, most African Americans who consider drums and drumming as symbolic artifacts and heritage practices of their ancestral roots remain thankful for the groundbreaking efforts of Dafora Horton, Katherine Dunham, Pearl Primus, Babatunde Olatunji, and Kofi Ghanaba in popularizing African dance and/or drumming in the United States of America. Some African Americans view drums and drumming as a tool of empowerment, and they often invoke the use of drums during the Stono Rebellion as an archetypal case. UNESCO has advocated for the prevention of the extinction of intangible forms of knowledge in the world; drums in the African American experience is often cited as an unfortunate example. As such, the United Nations organized an exhibition on March 3, 2009, in New York with the theme "Breaking the Silence, Beating the Drum," as part of the International Day of Remembrance of the Victims of Slavery and the Transatlantic Slave Trade. It is therefore rewarding for informed African Americans that West African dance can now be accessed by their children in the academy. Unfortunately, however, the generational gap and the negative media representation of Africa in America seem to account for the lack of participation in West African ensembles by most African American students. Most informants believe that change in this attitude can occur with education.

Sociological and communal dimensions of these university ensembles cannot be overemphasized. The effects of a vibrant West African dance-drumming ensemble on a campus can be transformational with respect to shaping the general multicultural landscape of the university as well as promoting the building of relationships among ensemble members through symbolic interactions. While the existence of a world music ensemble may simply replicate the multicultural demographic aura of particular cities, the West African ensemble contributes toward the process of constructing, nurturing, or intensifying cultural diversity on other campuses located at different regions. Why should "Ole Miss acquires unique drums from Ghana" be considered "Noteworthy News" and "University of Mississippi promotes African drumming" be given prominence in the June 19, 2003, issue of *Black Issues in Higher Education*? I argue that locating the acquisition within the history of drums in the American South provides a novelty and a pointer to a change of landscape in which diversity is being promoted.

As can be seen, this book has relevancy for the larger cultural and academic community that includes students' parents, other aficionados, and general lovers of world music, and although approached from an ethnomusicological perspective, the study targets a broader readership beyond ethnomusicologists. To presume that such a critical world music book should demonstrate theoretical perspectives engaging only to cosmopolitan ethnomusicologists may be regarded as disciplinary dogmatism. I am positive that some readers have found my use of combined Western and African interpretive perspectives equally engaging. Certainly, a world-minded reader will enjoy the parallel between Appadurai's explanation of "ephemeral pleasure" and the more-than-a-century-old Ewe metaphor of "the sumptuous soup pulling the stool."

It is gratifying that the quintessential roles that administrators play in the lives of these ensembles have been acknowledged. I believe such recognition will motivate other administrators who may be considering founding an ensemble in the future, for they will be ensured that their efforts will not be in vain. My informants observed that the most esteemed administrators are those who seek the growth of all ensembles on equal footing. Administrators' support for ensemble directors' professional development and growth, promotion, funding for the ensemble's programs and activities, and attitudes that present the ensemble as significant within the broader program are desirable. Contrarily, it is deplorable when directors metaphorically describe their ensembles as "orphans" because an apathetic administrator has replaced a former supportive one. Most of my informants think it may be over-tasking, if not also unethical, when credit-earning ensemble teaching does not count toward the workload of a faculty member. Also, it is appropriate when universities acquire their own musical instruments to replace those belonging to directors who started their drumming programs.

While the existence of West African dance drumming in some universities will soon be half a century old and even more, the life of this campus ensemble will be four, three, two decades or less in other institutions. No matter the span, I encourage all players/actors to take pride in your various accomplishments. As we take stock of the challenges that may confront our individual ensembles and courses, I remind everybody to explore the multiple and rich perspectives and experiences that this book has collated and shared. They offer useful lessons and suggestions that may chart the course of new directions that may ultimately foster the desired growth in this academic and cultural enterprise of ours. In addition, compelling insights, which abound in the study, may inform the decisions of institutions that may be considering founding a West African dance ensemble in the near future. Furthermore, the larger readership from the local and global academic and cultural communities that have a stake in the presence of West African dance drumming in North American communities will certainly find it gratifying that this book acknowledges, with deep appreciation, the contributions of different key players. Let me close by reiterating the wise Ewe saying *Detsivivi yehea zikpui* (It is the sumptuous soup that draws the stool closer to the table on which it is laid). By implication and extension, it can only be hoped that this study will awaken readers' interest in this genre in one way or another. Let us expect that the ways in which our activities on campus enrich the lives of people and fulfill university goals, liberal arts education ideals, and broader values should continue to provide us with a sustaining gratification of fulfillment.

APPENDIX A

Interviews: Consultants and Field Sites (University Campuses and Conferences)

Consultant/Informant	Consultant's Institution	Interview Sites	Date/Event
David Locke	Tufts University	Melford, MA	July 2007
Olly Wilson	University of California	Berkeley	July 2007
Christopher Ladzekpo	University of California	Berkeley	July 2007
Jacqueline DjeDje	University of California	Los Angeles	July 2007
Ama Oforiwaa Aduonum	Southern Illinois (Normal)	Columbus, OH	SEM 2007
James Burns	Binghamton University	Columbus, OH	SEM 2007
Samuel E. Nyamuame	Wesleyan University	Middletown, CT	December 2007
Eric Charry	Wesleyan University	Middletown, CT	December 2007
Damascus Kafumbe	Florida State University	Tallahassee	March 2008
Frank Gunderson	Florida State University	Tallahassee	March 2008
Gideon Alorwoyie	North Texas University	Middletown, CT	SEM 2008
Kobla Ladzekpo	University of California	Los Angeles	October 2009
Kwasi Ampene	University of Colorado	Boulder	November 2009
Kwasi Dunyo	York University/University of Toronto	Toronto	January 2010
Robert Simms	York University	Toronto	January 2010
Anna Melnikoff	York University	Toronto	January 2010
Modesto Amegago	York University	Toronto	January 2010
Russell Hartenberger	University of Toronto	Toronto	January 2010
Patricia Tang	MIT	Los Angeles	SEM 2010
Ricky Burkhead	University of Mississippi	Oxford [MS]	May 2011

APPENDIX B

A Survey for Student Members of Ensembles

Teaching, Learning, Performance, and Reception of West African Drumming and Dance in North American Universities: An Ethnomusicological Perspective

1) a) I am/was a female member of a college/university African drum-dance ensemble.
   b) I am/was a male member of a college/university African drum-dance ensemble.

2) Did you learn about this ensemble before enrolling at your ensemble's institution?
   a) Yes
   b) No

3) How did you first learn about this ensemble prior to joining it?
   a) From a friend
   b) Invitation from the ensemble's director
   c) Attendance of the ensemble's performance
   d) From university/college course catalog
   e) Other (please state)_____

4) Is African drumming and dance a credit earning activity in your institution?
   a) Yes
   b) No

5) What best describes your foremost motivation for joining the ensemble?
   a) To earn academic credit(s)
   b) To enrich my individual musical/artistic skills
   c) Just for fun
   d) To learn about another culture
   e) To sharpen my group and team skills

6) Presuming that all the preceding reasons (in No. 5) account for your decision to enroll in the ensemble, kindly match the numbers (5 to 1) with the above reasons in order of their importance to you. Please match the number 5 with the most important factor, and 1 with the least.

   Reasons   Number
   a) _____   _____
   b) _____   _____
   c) _____   _____
   d) _____   _____
   e) _____   _____

7) How long were you an active member of this ensemble?
   a) 1 semester
   b) 2 semesters
   c) 3 semesters
   d) 4 semesters
   e) 5 and more than 5 semesters

8) How will you describe your main artistic role in the ensemble?
   a) Drummer
   b) Dancer
   c) Singer
   d) Other percussionist

9) Did you play any administrative or organizational role in the ensemble?
   a) Secretary
   b) Disciplinarian
   c) Costume supervisor
   d) Instruments monitor
   e) Other (please name)_____

10) Did your artistic role in the ensemble change over time? If yes, please state the roles.
(For example, drummer to dancer)
_____

11) Which reason mainly sustained your interest and continued membership of the ensemble beyond a semester?
   a) Joy after a successful performance
   b) Joy for promoting multiculturalism and cultural life on campus
   c) Becoming very popular on campus
   d) The friendly nature of ensemble director and other members of the group
   e) Winning recognition for your school beyond campus and state
   f) Not applicable

12) If you took African drumming as a credit-earning course, was performance a course requirement?
   a) Yes
   b) No

13) How many times did you participate in a major performance as a member of the ensemble?
   a) 1 to 4
   b) 5 to 8
   c) 9 to 12
   d) 13 to 16
   e) more than 16 times

14) Please indicate which of these contexts do not apply to the performances in which you participated.
   a) Concert on campus
   b) Concert off-campus but in the city of your institution
   c) Other functions on campus
   d) Churches in the city of your ensemble
   e) Other schools in your city
   f) Festivals in your city but off-campus

15) Outreach performances of your group beyond campus did not include_____
    a) international dance festivals
    b) out-of-state/regional events
    c) symposia and conferences
    d) national celebrations

16) Did the ensemble sing all their songs in African languages?
    a) Yes
    b) No

17) Which approach did your director use most in teaching of songs?
    a) Completely rote
    b) Rote and written scores
    c) Mainly rote but song texts were written out as guidance
    d) Songs and texts were tape recorded and distributed to students

18) Was your director's approach completely new to you?
    a) Yes
    b) No

19) Would you consider the approach more African than Western?
    a) Yes
    b) No

20) Would you consider this approach a setback to your normal learning procedures?
    a) Yes
    b) No

21) Would you consider the approach of learning songs an enhancement of your pedagogical procedures?
    a) Yes
    b) No

22) Would you consider using the same approach should you become a director in the near future?
    a) Yes
    b) No

23) Please show your preference by selecting one of the following considerations in teaching West African drumming:
   a) African dance drumming must be taught and learned strictly according to the dictates of its indigenous practices for the sake of authenticity.
   b) African dance drumming must be taught by using pedagogical approaches with which students are already familiar.
   c) African dance drumming must be taught from indigenous African perspectives with mild modifications necessary for new contexts.
   d) Excessive concern for tradition must give way to the teacher's sensitivity to modernity.

24) As a youth who is at home with popular culture and its attendant dances, what best describes your feelings when doing traditional African dances?
   a) Ashamed
   b) Connected to nature
   c) Connected to another cultural community
   d) "Jungle" life
   e) Connected to the older generation

25) Did your director use African mnemonic devices (such as utterances that simulated the sound of drum rhythms or motives) in teaching drumming?
   a) Yes
   b) No

26) If yes and you are/were a drummer, how did these devices aid your mastery of the rhythms?
   a) Significantly
   b) To a large degree
   c) A little bit
   d) Not at all

27) Did your director sometimes delegate the teaching of some aspects of the ensemble to members?
   a) Yes
   b) No

28) If yes, then, did you consider that as effective in some ways?
   a) Yes
   b) No

29) If your answer to question 27 was yes, did you think that it undermined the control and authority of the director?
   a) Yes
   b) No

30) If your answer to question 27 was no, do you think that it could have enhanced the competence, confidence, and the level of trust in the ensemble?
   a) Yes
   b) No
   c) It would have made no difference

31) Are all the dances of your ensemble chosen from a single sub-Saharan African country?
   a) Yes
   b) No

32) If yes, which country?
   a) Ghana
   b) Senegal
   c) Nigeria
   d) Mali
   e) Other (Please state the name of country) _____

33) Please provide further information on the origin of the dances.
   a) A single ethnic group from the same country
   b) Multiple ethnic groups from the same country
   c) A single ethnic group from different countries
   d) Multiple ethnic groups from different countries

34) If applicable to your group, how best would you describe learning to sing songs in different ethnic languages?
   a) Challenging
   b) A novelty
   c) Too difficult

d) Fun
e) Easy to learn

35) Has your group had international performances in which you participated?
    a) Yes
    b) No

36) If yes, please list the country or countries.
    _____

37) Did you notice any difference(s) in the receptivity (responses) of international audiences from that of local audiences that attended your performances?
    a) Yes
    b) No
    c) Not really

38) Did your director sometimes modify the choreography, teach or select specific songs to match the needs of specific performance contexts?
    a) Yes
    b) No

39) Indicate the type of outreach activities in which your group has previously engaged.
    a) Workshops for County Middle and High Schools
    b) Teaching schools dances to be performed during their own concerts
    c) Joint performances with Middle and High Schools that your group's director had worked with
    d) Educational performances during Black History Month, festivals, and other celebrations

40) What do you consider the most common membership trend in your institution's ensembles?
    a) Belong to only one ensemble (jazz, African drum-dance ensemble, gamelan)
    b) Combine African drum-dance with jazz
    c) Combine African drum-dance with gamelan
    d) Combine steel band with African drum-dance
    e) It varies from time to time and from student to student

41) What percentage of your ensemble's percussionists are music majors?
   a) 1%–19%
   b) 20%–29%
   c) 30%–49%
   d) 50%–70%

42) What percentage of your ensemble's dancers are dance majors?
   a) 1%–19%
   b) 20%–29%
   c) 30%–49%
   d) 50%–70%

43) In order to know that administrators really support your group, arrange these activities in order of importance to you and which you may want them to do as much as possible. Please match the number 6 with the most important factor, and 1 with the least.
   a) Help in acquiring more or new musical instruments every five years.
   b) Help in acquiring new costumes every two-three years
   c) Attend concerts regularly
   d) Send congratulatory e-mails to members of the ensemble after an outstanding performance
   e) Help organize a reception for ensemble members at the end of every two or three years
   f) Help the ensemble embark on a recording project

Activities	Number
a) _____	_____
b) _____	_____
c) _____	_____
d) _____	_____
e) _____	_____
f) _____	_____

44) As in question 43, arrange the following motivational behaviors/moments/activities in the order of importance to you as a member of your ensemble. Please match the number 6 with the most important factor, and 1 with the least.
   a) Self-awareness of a well-executed performance by your group
   b) Wearing of gorgeous costumes during performance

c) Being your individual best during a specific performance
d) A long applause from a seated audience after every item
e) A standing ovation after the final item
f) A positive post-concert story in a popular newspaper

Moments	Number
a) ____	____
b) ____	____
c) ____	____
d) ____	____
e) ____	____
f) ____	____

45) What percentage would you assign the following societal blocks of your community that constitute the aficionados of your local concerts?

    a) Students of your institutions----------------%
    b) Students from other institutions------------%
    c) Staff/faculty from institutions--------------%
    d) People from the city community-----------%
    e) Followers from the county and state-------%
    f) Adults--%
    g) Youth--%

46) Do you think your membership of the ensemble affects your academic performance in other areas?
    a) Yes
    b) No

47) Showing your opinion on why African drum and dance should be encouraged in American universities, arrange the following reasons in order of importance. Place the number 6 against the most important reason and 1, the least important consideration.
    a) African drumming and dancing is a multicultural activity in which we acknowledge the importance of the plurality of cultures, and how such knowledge and participation can broaden our cultural and academic horizons.

b) African drumming and dancing provide insights necessary for a better understanding and appreciation of some aspects the music of the African diaspora, African American music, for example.
c) African drumming and dance enhance the bi-musicality of the American (music) student as Mantle Hood had advocated.
d) In this age of globalization, it is important to learn to perform any kind of music genre from any part of the world, including West Africa.
e) Cultural life on campuses must be enhanced through the performance of diverse musical forms.
f) African drumming and dance is part of humanity's expressive art forms to which anybody may instinctively be aesthetically drawn.

Consideration	Number
a) ___	___
b ___	___
c) ___	___
d) ___	___
e) ___	___
f) ___	___

48) What best describes your desires after participating in your African drum-dance ensemble?
   a) Would like to travel to Africa to understudy a traditional master drummer for a semester.
   b) Would like to travel to Africa on a short-term study-abroad program that will deepen your contextual understanding of African drumming and dance.
   c) Would like to work with an arts agency through which you could help promote the visits of African national dance troupes to America.
   d) Your membership of an African drum-dance ensemble has provided you with all that you need.

49) Do you think that one's ethnic and/or racial background influences one's level of mastery of and affect for African drumming and dance (movement)?
   a) Yes
   b) No

50) Should a book be written on your institution's ensemble, which areas would you like to see emphasized? Please arrange in your order of importance. Scale from 6–1 to represent the most to least important theme.
   a) Effect of the ensemble on the individual student-participant
   b) Ensemble's effect on the cultural life of the university's immediate community
   c) A brief history of West African dance drumming in the USA
   d) Pedagogical approaches and how they relate to issues of authenticity and cultural transmission within modern contexts
   e) Philosophical underpinnings of the promotion of African drumming dance in American universities
   f) Effects that field research on African rhythm have on the practice of West African dance drumming in American universities

Consideration	Number
a) ___	___
b ___	___
c) ___	___
d) ___	___
e) ___	___
f) ___	___

NOTES

INTRODUCTION

1. Under Willard Rhodes (Kobla Ladzekpo interview, November 2009; Charry 2005: 13).

2. Wesleyan University at Middletown, CT.

3. See table in chapter 2 on higher academic institutions in North America that have West African dance drumming ensembles and/or give instructions in the genre.

4. Patricia Tang and Daniel Reed were presenters; Ruth Stone and Kay Shelemay responded as discussants.

5. Akin Euba partly popularized his concept of "African Pianism" and other theories during the symposia and festivals he organized. See Omojola and Dor 2005 on Euba.

6. Seachrist (2003) on Halim El-Dabh.

7. Kimberlin and Euba (2005) on "African Pianism: Keyboard Music of Africa and the African Diaspora."

8. Chapman Nyaho (2009) on the piano music of Africa and the African diaspora.

9. Omojola (2009) on Fela Sowande.

10. My participation in the 12th Annual Conference of the Association of Ghana Methodist Church Choirs in North America in May 2010 as the guest of honor and the sole adjudicator provided revealing insights that have engaged my attention. I have already presented a conference paper on this event and will soon be publishing an article on it.

11. By 2011 when this book was being written.

12. Teaching multiple dances within a semester is the dance ensemble model and most common practice among the ensembles studied.

13. David Locke is the key advocate for teaching fewer dances aimed at promoting a more comprehensive study of a dance and for an ethnomusicologist's focused research to reinforce his teaching.

14. A metaphor contains two complementary ideas. The source domain is the idea used to facilitate the understanding of the other idea, which is the target domain. Hence, characteristics of a plant become the source domain used to enhance cognition of similar tendencies in a musical genre, the target domain.

15. Landscapes discussed in chapters 1, 2, and 6.

16. Various agencies explored in chapters 3, 4, 5, and 7.

17. As noted in chapter 6.

18. 12th Annual Conference of the Association of Ghana Methodist Church Choirs (North America).

19. At SEAN Regional Conference of African Studies held at the University of Florida, Gainesville.

20. At AMNA (Africa Meets North America) Symposium held at UCLA in October 2009.

21. In a speech at Lara Olatunje's graduation dinner. Lara was a former founding member of Ole Miss African Drum-Dance Ensemble.

CHAPTER 1

1. See also Nketia 1963; Olatunje 2005.

2. This factor of reinforcement is an important point to consider even when discussing Africanisms in cultures of the African diaspora.

3. From UN Web Services Section/Department of Public Information, United Nations.

4. See Levine (1982); Holloway (2005).

5. See George Shepperson's essay on "African Diaspora: Concept and Context," in Harris (1982).

6. I attended such Ghanaian churches in America sporadically between 1998 and 2010.

7. This Crummell dictum is from his "English Language in Liberia."

8. *Atumpan* implies a set of two drums and I believe the author does not imply four pieces of drums.

9. Some use "hooked" instead of "curved" to describe the drumsticks used in playing the atumpan.

10. Nketia (1963) explains the symbolism of these Akan drums.

11. Arom 1991 discusses a body of such dicta.

CHAPTER 2

1. Though called Gamelan Room because of Mantle Hood's first world music ensemble, it is used by other world music ensembles.

2. The tall Anlo Ewe master-drum.

3. These graduates include Dr. Asiamah and Dr. Asante-Darkwa, my professors at the University of Ghana, Legon.

4. "All" here refers to the major Ghanaian ethnic dance-drumming genres that the national ensemble performed.

5. Diane Thram is the editor of the *Journal of the International Library of African Music*.

6. Lunga is the tension and hourglass-shaped drum, which is also used as a speech surrogate. The same drum is called dundun (Yoruba), *donno* (Akan), and *dondo* (Ewe).

7. See also Locke/Titon (2009: 93–124). The citation above is from the *Shorter Version*.

8. The Agbekor Society performed during SEM's 50th Anniversary, held in Atlanta in 2005. The African Music Section of SEM organized the performance.

9. Professor Cliff Ochs and his wife Lucile McCook, both of the department of biology, and Professor Gerald Buskes of the mathematics department and his spouse Laura Boughton comprised the team that went to Ghana with me.

10. Professor Steve Brown briefly served as associate dean of the College of Liberal Arts before relocating.

11. Diedra Jackson was then working with University Media Services, but now is a lecturer at the University of Mississippi's Meek College of Journalism.

CHAPTER 3

1. Besides drumming, *no* or mother is used in Ewe creative conception to label the generative source of songs as well. As such, a composer-poet is a heno, with *he* or *ha* meaning song. (See Dor 2001: 67–70).

2. The discussion of such musical roles abounds in the works of Nketia, Jones, Arom Pantaleoni, Anku, Agawu, Chernoff, and Locke.

3. Nana Opoku Ware V.

4. A building since the Nkrumah regime having several governmental offices near the modern Accra Conference Centre.

5. Professor Opoku was a world-renowned authority in African dance who taught mostly at the University of Ghana, and partly at Brockport State University.

6. The informant did not give the real name of Opoku's sister.

7. Perhaps for ethical reasons, Locke withheld the name of this participant.

8. Dor (2004) provides insights on the concept of communal creativity.

9. David Locke's preferred phrases that replace the so-called "literate" and "non-literate."

10. The three co-chairs of the African Music Section of SEM in 2010 were George Dor, Daniel Reed, and David Locke.

11. Hometown of the Ladzekpos.

12. Hometown of Alorwoyie.

13. *Zigi* is a Northern Ewe social dance. See Agawu (1995: 67, 133–138).

14. Agawu (2003) explicitly illuminates and contests this practice of using data from an African ethnic cultural practice to suggest its applicability to the entire continent.

CHAPTER 4

1. Question 5 of the survey.

CHAPTER 5

1. This instrument was still in perfect shape in 2009 when I gave a paper on this book project at Africa Meets North America: Music Dialogue Project symposium, held at UCLA.

2. This grant has enabled world music programs ca. 2006–2010, and probably beyond.

CHAPTER 6

1. I rode with Kwasi Ampene, who also was a graduate student at Pitt and UWV alum, to these concerts.
2. English-speaking regions.

CHAPTER 7

1. This quotation is from Azagonǫ's website.
2. Although John Chernoff did not go to Wesleyan, he participated in Abraham Adzinya's Wesleyan African Ensemble.
3. Although Willie Anku is a Ghanaian, it was his continuous engagement with teaching West African drumming that led to his graduate theses.
4. Names of these colleges are from the center's website.
5. I said "official" because a few have contested his authorship of the anthem.
6. Both Kobla and Christopher Ladzekpo have affirmed Husunu Adonu as one of the greatest Anlo Ewe master drummers of his time. Sadly, however, he died an untimely death. Zadonu, the name of Kobla's Los Angeles African dance ensemble, is an acronym from his father's and brother's names.
7. If 1961 was the correct date of Alorwoyie's narrative, then Husunu Adonu was likely performing with a local group from Anyako prior to becoming the master drummer of the Ghana National Dance Ensemble, which was formed in 1962.
8. See Dor (2004: 32) for registering of appreciation during performance.
9. This master drummer would later leave for UCLA as a founding African drum instructor.
10. See Akrofi (2002: 33–36).
11. The dedication has the photo of Opoku as well.
12. Resonates with the symbolic interactionism among performers discussed earlier in this book.
13. Paramount King of the Ashanti Kingdom.
14. Interview with Kobla Ladzekpo, October 2009.
15. See DjeDje (2005: 267) for detailed information on "African Musicology."
16. The mediation of diasporic identities through West African dance drumming among immigrants in Canada is the thematic focus of Friesen (2009), an Indiana University masters thesis.

GLOSSARY

Adowa   Originally a funeral dance of the Akan ethnic group of Ghana.

Adzogbo   A war dance of the F<u>o</u>n people of Benin (formerly Dahomey). Men still use it to demonstrate their military and spiritual prowess.

Afiadenyigba   An Anlo Ewe city in the Volta region of Ghana, a few miles south of the Accra-Lome road. It is noted for its sub-regional styles of dance drumming and gifted drummers, including Gideon Alorwoyie.

African diaspora   Descendants of Africans coexisting as large recognizable ethnic groups outside Africa—located in the Americas, the Caribbean, Europe, and parts of Asia.

Africanism   The survival of African cultural elements in the heritages—music, religion and worldview, dance, language, philosophy and ethos, as well as behavioral mannerisms—of diasporic Africans after centuries of cultural change and assimilation in the New World.

Africanist   A scholar who specializes in the study of Africa and Africans, and also how they intersect with the rest of the world.

Afrostuds   A popular label for African studies courses that a student pursuing a bachelors degree at the University of Ghana must take and pass prior to receiving a diploma.

Agahu   A social dance originated by the Egun of Benin, and later spread to parts of Nigeria and Eweland through fishermen. As such, song texts of this genre are a mix of Egun, Yoruba, Ewe, French, and English languages.

Agbadza   The most popular inclusive recreational dance of the Anlo Ewe, believed to have been derived from an old war dance genre. The Anlo also perform variants of *Agbadza* including *Akpoka* and *Ageshi*, differentiated by tempo or characteristic drum and dance motives.

Agbedidi   [Ewe] Lit., longevity. Name that Godwin Agbeli gave to his University of Florida African dance drumming ensemble when he directed it.

GLOSSARY

Agbekor A stylized choreographed war dance of the Anlo Ewe that articulates their invincibility. Agbekor songs, dance movements, and drum languages are encoded texts of local militarism.

agency A term used in sociology to imply a deliberate action taken by an individual or group of individuals aimed at bringing about social change. Opposite of things attributed to nature and happenstance.

agoro Akan [Twi] word for "play." After a groovy musical performance the Akans can say, *agoro ye de*, meaning the play or performance was "sweet."

Akan The predominant ethnic group of Ghana, consisting of a confederacy of subcultural groups including Ashanti, Fante, Akwapim, Kwawu, Denkyira, Nzema, Brong, and Ahafo.

Amadinda A twelve-keyed xylophone played in Uganda. Four instrumentalists may play on a single instrument.

Anloga The paramount city of the Anlo Ewe, where Hogbetsotso, the festival that commemorates the Anlo Ewe migration, is also held.

Anyako Name of an Anlo city famous for lagoon and sea fishing. Musically, it is the home of the Ladzekpos, and of Hesino Vinoko Jeremiah Akpalu, the great Anlo composer-poet-singer.

Asantehene The King of the Asante kingdom, the highest political figure of the hierarchical political system. He rules from the Manhyia Palace in Kumasi.

atenteben The smallest of a family of Akan flutes. Made from a bamboo tube, it has been revitalized and redesigned by Ephraim Amu for use in the academy. Amu constructed the *atenteben* in Bflat as a transposing instrument like the clarinet; however, a C version also exists. They may be used to play dirges during funerals, or pieces composed for them.

Atrikpui Believed to be one of the oldest Anlo Ewe war dances.

Atsiagbekor The same as *agbekor*, the Anlo Ewe war dance. The prefix, *atsia*, which means style, emphasizes the showy, stylized character of the dance.

Atsimewu Longest or tallest Anlo drum, used as the master drum in *Atsiagbekor, Gahu, Gadzo*, and other genres.

Atumpan A set of two large carved Akan drums tuned about a fifth apart and always played together. They feature prominently in some Akan dances, and as speech surrogates (talking drums) used in conveying simulated verbal texts, depending on specific contexts.

Azaguno A recognized Ewe drummer. Literally, mother drummer, but also may be applied to master or lead drummer.

Baaksimba A dance-drumming genre of the Baganda of Uganda.

286 GLOSSARY

balafon A Mande xylophone used together with or in the place of the *kora* by *jalolu* (bards). Also called *bala*, it has wooded slats as keys that are laid over gourd resonators and stuck by beaters.

"ballet style" Modernized and choreographed African dances intended for stage performances for urban, national, and international target audiences.

Bambaya Also the name of a Guinean city, *Bambaya* is the name of a dance-drumming genre performed by the Dagbamba of the Northern region of Ghana. Since the first *Bambaya* performance was allegedly done after a heavy rainfall, dancers behave as though they are avoiding splashing collected water.

Bata A double-headed, hourglass-shaped Yoruba drum with one playing end of the pseudo conical shape bigger than the other. Since the Oyo king Shango's reign, it has been inextricably linked with Lukumi or Santeria religious practices and court music.

Bawa An athletic dance of the Lobi of northeastern Ghana. Male dancers hold castanets with their left hands, which they play in unison to activate the main pulse of the dance music provided on xylophones. The high level of activity of this dance is distributed over the entire body with vigorous movements in dancers' limbs and torsos.

Borborbor An intercultural traditional popular music genre of the Ghanaian Ewe, which combines hymn-like songs, typical traditional African dance-drumming procedures, and features from military music.

Cabildos African ethnic associations formed in Cuba in the late sixteenth century under the auspices of the Catholic Church. The associations helped perpetuate ethnic identity, solidarity, and communality in the New World through performances of African dances, music, and practice of other expressive cultural forms.

Candomble An African-derived religion practiced mainly by blacks in Brazil.

Chopi An ethnic group in Mozambique.

conditionalities Austerity measures imposed by aid-granting agencies or organizations on their underprivileged beneficiaries.

Congo Square An open ground in American Southern cities on which slaves used to meet and interact through music, dance, and other cultural performances. New Orleans' Congo Square has been the most documented.

Dagara An ethnic group in Northern Ghana and Burkina Faso. Also called Dagaaba, Dagarti, Dagara, and Dagao, these people speak the Gagare language and are famous for their dynamic xylophone traditions.

Dagbamba The people of the Dagbon kingdom in northern Ghana. They are also called the Dagomba.
Dagbon Name of a northern Ghanaian ethnic kingdom.
Damba takai A Dagbamba royal dance for kings and princes normally performed during the Damba festival. The drum ensemble comprises a team of *lunga* and *gung-gong* drummers. Dancers swirl their smocks and clash iron rods.
dance drumming Drumming that involves dancing or total performance including singing. While not all drumming in Africa are intended for dancing, dance drumming is not about drumming alone.
detsivivi "Delicious soup," used metaphorically for the magnetizing force from anything that may be appealing.
djembe A Mande single-headed, carved hand drum that is widespread in the whole of Africa and the world.
Doagbe Name of the cultural center that Godwin Agbeli founded at Kopeyia, his hometown, before his untimely death.
donno Akan name and version of the hourglass-shaped, double-headed tension drum.
drum circle(s) An American development from the 1970s of hand drumming without dance (movement), in which people from diverse racial backgrounds come together with different types of drums to engage in collective performance to cultivate a sense of world peace and harmony. Drumming is not polyrhythmic.
dùndún Yoruba name and version of double-headed, hourglass-shaped tension and their talking drum.
enculturation Gradual process of imbibing culture throughout one's life span.
enstoolment The social and cultural processes of making a chief or king.
Ethiopianism A Rastafarian concept that views the Ethiopian empire as a source of inspiration for the liberation of black people, since Ethiopia has not really been colonized and has had a different history of civilization.
Ewe A major West African ethnic group found in southern Benin, Togo, and Ghana.
fefe Ewe word for the noun "play," which may be contextually applied to a musical performance.
Fontomfrom An Akan court dance-drumming ensemble with huge drums including two *boma* and *atumpan*. The size of the instruments and the ensemble originally were emblems of power.
Francophone French-speaking, referring to modern nation-states that are former French colonies.

Fulbe   An ethnic group found in Gambia.

Fume-fume   A contemporary Ghanaian dance-drumming genre believed to have been created by Mustapha Dataade in the late 1950s.

Ga   An ethnic group in southeastern Ghana where Accra is located.

Gahu   An Anlo Ewe social (courtship) dance appropriated from Benin and Nigeria. A domesticated Anlo version of *agahu*.

Gamelan   Indonesian equivalent of "ensemble" or "orchestra," used for the specific name of their orchestra of gong chimes or tuned metallophones, with a flute, a few drums and stringed instruments, and occasional voices.

goje   A one-stringed bowed fiddle widely distributed in West Africa, prominently among the Dagbamba, Fulbe, and the Hausa.

Gota   An Anlo Ewe courtship dance that encourages couple dancing. The lead drummer plays cues on the *sogo* to signal the entry, intensified dancing, closure, and exit of each pair of dancers.

griot(s)   A general term introduced by French travelers in the sixteenth century to designate various West African bards found among ethnic groups, including *jalolu* (Mande), *lunsi* (Dagbon), *gewel* (Fulbe), and *marok'a* (Hausa).

Guinea Coast   The geographical region of present-day Ivory Coast, Ghana, Togo, Benin, and Nigeria, a source of slaves in the transatlantic trade, but also famous for vibrant and heavy dance-drumming ensembles and genres.

gung-gong   A Dagbamba double-headed, barrel-shaped bass drum with a snare on each head, played with a curved stick.

gyile   Xylophones of the Sisala, Dagara, and Lobi of northern Ghana.

ha   Ewe word for song, peer mate, and group. The selected meaning depends on the spoken tonal band and the context in a sentence.

habobo   [Ewe] Lit., organized musical or social group or association, with well-defined structures and roles.

Hausa   A large ethnic group predominantly located in Northern Nigeria, who are also found in other countries including northern Ghana.

Heno   A competent lead singer with a substantial mastery of a body repertoire of songs of his specialized genre. *Heno* is at times used interchangeably with *hesino*, although there are subtle semantic nuances between the two.

Hesino   Distinguished, prolific composer-poet, an epitome of multiple artistry who sings his own songs and earns the recognition of the Anlo as an authoritative custodian of Ewe knowledge.

Hogbetsotso A historical and socio-political festival observed by the Anlo Ewe of Ghana in commemoration of their migration westward from Notsie in present-day Togo. Anloga, the paramount city of the Anlo, is the site for the festival that involves a host of symbolic cultural performances and reenactment.

homeland The original place or ancestral home of dispersed people in the diaspora. This geo-cultural space lives in the collective memories, consciousness, and imaginations of migrants who now live in the New World. For example, Africa is the homeland for African Americans.

Jali A Mande professional bard who is a music and speech artisan, verbal artist, historian, counselor to royalty, entertainer, and guardian of indigenous knowledge.

Kenka A recreational dance of the Anlo Ewe in which the *bomba*, a large barrel-shaped hand drum, features prominently together with the *atsimewu* and other Anlo instruments.

kente An exquisite multicolored Ghanaian cloth that unequivocally epitomizes the classiest of Africans' sublime artistic expressions. This beautiful traditionally woven bodywear is imbued with symbolic cultural and political codes.

Keta A coastal Anlo Ewe town famous for maritime trade with European merchants especially between the sixteenth and nineteenth centuries; sea and lagoon fishing; a major trading center and district administrative town of the Volta region of Ghana.

Kete An Akan court dance consisting of suites often performed during funerals the royalty may attend. Shells of *kete* drums are covered with red and black multicolored cloths, the regular mourning colors of the Akan.

kora A twenty-one-stringed harp-lute often played by Mande *jalolu* to accompany their verbal art. It is now used in popular music and performed by virtuosic expatriate instrumentalists living in the Americas and Europe.

Kpanlogo Main social dance of the urban Ga, the indigenous citizens of Accra, Ghana's capital. Dance movements are concentrated at the waist, and songs are on topical themes including love, food, and politics.

Kpatsa The most popular social dance of the Ga-Adamgbe of southern Ghana.

lunga Dagbamba hourglass-shaped, double-headed tension drum used by the *lunsi*, verbal artists, as their lead instrument and a speech surrogate.

Mande A cluster of culturally related ethnic groups in Mali, Guinea, Gambia, and Senegal.

mbira A tuned lamellophone of the Shona in Zimbabwe, whose timbre and old tunes are used to mediate the visible and invisible spiritual worlds, thereby inducing spirit possession and ritual efficacy during *mapira*, family ceremonies.

Middle Passage(s) The journey and unpleasant experiences of slaves from Africa through Europe to the Americas during the transatlantic slave trade. Some view the collective return to Africa by some freed slaves as the second Middle Passage.

mpentemma A medium-sized, bottle-shaped, single-headed, carved Akan drum used in most Akan dance ensembles.

Nagla Athletic dance of the Kasene Nankane of Northern Ghana to flute and drum music.

Negritude A literary and ideological movement developed by francophone black intellectuals, writers, and politicians in France in the 1930s. Originally from Africa and the French Caribbean, these advocates used their writings to celebrate their shared black heritage as a counter-hegemony to French political and intellectual dominance.

New World New place of settlement (home) for dispersed races. The opposite of the homeland.

Nexus A world-renowned Toronto-based percussion ensemble founded and directed by Russell Hartenberger.

Ogun Yoruba *orisha* or divinity for iron and energy.

Open Doors A University of Mississippi event planned by the William Winter Institute of Racial Reconciliation to advocate increased interracial interactions, tolerance, and healthy diversity at that university.

PANAFEST A biannual Pan-African festival held in Ghana (Cape Coast and Accra) with the aim of uniting and celebrating black people of the world and redefining future directions for joint agency toward development of their people. The festival's cultural, artistic, and intellectual activities draw participation from Africans, diasporic Africans, and their friends.

Sabar A dance-drumming tradition practiced by the Wolof of Senegal, led by master drummers from hereditary families of *griots*.

Sankofa An Akan phrase which means "Go and retrieve it." A Ghanaian concept and advocacy for revitalizing the positive aspects of Africans' past that have been deconstructed by foreign forces and apparatuses. This conceptual metaphor is based on the behavior of the *sankofa* bird, which flies in a retrograde direction with its head downward as though picking something.

Santeria A Yoruba-derived religion practiced mainly in Cuba.
Sekyi A lively Akan social dance that involves dancers' swift alternation of forward and backward foot movements.
Shona A major ethnic group in Zimbabwe.
steel band A Caribbean (Trinidad and Tobago) ensemble of pans and empty containers of various sizes tuned to definite pitches, played in multiple parts and rhythmic veins similar to sub-Saharan African polyrhythmic ensemble drumming.
tabla Twin drums played in Hindustani classical music of North India.
Taiko A Japanese drum ensemble and music genre.
tambouritza An orchestra of chordophones (stringed instruments) belonging to people of and from the Balkan region of southeastern Europe.
tokoe A puberty dance of the Ga-Adamgbe of southern Ghana, normally performed by girls who have instruction and training prior to being culturally granted womanhood.
Venda A South African ethnic group.
"village style" A term often used to refer to the indigenous music genres performed in the village vein by cultural custodians who are deemed to practice and perpetuate what has been handed down by their ancestors with little or no urban, modern, and foreign influences.
Voudun African-derived religion practiced by Haitians and some African Americans in the New Orleans region.
Wolof An ethnic group in Senegal.
wudodo Lit., "planting of genre," the Ewe conception of establishing a musical genre as something that is metaphorically planted like a tree.
Wuno Literally in Ewe, drum mother or mother of drum, a general label used to designate an established drummer among an Anlo cultural community.
Yoruba A major cultural community located in northwestern Nigeria.
ZADONU The name of Kobla and Beatrice Ladzekpo's African music and dance company based in Los Angeles. The name is an acronym of Kobla's father's and brother's names, which he uses to immortalize them.
Zigi A northern Ewe (Ewedome) recreation dance-drumming genre that is almost synonymous with Ho Ziavi, the town that revitalized this near-defunct genre.
zikpui Ewe word for a "stool," be it for the royalty or ordinary use.

REFERENCES

Agawu, V. Kofi. *African Rhythm: A Northern Ewe Perspective*. Cambridge: Cambridge University Press, 1995.
———. *Representing African Music: Postcolonial Notes, Queries, Positions*. New York: Routledge, 2003.
Akrofi, Eric. *Sharing Knowledge and Experience: A Profile of Kwabena Nketia*. Accra: Afram Publications, 2003.
Akrofi, Eric, and James Flolu. "The Colonial Influence on Music Education in Ghana and South Africa." In *Music and Identity: Transformation and Negotiation*, ed. Eric Akrofi, Maria Smit, and Stig-Magnus Thorsen, 143–157. Stellenbosch, South Africa: Sun Press, 2007.
Ames, David W., and Anthony V. King. *Glossary of Hausa Music and Its Social Contexts*. Evanston, IL: Northwestern University Press, 1971.
Anku, William. "Principles of Rhythmic Integration in African Drumming." *Black Music Research Journal* 17 (1997): 211–238.
Appadurai, Arjun. *Modernity at Large: Cultural Dimensions of Globalization*. Minneapolis: University of Minnesota Press, 2005.
Appiah, Kwame Anthony. *In My Father's House: Africa in the Philosophy of Culture*. New York: Oxford University Press, 1992.
Arom, Simha. *African Polyphony and Polyrhythm: Musical Structure and Methodology*. Translated by Martin Thom, Barbara Tuckett, and Raymond Boyd. Cambridge: Cambridge University Press, 1991[1985].
Avorgbedor, Daniel. "Rural-Urban Interchange." In *The Garland Encyclopedia of World Music: Africa*, ed. Ruth Stone, 389–399. New York: Garland, 1998.
Asante, Molefi Kete. *An Afrocentric Manifesto*. Cambridge: Polity Press, 2007.
Azaguno. http://www.azaguno/
Bakan, Michael. *World Music: Traditions and Transformations*, 2nd ed. New York: McGraw-Hill, 2012[2007].
Barber, Karin. "Praise Poetry: Yoruba Oriki." In *African Folklore: An Encyclopedia*, ed. Phillip Peek and Kwesi Yankah, 364–365. New York: Routledge, 2004.
———. "Text and Performance in Africa." *Oral Tradition* 20 (2005): 264–277.
Bebey, Francis. *African Music: A People's Art*. Translated by Josephine Bennett. New York: Lawrence Hill, 1975[1971].
Berliner, Paul. *The Soul of Mbira: Music and Tradition of the Shona People of Zimbabwe*. Chicago: University of Chicago Press, 1993.

Blacking, John. *How Musical Is Man?* Seattle: University of Washington Press, 1973.

Blummer, Herbert. *Symbolic Interactionism: Perspective and Method.* Englewood Cliffs, NJ: Prentice Hall, 1969.

Boas, Franz. "Human Faculty as Determined by Race." In *The Shaping of American Anthropology 1883–1911: A Franz Boas Reader,* ed. George Stocking, 221–242. Chicago: University of Chicago Press, 1894.

Brandon, George. *Santeria from Africa to the New World: The Dead Sell Memories.* Bloomington: Indiana University Press, 1998.

Campbell, James. *Middle Passages: African American Journeys to Africa, 1787–2005.* New York: Penguin, 2006.

Charry, Eric. "A Guide to the Jembe." (a) In *Percussive Notes* 34 [1996](2): 66–72. (b) At http://echarry.web.wesleyan.edu/jembearticle/article.html

———. *Mande Music: Traditional and Modern Music of Maninka and Mandinka of Western Africa.* Chicago: University of Chicago Press, 2000.

———. "Introduction." In *The Beat of My Drum: An Autobiography.* Philadelphia: Temple University Press, 2005.

Corney, Laura. "Teaching and Learning within the Cross-Cultural Transmission of West African Music in Australian Community Setting." Thesis, University of Sydney, 2007.

Crummel, Alexander. *The Future of Africa.* New York, 1862.

Curtin, Philip. *The Atlantic Slave Trade: A Census.* Madison: University of Wisconsin Press, 1969.

DjeDje, Jacqueline Cogdell, ed. *African Musicology: Current Trends. Volume II. A Festschrift Presented to J. H. Kwabena Nketia.* Los Angeles: UCLA International Studies and Overseas Program/The James Coleman African Studies Center and Crossroads Press/African Studies Association, 1992.

———. "African Musicology: Current Research and Future Directions." In *Multiple Interpretations of Dynamics of Creativity and Knowledge in African Music Traditions: A Festschrift in Honor of Akin Euba on The Occasion of His 70th Birthday,* ed. Bode Omojola and George Dor, 267–303. Point Richmond, CA: Music Research Institute Press, 2005.

———. *Fiddling in West Africa: Touching the Spirit in Fulbe, Hausa, and Dagbamba Cultures.* Bloomington: Indiana University Press, 2008.

DjeDje, Jacqueline Cogdell, and William G. Carter, eds. *African Musicology: Current Trends. Volume I. A Festschrift Presented to J. H. Kwabena Nketia.* Los Angeles: UCLA African Studies Center and African Arts Magazine and Crossroads Press/African Studies Association, 1989.

Dor, George Worlasi Kwasi. "Tonal Resources and Compositional Processes in Ewe Traditional Vocal Music." Diss., University of Pittsburgh, 2001.

———. "Communal Creativity and Song Ownership in Anlo Ewe Musical Practice: The Case of Havorlu." *Ethnomusicology* 48 (2004): 26–51.

———. "Drumming." In *The Greenwood Encyclopedia of African American Folklore,* ed. Anand Prahlad, 356–363. Westport, CT: Greenwood Press, 2006.

———. "Life is Short, Art and Scholarship Are Long: A Tribute in Memory of Professor Willie Anku." *African Music* vol. 8(4) (2010): 110–123.

Drake, St. Clair. "Diaspora Studies and Pan-Africanism." In *Global Dimensions of the African Diaspora*, ed. Joseph Harris, 341–402. Washington: Howard University Press, 1982.

Dunham, Katherine Mary. *Island Possessed*. Chicago: University of Chicago Press, 1969.

Edwards, Bryan. *The History, Civil and Commercial, of the British Colonies in the West Indies*. London: J. Stockdale, 1793.

Emery, Lynne Fauley. *Black Dance: From 1619 to Today*, 2nd rev. ed. Princeton, NJ: Princeton, 1988.

Epstein, Dena. "African Music in British and French America." *Musical Quarterly* 50(1) (1971): 61–91.

Euba, Akin. *Yoruba Drumming: The Dùndún Tradition*. Bayreuth: African Studies Series; and Lagos: Elekoto Music Centre, 1990.

———. "Issues in Africanist Musicology: Do We Need Ethnomusicology in Africa?" In *Proceedings of the Forum for Revitalizing African Music Studies in Higher Education*, ed. Frank Gunderson, 137–139. Ann Arbor: U.S. Secretariat of the International Center for African Music and Dance, International Institute, University of Michigan, 2001.

———. "Gods and Deputy Gods: Music in Yoruba Religions and Kingship Traditions." In *The Interrelatedness of Music, Religion, and Ritual in African Performance Practice*, ed. Daniel Avorgbedor, 39–64. Lewiston, NY: Edwin Mellen Press, 2003.

Fiagbedzi, Nissio. "The Music of the Anlo-Ewe of Ghana: An Ethnomusicological Enquiry into Its History, Cultural Matrix and Style." Diss., University of California at Los Angeles, 1977.

Feld, Steve. *Sound and Sentiment: Birds, Weeping, Poetics, and Song in Kaluli Expression*. Philadelphia: University of Pennsylvania Press, 1982.

Floyd, Samuel. *The Power of Black Music: Interpreting its History from Africa to the United States*. New York: Oxford University Press, 1995.

Foucault, Michel. *The Order of Things: The Archaeology of the Human Sciences*. New York: Pantheon, 1970.

———. *The Archaeology of Knowledge*. Translated by A. M. Sheridan Smith. New York: Pantheon, 1972.

Foulkes-Levy, Laurdella, and Burt J. Levy. *Journeys Through the Life and Music of Nancy Van De Vate*. Toronto: Scarecrow Press, 2005.

Friedberg, Lilian. "Rare German Interviews with Famoudou Konate." *Percussive Notes* 39 (6) (2001).

Friedson, Steven. *Dancing Prophets: Musical Experience in Tumbuka Healing*. Chicago: University of Chicago Press, 1996.

———. *Remains of Ritual: Northern Gods in a Southern Land*. Chicago: University of Chicago Press, 2009.

Galeoto, Joseph. "Drum-Making among the Southern Ewe People of Ghana and Togo." Thesis, Wesleyan University, 1985.

Gaston, Jessie Ruth. "The Case of Voodoo in New Orleans." In *Africanisms in American Culture*, 2nd ed., ed. Joseph Holloway, 111–151. Bloomington: Indiana University Press, 2005.

Gbolonyo, J. Stephen Kofi. "Indigenous Knowledge and Cultural Values in Ewe Musical Practice: Their Traditional Roles and Place in Modern Society." Diss., University of Pittsburgh, 2009.

Giddens, Anthony. *The Constitution of Society*. Cambridge: Polity Press, 1984.

Green, Doris. "Preservation and Presentation of African Music and Dance." *Percussive Notes* 42(3) (2004): 30–35.

Hartigan, Royal. "Ghanaba and the Heritage of African Jazz." *Annual Review of Jazz Studies* 9 (1999): 145–164.

Harris, Joseph, ed. *Global Dimensions of the African Diaspora*. Washington: Howard University Press, 1982.

Heard, Marcia E. "Asadata Dafora: African Concert Dance Traditions in American Concert Dance." Diss., New York University, 1999.

Heard, Marcia E., and Mansa K. Mussa. "African Dance in New York City." In *Dancing Many Drums: Excavations in African American Dance*, ed. Thomas F. DeFrantz, 143–167. Madison: University of Wisconsin Press, 2002.

Hegel, Georg Wilhelm Friedrich. *Lectures on the Philosophy of World History*, translated by H. B. Nisbet. Cambridge: Cambridge University Press, 1975 [1822–28].

Herdon, Maria, and Norma McLeod. *Music as Culture*. Point Richmond, CA: Music Research Institute Press, 1990 [1980].

Hill, Matthew Edward. "The Dancing Djembe: Resources for Exploring Guinean Drum and Dance Connections." *Percussive Notes*, 2011.

Hirt-Manheimer, Isaac. "Understanding 'Fast *Agbekor*': A History of Ghana's National Dance Company and an Analysis of Its Repertoire." Thesis, Wesleyan University, 2004.

Hobsbawm, Eric, and Terence Ranger. *The Invention of Tradition*. Cambridge: Cambridge University Press, 1983.

Holloway, Joseph. *Africanisms in American Culture*. Bloomington: Indiana University Press, 2005.

Jones, A. M. *Studies in African Studies*. 2 vols. Oxford: Oxford University Press, 1959.

Keil, Charles. *Tiv Song: The Sociology of Art in a Classless Society*. Chicago: University of Chicago Press, 1979.

Kimberlin, Cynthia, and Akin Euba, eds. *Toward an African Pianism: The Keyboard Music of Africa and the Diaspora, Essays*, 2 Vols. Point Richmond, CA: Music Research Institute Press, 2005.

Kisliuk, Michelle, and Kelly Gross. "What Is the 'It' that We Learn to Perform?: Teaching BaAka Music and Dance." In *Performing Ethnomusicology: Teaching and Representation in World Music Ensembles*, ed. Ted Solis, 249–260. Berkeley: University of California Press, 2004.

Kly, Y. N., ed. *The Invisible War: The African American Anti-Slavery Resistance from the Stono Rebellion through the Seminole Wars*. Atlanta: Clarity Press, 2006.

Knight, Roderic. "Towards a Notation and Tablature for the Kora." *African Music* 5(1) (1971): 23–36.

———. "Mandinka Drumming." *African Arts* 7 (1974): 24–35.

———. *Kora Manding: Mandinka Music of the Gambia*. Sound recording and booklet. Tucson, AZ: Ethnodisc, 1972.

Koetteng, James. "Analysis and Notation of West African Drum Ensemble." *Selected Reports in Ethnomusicology* 1 (1970): 115–146.

Kubik, Gerhard. *Africa and the Blues*. Jackson: University Press of Mississippi, 1999.

Levine, Lawrence. "African Culture and US Slavery." In *Global Dimensions of the African Diaspora*, ed. Joseph E. Harris, 127–135. Washington: Howard University Press, 1982.
Locke, David. "The African Ensemble in America: Contradictions and Possibilities." In *Performing Ethnomusicology: Teaching and Representation in World Music Ensembles*, ed. Ted Solis, 168–188. Berkeley: University of California Press, 2004.
Maultsby, Portia. "Africanisms in African Music." In *Africanisms in American Culture*, ed. Joseph Holloway, 326–355. Bloomington: Indiana University Press, 2005.
McCall, Sarah Rachael. "A Case Study of Music-Making in a Ghanaian Village: Application For Elementary Music Teaching and Learning." Thesis, Louisiana State University and Agricultural and Mechanical College, 2010.
Mensah, Atta-Annan. "The Polyphony of Gyil-gu, kudzu and Awutu Sakumo." *Journal of the International Folk Music Council* 19 (1967): 75–79.
Merriam, Alan. *Anthropology of Music*. Evanston, IL: Northwestern University Press, 1964.
Meyer, Bright. *Translating the Devil: Religion and Modernity among the Ewe in Ghana*. Trenton, NJ: Africa World Press, 1999.
Monson, Ingrid. *Freedom Sounds: Civil Rights Call Out to Jazz and Africa*. Oxford: Oxford University Press, 2007.
Monts, Lester. "Islam in Liberia." In *The Garland Handbook of African Music, 2nd Ed.*, ed. Ruth Stone, 63–87. New York: Routledge, Taylor and Francis Group, 2000.
Mulvey, Laura. 1975. "Visual Pleasure and Narrative Cinema." *Screen* 16(3): 6–18.
Nketia, Kwabena J. H. *Drumming in Akan Communities of Ghana*. Edinburgh: University of Ghana and Thomas Nelson and Sons, 1963.
———. *Music, Dance and Drama: A Review of Performing Arts of Ghana*. Accra, 1965.
———. *Our Drums and Drummers*. Accra: Ghana Publishing House, 1968.
———. *Ethnomusicology in Ghana*. Accra: Universities Press, 1970.
———. *The Music of Africa*. New York: W. W. Norton, 1974.
———. *The Play Concept in African Music*. Laura Boulton Lectures. Ed. Tom Venum. Tempe Ariz.: Hurd Museum, 1991.
———. "The Scholarly Study of African Music: A Historical Review." In *The Garland Encyclopedia of World Music: Africa*, ed. Ruth Stone, 1: 13–73. New York: Garland, 1998.
———. *African Art Music/The Creative Potential of African Art Music in Ghana*. Companion booklet to ICAMD CD recordings (ICAMD/DMVI/ICAMD/DMV4). Accra: Afram Publications, 2004.
Nketia, Kwabena J. H., and Jacqueline Cogdell DjeDje. "Introduction: Trends in African Ethnomusicology." In *Selected Reports in Ethnomusicology, Vol. 5: Studies in African Music*, ed. J. H. Kwabena Nketia and Jacqueline Cogdell DjeDje, ix–xx. Los Angeles: UCLA Program in Ethnomusicology, Department of Music, [YEAR].
Nyaho, Chapman William. *Piano Music and the African Diaspora*. 6 Vols.. Oxford: Oxford University Press, 2007, 2007, 2008, 2008, 2008, and 2009.
Nzewi, Meki. "The Rhythm of Dance in Igbo Music." *Conch* 3 (1971): 104–108.
———. "The Igbo Concept of Mother Musicianship." In *Musical Sense and Meaning: An Indigenous African Perception*, ed. Meki Nzewi, Israel Anyahuru, and Tom Ohiaraumunna, 33–47. Pretoria: UNISA Press, 2009.
Nzewi, Meki, Kofi Agawu, and Anri Herbst, eds. *Music Arts in Africa: Theory, Practice, and Education*. Pretoria: UNISA Press, 2003.

Olatunji, Babatunde, and Robert Atkinson. *The Beat of My Drum: An Autobiography*. Philadelphia: Temple University Press, 2005.

Omojola, Bode. *The Music of Fela Sowande: Encounters, African Identity and Creative Ethnomusicology*. Point Richmond, CA: Music Research Institute Press, 2009.

Pantaleoni, Hewitt. "The Rhythm of *Atsia* Dance Drumming among the Anlo (Ewe) of Anyako." Thesis, Wesleyan University, 1972.

Perpener, John. *African-American Concert Dance: The Harlem Renaissance and Beyond*. Urbana: University of Illinois Press, 2001.

Polak, Rainer. "A Musical Instrument Travels around the World: *Jembe* Playing in Bamako." *World of Music* 42(3) (2000): 7–46.

Rasmussen, Anne. "Bilateral Negotiations in Bimusicality: Insiders, Outsiders, and the 'Real Version,' in Middle Eastern Music Performance." In *Performing Ethnomusicology: Teaching and Representation in World Music Ensembles*, ed. Ted Solís, 168–188. Berkeley: University of California Press, 2004.

Rice, Timothy. *May It Feel Your Soul: Experiencing Bulgarian Music*. Chicago: University of Chicago Press, 1994.

Roberts, Storm John. *Black Music of Two Worlds: African, Caribbean, Latin and African-American Traditions*. New York: Schirmer, 1998.

Rouget, Gilbert. *Music and Trance: A Theory of the Relations between Music and Possession*. Chicago: University of Chicago Press, 1985.

Schauert, Paul. "Staging Nationalism: Performance, Power and Representation in Ghana's State Dance Ensembles." Diss., Indiana University, 2011.

Schuler, Jack. *Calling Out Liberty: The Stono Slave Rebellion and the Universal Struggle for Human Rights*. Jackson: University Press of Mississippi, 2009.

Scott, James. *Domination and the Arts of Resistance: Hidden Transcripts*. New Haven: Yale University Press, 1990.

Seachrist, Denise. *The Musical World of Halim El-Dabh*. Kent, OH: Kent State University, 2003.

Seeger, Anthony. *Why Suya Sing: A Musical Anthropology of an Amazonian People*. Urbana: University of Illinois Press, 2004 (1987).

Shelemey, Kaufman. *Soundscapes: Exploring Music in a Changing World*, 2nd ed. New York: W. W. Norton, 2006.

Shepperson, George. "African Diaspora: Concept and Context." In *Global Dimensions of the African Diaspora*, ed. Joseph E. Harris, 46–53. Washington: Howard University Press, 1982.

Skinner, Elliot F. "The Dialectics between Diasporas and Homelands." In *Global Dimensions of the African Diaspora*, ed. Joseph E. Harris, 17–45. Washington: Howard University Press, 1982.

Smith, Mark M., ed. *Stono: Documenting and Interpreting a Southern Revolt*. Columbia: University of South Carolina Press, 2005.

Solís, Ted, ed. *Performing Ethnomusicology: Teaching and Representation in World Music Ensembles*. Berkeley: University of California Press, 2004.

Southern, Eileen. *The Music of Black Americans: A History*, 3rd ed. New York: W. W. Norton, 1997 (1971).

Stanley, Henry Morton. *Through the Dark Continent*. New York: Dover, 1988 (1878).

Strumpf, Mitchel. "Ghanaian Xylophone Studies." *Review of Ethnology* 3(6) (1970): 41–45.
Stone, Ruth. *Let the Inside Be Sweet: The Interpretation of Music Event among the Kpelle of Liberia*. Bloomington: Indiana University Press, 1982.
Sunkett, Mark. *Mandiani Drum and Dance: Djembe Performance and Black Aesthetics from Africa to the New World*. Tempe, AZ: White Cliffs Media, 1995.
Tang, Patricia. *Masters of the Sabar: Wolof Griot Percussionists of Senegal*. Philadelphia: Temple University Press, 2007
Tompkins, William David. "Afro-Peruvian Traditions." In *The Garland Encyclopedia of World Music, Vol. 2: South America, Mexico, Central America and the Caribbean*, ed. Dale A. Olsen and Daniel E. Sheehy, 491. New York: Garland, 1998.
Tracey, Andrew. "The Matepe Mbira Music of Rhodesia." *African Music* 4(4) (1970): 37–61.
———. *Chopi Musicians: Their Music, Poetry, and Instruments*. London, 1948.
Trimollos, Ricardo D. "Subject, Object, and the Ethnomusicology Ensemble: The Ethnomusicological 'We' and 'Them.'" In *Performing Ethnomusicology: Teaching and Representation in World Music Ensembles*, ed. Ted Solis, 4: 23–52. Berkeley: University of California Press, 2004.
Uya, Okon Edet. "Conceptualizing African-American/African Relations: Implications for African Diaspora Studies." In *Global Dimensions of the African Diaspora*, ed. Joseph E. Harris, 69–84. Washington: Howard University Press, 1982.
Volk, Terese M. *Music, Education, and Multiculturalism: Foundations and Principles*. New York: Oxford University Press, 1998.
Wachsmann, Klaus. "The Trend of Musicology in Africa." *Selected Reports* 1(1) (1966): 61–65.
———. "The State of African Musicology." In *African Studies of Makerere 1961–66. A Report*, 82–93. Kampala: Makerere University College, 1967.
———. "Ethnomusicology in African Studies: The Next Twenty Years." In *Expanding Horizons*, ed. Gwendolen M. Carter and Ann Paden, 131–142. Evanston: Northwestern University Press, 1969.
———. "Ethnomusicology in Africa." In *The African Experience, Volume I: Essays*, ed. John N. Paden and Edward Soja, 128–151. Evanston: Northwestern University Press, 1970.
Wade, Bonnie C. *Thinking Musically: Experiencing Music, Expressing Culture*. New York: Oxford University Press, 2004.
Welsh-Asante, Kariamu, ed. *African Dance: An Artistic, Historical, and Philosophical Inquiry*. Trenton, NJ: Africa World Press, 1998.

VIDEOGRAPHY

Binghamton University [New York] "Nukporfe" African Performance Ensemble, directed by James Burns, and assisted by Pierrette Aboadji.
Agbekor: http://youtu.be/JOhQfILnq24
http://youtu.be/MgtEBbOxoSQ
Kinka: http://youtu.be/vWizEFi2Rto
Kpatsa: http://youtu.be/wikW74jLkwU

CalArts African Drumming and Dance Ensemble. "Kobla Ladzekpo Farewell Concert 2007." http://www.youtube.com/watch?v=10RGDLy3054. Uploaded by Jahian L. Price.

CalArts African Drumming and Dance Ensemble. "Alfred Ladzekpo Farewell Concert 2011 Speeches Part 6." http://www.youtube.com/watch?v=KV-t-yXuCjY. Uploaded by Jahian L. Price.

CalArts African Drumming and Dance Ensemble. "Alfred Ladzekpo Farewell Concert 2011 Agbekor Part 2." http://www.youtube.com/watch?v=EZNmJNifQ4I. Uploaded by Jahian L. Price.

CU-Boulder West African Highlife Ensemble, directed by Kwasi Ampene and Adjei Abankwah. "5th Annual Highlife Concert Featuring CU-Boulder West African Highlife Ensemble," with guest artists Okyerema Asante, Kwame Seth Asiedu, John Galm, 2005.

Gates, Henry Louis, Jr. *Wonders of the African World*. Directed by Nick Godwin and Helena Appio. Alexandria, VA: PBS Home Video, 2000.

Hood, Mantle. *Atumpan: The Talking Drums of Ghana* [DVD]. Los Angeles: Institute of Ethnomusicology, University of California (UCLA), 1964.

Ole Miss African Drum and Dance Ensemble (OMADDE), directed by George Dor. "Rhythms of Liberation: A Concert In Commemoration of Ghana's 50th Independence Anniversary 1957–2007." DVD produced by the Center for Media Production, Matthew Graves, editor, Andy Harper, executive producer. Oxford, MS: University of Mississippi.

———. "2012 Black History Month Concert Celebrating 50 Years of Integration." http://vimeo.com/37604609, UM Documentary Project.

JVC/Smithsonian Folkways Video Anthology of Music and Dance of Africa, Vol. 2 (The Gambia, Liberia, Ghana, and Nigeria), No. 16: *Fontomfrom*, No. 17: *Adowa*, and No. 18: *Kete*. Hiroshi Yamamoto, director; J. H. Kwabena Nketia, Africa editor (book), 1996.

Wesleyan West African Drumming and Dance Ensemble. "Adzenyah in Three: A Tribute Concert DVD," by Current and Former Students of Abraham Adzenyah. Middletown, CT: Center for the Arts, Wesleyan University, 2002.

West Virginia University African Drumming and Dance Ensemble, directed by Pascal Younge. "A Concert of World Music" (videorecording). Morgantown: WVU Television Productions, 2000.

INDEX

Page numbers in **bold** indicate illustrations.

Aboadji, Pierrette, 93, 94–95, 111
Abraham Adzinya Tribute Concert CD, 53. *See also* Adzinya, Abraham
Academic Initiatives Fund (AIF), 182
Academy of Arts (Berlin), 227
Acheampong (general), 244
Addo, Akosua, 234
Addo, Beatrice, 105
Addy, Yakobo, 242
Adinku, 105
Adjaye, Joseph, 195
administrators, 97, 157–58, 159, 161; agency of, 10, 63, 66, 156, 160; and authenticity, 140; categories of, 9; greetings by, 198; and orphan ensembles, 162, 265
Adowa, 104, 245
Aduonum, Ama Oforiwaa, 9, 145, **181,** 208
Aduonum, Kwasi, 246
Adzido Pan-African Dance Ensemble, 241
Adzinya, Abraham, 5, 45, 98; and John Chernoff, 283ch7n2; and Freeman Donkor, 54; and Ghana Dance Ensemble, 56; and Isaac Hirt-Manheimer, 231; and Samuel Elikem Nyamuame, **54;** and sabbatical, 57, 180; and "teaching the right thing," 121; and tribute concert, 58, 194; visits Toronto, 69; at Wesleyan University, 53, 55, 78–79, 128, 137. *See also* Abraham Adzinya Tribute Concert CD
Adzogbo, 47

Afa, 19
Africa and the Blues (Kubik), 22
Africa Meets Asia, 227
Africa Meets North America (AMNA), 4, 5, 46, 47, 134, 191
Africa Speaks, America Responds, 37
African Academy of Arts and Research, 31, 47
African Art Music (Nketia), 242
African Drumming and Dance Ensemble, 193, 195, 211
"African Fantasy," 35
African Festival, 67, 193
African Methodist Episcopal Church. *See* AME Church
African Methodist Episcopal Zion Church. *See* AMEZ Church
African Music and Dance Ensemble, 130, 194
African Music Ensemble, 73, 77, 82, 161, 185, 217
African Music Journal, 82
African Music Section, 4, 119, **122,** 281ch2n8, 282ch3n10
African musicology, 252
African Personality, 249
African Students Association, 85
African Year, 50
Africanaise, 95
Africanisms, 17, 19, 25, 26, 39
Africanisms in American Culture (Holloway), 20
Afro-Caribbean Ensemble, 45

301

AfroStuds, 246
"Agahu," 48
Agawu, Kofi, **184**, 191, 206, 250
Agbadza, 82
Agbedidie African Music and Dance Ensemble, 185
Agbekor, 80, **93**
Agbekor Drum and Dance Society, 78, 82, 84, 113, 114, 281ch2n8
Agbeli, Godwin, 82, 98, 207; and Agbedidie African Music and Dance Ensemble, 208; and Asiedu Keteke Cultural Troupe, 241; and Dagbe Cultural Institute and Arts Centre, 231; and David Locke, 79, 80, 81, 112, 242; and Patricia Tang, 84; and "teaching the right thing," 121; visits Toronto, 69
Agbeli, Nani, 45, 82
Agbeli family, 232
"agro ye de," 197
Ahima, Kwame, 45
AIF (Academic Initiatives Fund), 182
Akan chiefs, 104
Akan dances, 70, 104, 195, 244, 245
Akan drums, 38, 47, 231
Akan master drummers, 100
Akan musical instruments, **55**
Akan sayings, 197
Akan study-abroad program, 234
Akan tradition, 51
Akrong, Isaac, 45, 64, 158, **184**
Alabi, Buki, **148**, 149, **154**
Alabi, Kemi, **148**, 149, **154**
Alford, Jeff, 174
All-African Students Union in the Americas, 35
Alorwoyie, Gideon Foli, 98; and Asiedu Keteke Cultural Troupe, 242; and authenticity, 8; career of, 240; childhood of, 239–40; at College at Brockport, State University of New York, 221; education of, 240; and Philip Gbeho, 238, 240; and Ghana Dance Ensemble, 80, 242; and Kobla Ladzekpo, **123**; and David Locke, 79, 81, 82, 114, 120; and OMADDE, 92; and Albert Mawere Opoku, 244; pedagogical approach of, 107; and professional ensembles, 62; and Steve Reich, 138, 229; at SEM 2008, **184**; at SEM 2010, **183**; and "teaching the right thing," 121, 122; and "Teaching the Right Thing," 8
AME Church, 18. *See also* churches
Ameanyo, Togbui, II. *See* Alorwoyie, Gideon Foli
Amegago, Modesto, 5, 67, 144, 145, 194, 246
Amepene, Kwesi, 233
Amevuvor, Kwasi, 244
AMEZ Church, 18. *See also* churches
Ameze, 149
AMNA (Africa Meets North America), 4, 5, 46, 47, 134, 191
Amoako, William, 98, 128, 246
Amoh, 88
Ampene, Kwasi: at Africa Meets Asia, 227; at concerts, 283ch6n1; and DVDs and VHS recordings, 186–87; and West African Highlife Ensemble, 131, 171–72, **182**, 194
Amu, Ephraim, 245
Ananse, 80
Anansekrom, 80
Andrew Mellon Grant, 82
Andrew Mellon Tuition Fellowship, 77, 181
Angelou, Maya, 216, 247
Anglophone countries, 165, 206, 209, 261
Anku, William Oscar, 45, 98, 128, 230, 246, 250, 283n3; and African Music Ensemble, 73, 171, 208; at AMNA, **74**; remembered at SEM 2010, **183**
apentemma, 38
Appadurai, Arjun, 225, 226, 264; "Consumption, Duration, and History," 196
Appiah, Kwame, 29
Arizona State University, 85
Armstrong, Cathy, 68, 158
Armstrong, Louis, 38, 216, 240. *See also* Louis Armstrong Park

INDEX 303

Arts Centre, 240, 241, 242
Arts Council of Ghana, 12, 80, 238, 240, 241, 261
Asante, Molefi Kete, 40
Ashanti music, 51
Ashong, Joseph, 68, 158
Asiedu Ketete Cultural Troupe, 241
atenteben, 77
Atsimewu, 46, **47, 48, 50,** 90, 91, 121, **187**
atumpan, 38, 281n9
audiences, 114, 195–96; and Ghanaian storytelling, 87; participation by, 196, 203–4; and prejudices, 145
authenticity, 8, 17, 119, 121, 136, 140, 257, 259; and drum circles, 123; and Isaac Hirt-Manheimer, 231; and notation, 115; and Albert Mawere Opoku, 244; and Ricardo Trimillos, 127
Avorgbedor, Daniel, 233
Ayitee, Robert Anane, 45, 47, 240, 261
Azaguno, 227
azaguno, etymology of, 100–102

Badu, Kwasi, 47, 51, 159
Bagandan instruments, **187**
Bain, Kevin, 89
Baksimba, 77
Ballet National du Mali, 228
Ballet Negres, 32
ballet style, 141, 142, 143, 144
Ballets Africains, Les, 12, 38, 228
Bambaya, 203
Bangoura, Fana, 45
Barz, Greg, 45
Beat of My Drum, The (Olatunji), 34
Becker, Bob, 68–69
Beeko, Eric, **74**
Beijing Central Conservatory of Music, 227
Berklee College Ensemble, 237
bi-musicality, 52, 133, 134, 170, 230
binarism, 119–20, 121, 124, 127
Binghamton University, 107, 172
Black Brotherhood, 28
Black History Month, 193, 202

"Black Kingdoms of the Nile," 40
Blacking, John, 117; *How Musical Is Man*, 42, 133
Blakey, Art, 35, 38
Blumer, Herbert, 153
Boas, Franz, "Human Faculty as Determined by Race," 41
Bonsu, Robert Osei, 45, 47, 261
Borborbor, **154**
Bordieux, Pierre, 125
Boughton, Laura, 282ch2n9
Bramlett Elementary School, 218
Brandon, George, 19
"Breaking the Silence, Beating the Drum," 23, 264
Brockport State College, 221, 244, 282n5
Brown, A. R. Radcliffe, 32
Brown, Steve, 88, 89, 198, 282ch2n10
Brown University, 83, 207
Buhaina, Abdullah Ibn. *See* Blakey, Art
Burkhead, Ricky, 87, 89, 90, 92, 138–39, 214–15; and OMADDE, **186,** 213, **236**
Burkhead, Tim, **186**
Burns, James, 98, 107, 111; and *Africanaise,* 95; agency of, 172–73; and George Dor, **94;** and listening, 117; and Nukporfe African Dance/Drumming Ensemble, 92–93, **93,** 94, 96, 237; pedagogical approach of, 117, 118; visits Ghana, 169
Buskes, Gerald, 282ch2n9

cabildos, 19
California College of the Arts, 106
California School of Performing Arts, 194
call-and-response, 18, 39, 147, 199, 203
Campbell, James, 40, 41
Candomble, 20
Caribbean Carnival (Manning and Thenstead), 34
Carlisle, David, 92, **186**
Carter, William, 247
"Case of Voodoo in New Orleans, The" (Gaston), 24
Cathedral of Learning, 219–20

Catholic Church, 19. *See also* churches
CDs, 186, 217
Center for Intercultural Musicology, 227
Charry, Eric, 5, 180; on *djembe* drum, 228–29; and George Dor, **57**; on funding, 182–84; on Babatunde Olatunji, 34; at Wesleyan University, 53–54, 57, 58, 159
Cheers, Michael, 153
Chernoff, John, 75, 138, 230, 250, 283ch7n2
chordophones, 14, 24, 207, 208
Christianity: conversion to, 17, 18, 20; and intellectualism, 26; and missionaries, 27; and suppression of drumming, 17, 255; and Western music, 134
churches, 17–19, 25–26. *See also* AME Church; AMEZ Church; Catholic Church; Community of Reconciliation Church; Ethiopian Orthodox Christian Church
civil rights movement, 35, 41, 42, 248
Civil War, 17
clapping/handclapping, 18, 19, 24, 25, 39, 203–4
Clarksdale, Mississippi, 149, 201
Clarksdale High School, 149; workshop at, **202**
Clinton, Bill, 194
coffee and milk, 130
cofrados, 19
Cole, Don, 174
College at Brockport, State University of New York, 221, 244, 282n5
colonialism, 134, 205
Coltrane, John, 35, 36
Columbia University, 45; and Ewe dances, 261; and Kobla Ladzekpo, 221; and David Locke, 78; and West African drumming, 3, 47, 220; and Philip Yopovsky, 221
communal creativity, 116, 147, 204
communality, 232; at Binghamton University, 117; at festival, 86; at Ghana50 concert, 222; at performances, 202; versus individualism, 249; at York University, 66

Community of Reconciliation Church, 77. *See also* churches
congas, 142
Congo Square, 21, **21, 22, 23,** 24
"Consumption, Duration, and History" (Appadurai), 196
Cornelius, Steven, 45
Cornell University, 95
costumes, 57, 70, 183
court drumming, 16
Crokett, I-nassah, 204
Crummell, Alexander, 27, 29, 30
Cuba, 19
culture/subculture at universities, 130, 188, 190, 192

DaCosta, Mohammed, 207, 208
Dagbe Cultural Institute and Arts Centre, 231
Dagbon musical instruments, **55**
Damba Takai dance, 48
Damm, Bob, 92
dance ensemble model, 111, 112, 280n12
dance troupe model, 111, 112
"Dance's Katherine the Great," 32
"Dancing Djembe, The" (Hill), 107, 228–29
Daniels-Smith, Dianne, 88
Dataade, Mustafa, 241
Denis (professor), 61
detsivivi yehea zipkui, 11
"Dialectics Between the Diasporas and Homelands, The" (Skinner), 28
diaspora, 15, 16–17, 25, 99, 233, 254
"Diaspora Studies and Pan-Africanism" (Drake), 248
Diop, Cheikh Anta, 40
DjeDje, Jacqueline Cogdell: and African Year, 50; and Kwasi Badu, 51; and George Dor, **52**; and Gamelan Room, 51–52; and summer world music programs, 217; *Touching the Spirits*, 42; at UCLA, 44, 46, 157, 159, 198
djembe: "The Dancing Djembe," 107, 228–29; at Harvard University, 85; and

Ladji Kamara, 39; and Anna Melnikoff, **66**, 142–43
"do not follow the path," 173
dondo, 281ch2n6
Donkor, Freeman, 54, 79, 137
donno, 281ch2n6
Dor, George: at AMNA, **74**; and James Burns, **94**; and Eric Charry, **57**; dancing, **235**; and Jacqueline Cogdell DjeDje, **52**; and drums, **199, 200**; and Christopher K. Ladzekpo, **61**; and OMADDE, **186, 236**; at SEM 2010, **183**, 282ch3n10
Dor, Shelter, 149, **186**
Dor, Yawa, **148**, 149, 150, **150, 154,** 200
Doudou, 105
Drake, St. Clair, "Diaspora Studies and Pan-Africanism," 248
drum circles, 123, 142, 144
drum languages, 100, 104, 105
drum lines, 39–40
drum substitutes, 18, 19, 25, 26
"Drum-Making Among the Southern Ewe People of Ghana and Togo" (Galeoto), 231
Drumming (Reich), 138
drumming: modes of, 20; on slave ships, 22–24; substitute for, 39; suppression of, 17, 20, 38, 209
drums: making and repairing, 136–37; purchased from Ghana, 88–90; as symbols, 14
Drums of Passion (Babatunde), 36
Du Bois, W. E. B., 213
dunduba, **66**
dundun, **65,** 281ch2n6
Dunham, Katherine Mary, 30, 32–33, 34, 38, 263
Dunyo, Kwasi, 45, 86; and authenticity, 8; class, **71, 153**; dancing, **72**; on drum circles, 123; on etymology of *azaguno*, 101–2; on master drummers, 99; and study-abroad programs, 124; as teacher, 66–67, 71, 107–9, 126, 131, 158, 218; teaching, **64, 70**; and "teaching the right thing," 121, 122; at University of Toronto, 69, 70; at York University, 63
Duquesne University, 219
DVDs, 186, 194

Ekwueme, Laz, "Structural Levels of Rhythm and Form in African Music," 261
El-Dabh, Halim, 191
Ellington, Duke, 37
Emancipation, 25, 27–28, 263
England, Nicholas, 78, 261
English language, 11, 206; command of, 10, 85, 165, 167; in Ghana, 261
ephemeral pleasure/ephemerality, 195, 196, 264
Ethiopian Christian chant, 4
Ethiopian Orthodox Christian Church, 27. *See also* churches
Ethiopianism, 213
ethnoscapes, 225
Euba, Akin: and Africa Meets Asia, 227; and African Pianism, 280n5; at AMNA, **74**; as composer, 230; and Symposium on African Pianism, 191; as teacher, 76, 77, 171
Ewe dances, 47–48, 94–95
Ewe drums, 36, 75, **199, 200**
Ewe musical instruments, **55**

"Factoring in Race" (Locke), 120
Fastrack Recording Studio, 139
Federal Theatre African Dance Troupe, 31
fefea vivi, 197
financescapes, 225
First All-African Peoples Conference, 35
Flaming Donos, 69
Folkloric Dance Company, 243
Folkloric Dance Company of the Arts Council, 80
fontomfrom, 38
foot stomping, 18, 19, 24, 25
Foulkes-Levy, Laurdella, 191
foundations, 168, 181, 186, 222

Fourth Symposium on the Music of Africa, 191
Francophone countries, 82, 206–7, 209
"Freedom Is a Constant Struggle," 153
Freeman, Donkor, 56
Frieberg, Lillian, 143
Frishkopf, Michael, 45
funding, 180, 181, 183, 184, 186

Gadamer, Hans-Georg, 125
Gahu dance: "Agahu," 48; and audience participation, 203; at University of Mississippi, 90, 92, 147, 153; at Wesleyan University, 56
Galeoto, Joseph: and Berklee College Ensemble, 237; "Drum-Making Among the Southern Ewe People of Ghana and Togo," 231
Gamelan Room, 46, 47, 51–52; and Kobla Ladzekpo, **49**; naming of, 192, 281ch2n1
Garvey, Marcus, 28, 213
Gaston, Jessie Ruth, "The Case of Voodoo in New Orleans," 24
Gates, Charles, 92, **160**, 161, 164; at Ghana50 concert, 198, 226; on liberal arts education, 162–63
Gates, Henry Louis: "Black Kingdoms of the Nile," 40; *Wonders of the African World*, 40, 211
Gbeho, Philip, 12, 216, 238; and Gideon Foli Alorwoyie, 240; "God Bless Our Homeland Ghana," 238. *See also* Gbeho Research Group
Gbeho Research Group, 240, 241
Gbolonyo, J. S. Kofi, 73, 75, 77, 128, **181**, 208, 246; at AMNA, **74**; and etymology of *azaguno*, 100; and OMADDE, 92; as teacher, 173; visits Ghana, 76; visits middle schools, 217
Georgia Slave Code of 1755, 21
Gertrude C. Ford Center for the Performing Arts, 191; and African Drumming and Dance Ensemble, 193–94; and Ghana50, 198, **224**; and OMADDE, 153, 173

Ghana, 7, 262; independence of, 35, 195. *See also* Ghana 50th Independence Anniversary Secretariat; Ghana50
Ghana Dance Company. *See* Ghana Dance Ensemble
Ghana Dance Ensemble, 165, 231, 246, 261; and Pierrette Aboadji, 93, 95; and General Acheampong, 244; and *fontomfrom*, 245; and Mantle Hood, 170; and J. H. Kwabena, **248**; and Beatrice Ladzekpo, 49; and Albert Mawere Opoku, 242; and Sulley, 48
Ghana 50th Independence Anniversary Secretariat, 223. *See also* Ghana: independence of; Ghana50
Ghana National Dance Ensemble. *See* Ghana Dance Ensemble
Ghana National Dance Troupe, 104, 105
Ghana National Symphony Orchestra, 238
Ghana50: flyer, **224**; and Charles Gates, 226; and Gertrude C. Ford Center for the Performing Arts, **91**, 173, 198; and Michael Johanssen, 222; and "Liberate the World," **91**; and OMADDE, **91**; proclamation, **223**; program notes, **177**; and "Rhythms of Liberation," **224**. *See also* Ghana: independence of; Ghana 50th Independence Anniversary Secretariat
Ghanaba, Kofi, 37, 38, 216, 263
Ghanaian hand drums, **63**
Giddens, Anthony, 10
Glisson, Susan, 91
globalization, 50, 139, 193, 198, 225–26, 251
"God Bless Our Homeland Ghana" (Gbeho), 238
gospel music, 39, 192, 213
Graham, Martha, 31
grants, 167–68, 169, 186, 220
Graves, Larry, 45, 63–64, 158
Gray, Bishop, 210
Gray Center, 210
greetings, 197–98, 199–200, 202
Gross, Kelly, 130
Grueschow, Andrew, **155**

Guggenheim Fellowship, 58, 133–34
Guinea Ballet Nationale. *See* Ballets Africains, Les
Guinea National Ballet. *See* Ballets Africains, Les
Gullah, 18
Gullah-Geechee Ring Shouters, 18
Gunderson, Frank, **185,** 208

habǫbǫ, 98, 113
Harding, Philip, 230
Harpur Chorale, 95
Harrison, L., 105
Hartenberger, Russell, 45, 53, 58, 68, **69,** 86, 157; education of, 137–38; on funding, 181–82; at University of Toronto, 158, 171; visits Ghana, 138
Hartigan, Royal, 37–38, 58
Harvard University, 84, 85
Heidegger, Martin, 125
Herskovits, Melville, 32, 213
Hill, Matthew Edward, "The Dancing Djembe," 107, 228–29
Hirt-Manheimer, Isaac, "Understanding 'Fast Agbekor,'" 231
Hogbetsotso Festival, 239
Holiday, Billie, 38
Holloway, Annette, **236**
Holloway, Joseph, *Africanisms in American Culture,* 20
Hood, Mantle, 46, 50, 132–33, 261; and bimusicality, 52, 170, 230; and Jacqueline Cogdell DjeDje, 157; *The Talking Drums of Ghana,* 136; at UCLA, 3, 192
Hopkins, Glenn, 96, **162,** 163, 164, 223–24
Horton, Asadata Dafora, 30–31, 33, 47, 263
How Musical Is Man (Blacking), 42, 133
Hughes, Langston, "The Negro Speaks of Rivers," 34
"Human Faculty as Determined by Race" (Boas), 41

"I was there . . . ," 87, 89
ICAMD. *See* International Center for African Music and Dance
ICTM. *See* International Council of Traditional Music
ideoscapes, 225
idiophones, 14, 26, 208
improvisation, 101, 110
Indiana University, 45
Institute of African Studies, 12, 60; and James Burns, 93; establishment of, 249; and Ghana Dance Ensemble, 242; and Kobla Ladzekpo, 105; and Kwabena Nketia, 245, 246
interactions, 145, 146, 147, 148
International Center for African Music and Dance (ICAMD), 211
International Conference on Racial Reconciliation, 91, 153
International Council of Traditional Music (ICTM), 5, 252
International Day of Remembrance of the Victims of Slavery and the Transatlantic Slave Trade, 23, 264
International Monetary Fund, 80
iPods, 229
"It is the sumptuous soup . . . ," 11, 96, 195, 251, 264, 265

Jackson, Diedra, 90, 282ch2n11
Jemmy, 20
Jenkins, Kendra, 39
Job 600, 105
Johanssen, Michael, 222
John Simon Guggenheim Fellowship, 32, 58
John Simon Guggenheim Memorial Foundation, 58
Johnson, Emanuel, 204
Jones, A. M., 261
Jones, Daniel, 192
Julius Rosenwald Fellowship, 32, 34
JVC & Smithsonian Video Anthology of Music and Dance, Vol. 2, 245

Kafumbe, Damascus, **185,** 208
Kamara, Ladji, 38–39
kebaro, 27

Kebede, A., 208
kenkeni, **66**
Kent State University, 191
kente cloth, 201, 211, 216
kidi, **199**
"kill the snake with the stick in his hands," 68
Kimberlin, Cynthia, 4
King, B. B., 191
Kiniwe African Music and Dance Ensemble, 45, **79,** 82, 251
Kippen, Jim, 68
Kisliuk, Michelle, 45, 130
Klottey, 105
Knight, Roderic, 45
Koetting, James, 230, 250
Konate, Famoudou, 143, 226–27, 228, 251
Konu, George, 241
Kpanlogo dance, 203
Kpatsa dance, 201, 204
Kpogo, Robert, 45
Kubik, Gerhard: *Africa and the Blues,* 22; "A Strange Absence," 22
Kuyate, Jali Madi, 228, 251
Kwabena Nketia Lecture Hall, 249. *See also* Nketia, Kwabena
Kwakwa, Patience, 105
Kwame Nkrumah Chair for Pan-Africanism, 249. *See also* Nkrumah, Kwame
Kykunkor, 31
Kyrema, Odomankoma. *See* Ghanaba, Kofi

Labanotation, 118. *See also* notation
Labi, Gyima, 230
Ladzekpo, Alfred, 78, 98, 121, 194, 220
Ladzekpo, Beatrice, **47,** 49, 106, 136, 243
Ladzekpo, Christopher K. (C. K.), 45, 58, 98; and Arts Council of Ghana, 240; and Asiedu Ketete Cultural Troupe, 241; and authenticity, 8; and George Dor, **61**; and Husunu Adonu Ladzekpo, 283n6; and orphan ensembles, 159, 162; and orphan programs, 61; as teacher, 115; and "teaching the right thing," 121; and Olly Wilson, 60, 158, 180

Ladzekpo, Husunu Adonu, 240, 283n6, 283n7
Ladzekpo, Kobla, 45, 51, 98; and Gideon Foli Alorwoyie, **123**; and authenticity, 8; at College at Brockport, State University of New York, 221; on etymology of *azaguno* and *wuno,* 100–101; in Gamelan Room, **49**; and Ghana National Dance Troupe, 105; and Beatrice Ladzekpo, **47**; and Husunu Adonu Ladzekpo, 283n6; pedagogical approach of, 107, 209; and John L. Price, 215; and professional ensembles, 62; retirement of, 194; at SEM 2010, 5, 119, **183**; at SEM 2012, **221**; on state drummers, 104–5; as teacher, 46, 104; and "teaching the right thing," 120, 121, 136, 140; and Philip Yopovsky, 221, **221**; and Zadonu, **155**
Ladzekpo, Kofi Zate, 251
Ladzekpo, Togbui Kobla, 46
Ladzekpo family, 61, 232
Ladzekpo-Cole, Yeko, **48,** 51, 106, **155**
Lafayette Lower Elementary School, 200, 218
language constraint, 207
Lawrence, Sidra, 45
lead drummers, 7, 100, 120, 135–36, 169, 255; Gideon Foli Alorwoyie, 239; defined, 102; David Locke, 78, 79, 99
Let the Inside Be Sweet (Stone), 42
Levy, Burt, 191
"Liberate the World," **91**
Ligeti, Gyorgy, 229
Liu, Karen, **155**
Living Blues Symposium, 191
Locke, David, 45, 58, **81**; and Agbekor Society, 113; and Godwin Agbeli, 242; and authenticity, 8, 119–20; on community service, 237; education of, 78–79, 116; and excerpts, 113; "Factoring in Race," 120; and festivals, 85–86, 194, 237, 263; and former teachers, 81–82, 120; and group model, 98, 113; and *habobo,* 98, 113; and Kiniwe Ensemble, **79**; and Alfred

Ladzekpo, 220; and lead drummers, 99, 102; and professional ensembles, 62; at SEM 2010, 282ch3n10; and study-abroad projects, 235; and Patricia Tang, 84; as teacher, 107, 111, 112, 113, 118–19, 127, 280n13; on teachers, 125, 129; at Tufts University, 78, 171; visits Ghana, 79–81, 82; and workshop, 82, 114

Louis Armstrong Park, **21, 23**. *See also* Armstrong, Louis

lunga, 82, 281ch2n6

Lunna, Abubakari, 79, 80, 82, 251

Lwanga, Charles, 45, 73, 75

Makubuya, James, 45, 49, 83, 171

Malinowski, Bronislaw, 32

Malm, William, 42

Mande dances, 207

Mande drumming, 63, 64, **66**, 67, 70, 141, 142

Mande music, 53, 227

Manning, Samuel L., *Caribbean Carnival,* 34

March, Marcel, 93

marching bands, 39, 146, 191

Mason, Major Albert, 210

Massachusetts Institute of Technology (MIT), 82–83, 84, 194, 206

master drummers, 7, 98, 99–100, 101, 102, 122, 255; Godwin Agbeli, 80; Gideon Foli Alorwoyie, 80, 82, 239; Robert Anani Ayitei, 240; Mustafa Dataade, 241; and Flaming Donos, 69; Famoudou Konate, 228; Husunu Adonu Ladzekpo, 240; Kobla Ladzekpo, 46; Sulley, 48

Masters of the Sabar (Tang), 84

Matiwre, Sleasby, 45

May, Elizabeth, 42

May It Feel Your Soul (Rice), 42

McAlester, David, 53, 78, 157

McAllister, David, 42, 157

McCook, Lucile, 282ch2n9

McDonnell-Barksdale Honors College. *See* Sally McDonnell Barksdale Honors College

McIntosh County, 18

McLead, James, 39–40

McLeod, James, 214

mediascapes, 225

Melnikoff, Anna, 45; on drum circles, 123; education of, 111, 141–43; and Famoudou Konate, 226; Mande drumming class, **66**; moves to Toronto, 142; as teacher, 63, 64, 66, 67, 109, 110, 144; teaching, **65**; visits Chicago, 143; visits Guinea, 143; visits Senegal, 143

Memphis Symphony Orchestra, 92

Mensah, 105

Mensah, Edna, 105, 244

Mensah, Helen, 54, 56, 183, 231

Mensah, Sowah, 45, 186, 217

metaphors, 5–6, 100, 188–89; coffee and milk, 130; defined, 280n14; orphan ensembles, 159, 265; plants, 11; soup, 195, 251, 264

Metropolitan Opera, 32

Middle Passage, 23–24

MIT (Massachusetts Institute of Technology), 82–83, 84, 194, 206

Monk, Thelonious, 38

Morehouse College, 34, 35

mother drummers, 7, 99, 100, 255; Kobla Ladzekpo, 46; Meki Nzewi on, 99, 100

multiculturalism, 152, 181, 190, 218, 219, 221–22; and festivals, 193; in Toronto, 67, 72–73

multi-musicality, 8–9, 131, 132, 133, 152

Mulvey, Laura, 196

Mundundu, Anicet, 73, **74,** 75, 77, 208

"Musical Instrument Travels Around the World, A" (Polak), 228

"musical performance as play," 197

Nannyonga-Tamusuza, Sylvia, 73, 75, 77, 208

National Dance Company. *See* Ghana Dance Ensemble

Nayo, Nicholas, 230

Negritude, 213

Negro Act of 1740, 20–21

Negro Freedom Rally, 34
"Negro Speaks of Rivers, The" (Hughes), 34
Negro worship music, 17
New Orleans slave rebellion, 21
Nexus, 138
Nketia, J. H. Kwabena, 46, 197, 230, 245–47, 249; and Abraham Adzinya, 78–79; *African Art Music*, 242; at AMNA, **74**; and Ghana Dance Ensemble, **248**; and Mantle Hood, 170; as teacher, 73, 76. *See also* Kwabena Nketia Lecture Hall
Nkrumah, Kwame, 36, 247, 248–49; and Ghana Dance Ensemble, 242, 243; and Pan-Africanism, 35, 213, 262. *See also* Kwame Nkrumah Chair for Pan-Africanism
Non-Aligned Movement, 243
notation, 103, 115, 166, 230; and Akin Euba, 77; and David Locke, 78, 79, 118. *See also* Labanotation
Nuatro, Kodzo, 251
Nukporfe African Dance/Drumming Ensemble, 92–93, 94, 95, 117–18; James Burns on, 95–96, 172; at festival, 194, 237; and funding, 184; performing *Agbekor* dance, **93**
Nutt Auditorium, 203
Nuxo, 239
Nwezi, Meki, 250
Nyaho, Chapman, 4, **184**
Nyamuame, Samuel Elikem, 203, 204, 207, 208; and Abraham Adzinya, **54,** 57, 180; on drum circles, 123; and Ghanaian drums, **56**; on "teaching the right thing," 140
Nzewi, Meki, 99, 100, 206

Obeng, 83
Oberlin Conservatory of Music, 45
Oberlin Mandinka Ensemble, 45
Ochs, Cliff, 282ch2n9
Odada, 242
Ogun, 134
Olatunje, Lara, 149, **149,** 150, **150,** 281n21

Olatunji, Kwame, 36
Olatunji, Michael Babatunde, 30, 262; *The Beat of My Drum,* 34; career of, 35; and drum circles, 123; *Drums of Passion,* 36; education of, 34–35; and Percussion Hall of Fame, 214; at World's Fair, 35. *See also* Olatunji Center for African Culture
Olatunji Center for African Culture, 36, 47. *See also* Olatunji, Michael Babatunde
Ole Miss. *See* University of Mississippi
Ole Miss African Drum and Dance Ensemble (OMADDE), **90**, 148, 150, 173, **186**, 222; and Ricky Burkhead, 139; and Ricky Burkhead, George Dor, and Annette Holloway, **236**; at Clarksdale High School, 201; Charles Gates on, 161, 226; and Kendra Jenkins, 39; and James McLeod, 214; and Lara Olatunje, **149,** 281n21; performing *Borborbor,* **154**; performing "Liberate the World," **91**; performing *Tokoe,* **88**; performs at Powerhouse, 204; and YOCONA Children's Festival, **89,** 201
Omojola, Bode, 4, **184**
Open Doors, 91, 92
Opoku, Albert Mawere, 221, **247**, 282n5; and Abraham Adzinya, 79; and Ghana Dance Ensemble, 242–43, 244; and *JVC & Smithsonian Video Anthology of Music and Dance,* Vol. 2, 245; Kobla Ladzekpo on, 105
oral-aural method, 108, 109, 110, 115, 117
Orff, Carl, 77
orphan ensembles, 159, 162, 265
O'Sullivan, Kevin, **155**
Oxford Middle School, 218
Ozah, Sister Marie Agatha, **74,** 76, **184**

PANAFEST, 216
Pan-Africanism, 34, 35, 36–37, 213, 216; and Katherine Mary Dunham, 33; and Kwame Nkrumah, 262. *See also* "Diaspora Studies and Pan-Africanism"; Kwame Nkrumah Chair for Pan-Africanism

Pantaleoni, Hewitt, 58, 230
Parker, Charlie, 37
Partners and Associates Grant, 87
patronage, 95, 215–16
Payne, Elizabeth, 87, 88
pedagogical approaches, 102–3, 115, 255, 258
Pedigo, Susan, 150
Percussion Arts Association, 139
Percussion Arts Society, 215
Percussion Hall of Fame, 214
Performing Ethnomusicology (Solis), 125
Perry and Marty Granoff Center for the Creative Arts, **80, 82**
Peru, 19
Piedra, Olman, 45
"play was sweet, the," 197
Polak, Raimer, "A Musical Instrument Travels Around the World," 228
Poro, 19
Powerhouse, 204, 211
praise drum poetry, 17
praise poetry, 15, 16
praise singing, 17
Pratt, John Thomas, 32
prejudices, 116; and Oforiwaa Ama Aduonum, 9, 145; and Franz Boas, 41; and Pearl Primus, 33
Price, John L., 151, **155**, 215
Primus, Pearl, 31, 33–34, 263
Princeton University, 95, 191
programming, 115, 140, 176, 257
Pwono, Damien, 73

Ramba, 84. See also *sabar* ensemble at MIT
Rambax MIT. See *sabar* ensemble at MIT
Rann, Lara Diane, **155**
Rasmussen, Anne, 130
Rawlings, Jerry John, 194–95
Redfield, Robert, 32
Reed, Daniel, 282ch3n10
Reich, Steve, 9, 138, 229; *Drumming*, 138
Reichl, Jun, **155**
Rencher, Ollie, 210
relationships, 16, 145, 148, 150, 152

religious behavior, regulated, 18
religious dance drumming, 17
religious dances, 17, 256
Rhodes, Willard, 157, 261
"Rhythms of Liberation," **224**
Rice, Tim, 68; *May It Feel Your Soul*, 42
Ricoeur, Paul, 125
Roach, Max, 38
Robert, Bob, 137

sabar drumming, 82–83, 109, 110
sabar ensemble at MIT, 85–86, 109, 194, 206, 237; and Patricia Tang, 83; and Lamine Toure, **83**. See also Ramba
Sackyefio, 105
Salima, 243
Sally McDonnell Barksdale Honors College, 87, 88
Salu, Jennifer, 149
Samonds, John, 88, 89
Sande, 19
Sanger, Annette, 68
Sankofa African Performing Ensemble, 45
Santeria, 19, 20
Sanvicente, Melissa, **155**
Sapir, Edward, 32
Schauert, Paul, 231
Schoenberg Music Building, **46**
School of Music, Dance, and Drama. See School of Performing Arts
School of Performing Arts, 245, 246, 261
Scott, James, 29
Seachrist, Denise, 4
Seeger, Charles, 42
SEM. See Society for Ethnomusicology
SEM Southeast/Caribbean Chapter Meeting, **185**
SEM 2006, 220
SEM 2008, 5, **184**
SEM 2010, 8, 119, 243; African Music Section, **122**; co-chairs, 282ch3n10; and John L. Price, 215; Sound Ecologies, 252; and Philip Yopovsky, 220
SEM 2011, 252

Senegal, 82, 84, 85, 86, 143, 206
Shanghai Conservatory of Music, 252
Shango/Spiritual Baptist faith, 33
Shelemay, Kay Kaufman, 27; *Soundscapes,* 4
Shogolo Oloba. *See* Federal Theatre African Dance Troupe
Simms, Robert, 45, 193, 204–5, 206, 216–17; on Anna Melnikoff, 111; at York University, 63, 66, 67, 158
Sims, Mark, **155**
Skinner, Elliot, "The Dialectics Between the Diasporas and Homelands," 28
slavery, 28; and Catholic Church in Peru, 19; and confiscation of drums, 210; slave ships, 22–24; and suppression of drumming, 15, 17, 20, 87, 173. *See also* International Day of Remembrance of the Victims of Slavery and the Transatlantic Slave Trade
Sloan, Mary, 148–49
Society for Ethnomusicology (SEM), 53, 252, 281ch2n8
Solis, Ted, *Performing Ethnomusicology,* 125
Sound Ecologies, 252
"Sounds of Blackness," 209
Soundscapes (Shelemay), 4
Southern, Eileen, 17, 247
Sowande, Fela, 230
space, 52, 65–66, 67, 176–78
speech surrogates, 14, 20, 132
Speranzeva, Ludtrilla, 32
Spiva, Derrick, Jr., **155**
Spring Festival, 50
Stanley, Henry Morton, *Through the Dark Continent,* 26
State University of New York at Binghamton. *See* Binghamton University
step dancing, 39, 209
Stone, Ruth, *Let the Inside Be Sweet,* 42
Stono Rebellion, 20, 24, 263
"Strange Absence, A" (Kubik), 22
Strayhorn, Billy, 37
Structural Adjustment Program, 80
"Structural Levels of Rhythm and Form in African Music" (Ekwueme), 261

Student Youth Travels Organization (SYTO), **233**
study-abroad programs, 12, 124, 235, 262, 263; long-term, 234; short-term, 232–34
"Subject, Object, and the Ethnomusicology Ensemble" (Trimillos), 127
Sulley, 48
Sullivan-Gonzalez, Douglas, 88
Sunkett, Mark, 84
SUNY Binghamton. *See* Binghamton University
Sutker, Neili, **155**
Swindall, Susan, **234**
symbiosis, 18, 32, 48, 104, 230, 248
symbolic interactionism, 153
Symposium on African Pianism, 191
syncretism, 32
SYTO (Student Youth Travels Organization), **233**

Tagoe, Emmanuel, 242
Talking Drums of Ghana, The (Hood), 136
Tamakloe, E., 105
Tambouritza Orchestra, 219
Tang, Patricia, **84**, 98, 111, 206; education of, 83–84; *Masters of the Sabar,* 84; and *sabar* ensemble, 83; as teacher, 109; visits Senegal, 84, 86
Tayo, **148**, 149
"Teaching African Music in the American Academy," 119
"teaching the right thing," 119, 120, 140, 141
"Teaching the Right Thing," 8
technoscapes, 225
Tenzer, Michael, 173
Thenstead, Adolph, *Caribbean Carnival,* 34
Thram, Diane, 82, 281ch2n5
Through the Dark Continent (Stanley), 26
Tokoe, 88
Toronto: and Anna Melnikoff, 142; and multiculturalism, 67, 72–73, 181, 205, 218, 220
Touching the Spirits (DjeDje), 42
Toure, Lamine, 83, **83**, 84–85, 86, 109–10

INDEX 313

Toure, Sekou, 228
Tower of Power, 39
Trimillos, Ricardo, 125; "Subject, Object, and the Ethnomusicology Ensemble," 127
Tufts University, 45; and Andrew Mellon Grant, 82; and David Locke, 171; and festival, 85–86, 237; and fundraiser concert, 82; and Kiniwe Ensemble, **79, 81**; and David Locke, 78; and study-abroad projects, 235
Turbyfill, Mark, 32
12th Annual Conference of the Association of Ghana Methodist Church Choirs in North America, 280n10

UCLA. *See* University of California at Los Angeles
UM Brand Photography, 89
"Understanding 'Fast Agbekor'" (Hirt-Manheimer), 231
UNESCO, 263
United Nations, 229
University of Alberta, 45
University of Bowling Green, 45
University of British Columbia, 173
University of California, Berkeley, 45, 58
University of California at Los Angeles (UCLA), 3, 44, 45, 46, 47, 131, 170, 209, 220, 261; and African Year, 50; and AMNA, 134; and Kwasi Badu, 51; and concerts, 194, 198; and multi-musicality, 8–9; and space, 52; and Spring Festival, 50; and study-abroad programs, 236; and summer workshops, 236; and summer world music programs, 217; and Year of African Music, 194
University of Chicago, 32, 150, 226
University of Colorado, 131, 171–72, 194
University of Florida, 69, 84, 186, 206–7
University of Ghana, 12; and Modesto Amegago, 144; and Ghana Dance Ensemble, 242; and Mantle Hood, 170; and David Locke, 79; and Albert Mawere Opoku, 282n5

University of Michigan, 211
University of Minnesota, 186
University of Mississippi, 161, 222; and Black History Month, 202; International Conference on Racial Reconciliation, 153; and Diedra Jackson, 282ch2n11; and Daniel Jones, 192; and Living Blues Symposium, 191; Open Doors, 92; purchases drums from Ghana, 88–90; and Nancy Van De Vate, 191; and workshop, 201
University of Pittsburgh, 45, 171; and Joseph Adjaye, 195; and African Drumming and Dance Ensemble, 195; and William Amoako, 128; and Andrew Mellon Tuition Fellowship, 181; and William Oscar Anku, 73, 128; and J. S. Kofi Gbolonyo, 128, 217; and Mark Sunkett, 85; and Symposium on African Pianism, 191
University of Rochester, 45
University of St. Thomas, 45
University of Toronto, 45; and West African dance/drumming, 68, 70, 73, 171; and world music ensembles, 73
University of Virginia, 45
University of West Virginia, 77, 192, 193, 195
Uya, Okon Edet, 26
Uzoigwe, Joshua, 230

Van De Vate, Nancy, 191
Vanderbilt University, 45
Venda music, 42
Venon, Ron, 91
Vidal, Olatunjie, 171
Vidal, Tunji, 49
village style, 141, 142, 143, 257–58
vocables, 108, 110, 115, 147
Volk, Teresa, 42
volunteer causes, 237
Voudoun, 20, 24

Wabash College, 45, 83
Wachsmann, Klaus, 46, 247, 252
Walmart, 178
Wamidan World Music Ensemble, 45

Warren, Guy. *See* Ghanaba, Kofi
Watson, John Fanning, 18
Watts, Isaac, 18
Weintraub (faculty member), 75
Wesleyan African Ensemble, 283ch7n2
Wesleyan University, 45; and Abraham Adzinya, 128, 194; and *Gahu* dance, 203; and Isaac Hirt-Manheimer, 231; and David Locke, 78–79; and West African dance/drumming, 53, 182–83
West African Drumming and Dance Ensemble, 45
West African Drumming Ensemble, 45
West African Highlife Ensemble, 131, **182,** 194
West African Music and Dance Ensemble, 45, **76**
West African Music Ensemble, 45, 47
William Winter Institute for Racial Reconciliation, 91, 153
Wilson, Olly, 9, 58, **59**, 158; and Guggenheim Fellowship, 133–34, 243; and Christopher K. Ladzekpo, 180
Winslow, Richard, 53
Woma, Bernard, 45
Wonders of the African World (Gates), 40, 211
Woodrow Wilson High School, 79
World Fest, 193
wudodo, 11, 188–89
wuga, **200**
wuno, etymology of, 100–102

Yartey, Nii, 244
Year of African Music, 194
Yewe, 19
YOCONA Children's Festival, **89,** 201
YOCONA International Folk Festival, **89,** 148–49, 211
Yopovsky, Philip, 220–21, **221**
York University, 45; and African Festival, 67, 193; and space, 65–66; and West African dance/drumming, 63–64, 67
Yoruba, 19, 35, 49

Young, Lester, 37
Younge, Pascal, 75, 128; and African Drumming and Dance Ensemble, 193, 195, 211, 212, 213; and Azaguno, 227; and middle schools, 217; and study-abroad programs, 234; at University of Pittsburgh, 77, 171
YouTube, 229

Zadonu, 121, **155,** 215, 283n6
zigi, 282n13

www.ingramcontent.com/pod-product-compliance
Lightning Source LLC
Chambersburg PA
CBHW021833220426
43663CB00005B/225